# Children's Literature

Volume 12

# Volume 12

*Annual of
The Modern Language Association
Division on Children's Literature
and The Children's Literature
Association*

Yale University Press
New Haven and London
1984

*Children's Literature*

*Editorial Correspondence should be addressed to:*
The Editors, *Children's Literature*
Department of English
University of Connecticut
Storrs, Connecticut 06268

Manuscripts should conform to the *MLA Handbook*. An original on non-erasable bond and a copy are requested. Manuscripts must be accompanied by a self-addressed envelope and return postage.

Volumes 1–7 of *Children's Literature* can be obtained directly from the Children's Literature Foundation, Box 370, Windham Center, Connecticut 06280.

Library of Congress catalog card number: 79-66588
ISBN: 0-300-03144-0 (cloth), 0-300-03179-3 (paper)

Set in Baskerville type by The Saybrook Press, Inc., Old Saybrook, Conn. Printed in the United States of America by Vail-Ballou Press, Binghamton, N.Y.

10    9    8    7    6    5    4    3    2    1

# Contents

*Articles*

Exploring the Levels of Childhood:
The Allegorical Sensibility of
Maurice Sendak     *Geraldine DeLuca*    3

"For the Instruction of the Young":
The Deerfield Captivity Narratives    *Alexander Medlicott, Jr.*    25

*Hans Brinker*: Sunny World,
Angry Waters     *Jerome Griswold*    47

"Men Sell Not Such in Any Town":
Christina Rossetti's Goblin Fruit
of Fairy Tale     *Jeanie Watson*    61

Tailpiece: *The Tale of Two Bad Mice*     *Suzanne Rahn*    78

The Literary Transformation
of a Sluggard     *Mary-Agnes Taylor*    92

The Narnia Books of C. S. Lewis:
Fantastic or Wonderful?     *Dennis B. Quinn*    105

Beyond Explanation, and Beyond
Inexplicability, in *Beyond Silence*     *Perry Nodelman*    122

A Response to Perry Nodelman's
"Beyond Explanation"     *Eleanor Cameron*    134

*Reviews*

Bringing Shakespeare to Young
People, and Young People
to Shakespeare     *Sidney Homan*    149

Childhood's Companions     *Gillian Avery*    154

The Grimm *German Legends*
in English     *Jack Zipes*    162

Illustrated Classics in Facsimile     *Feenie Ziner*    167

*Alice's Adventures*, the
Pennyroyal Press Edition     *Leonard S. Marcus*    175

Lives and Letters  *Elizabeth Segel*  185
Literature and the Child Reader  *Carol Billman*  192
Thirty Writers Talk about Writing  *Perry Nodelman*  200

*Varia*

A Blind Child's View of Children's
   Literature  *Craig Werner*  209
Dissertations of Note  *Rachel Fordyce*  217
Errata  224
Contributors and Editors  225

# Children's Literature

# Exploring the Levels of Childhood:
# The Allegorical Sensibility of Maurice Sendak

Geraldine DeLuca

Upon the publication of *Outside Over There*, released by Harper and Row in 1981 as a book for both adults and children, Maurice Sendak commented to Selma Lanes that he had "waited a long time to be taken out of kiddy-book land and allowed to join the artists of America."[1] One can understand the problem as Sendak sees it: perhaps in his eyes even the praise has missed the point. Children's literature critics—the "custodians of children's books" in Hilton Kramer's words—may not be thought capable of recognizing the symbolic nature and artistic origins of Sendak's work.[2] And the charges are, no doubt, sometimes justified. Children's literature is particularly subject to the thumbnail sketch that tends to take either a lighthearted or a moralistic approach toward the books reviewed. And works like Sendak's tend either to be reverentially overpraised—as, ironically, we see in Selma Lanes's book about him—or condemned for their experiments. But children's literature, as we all know, is a particularly difficult field in which to make judgments, encompassing as it does literature for various age groups—none of them our own—and including pictorial art as well. Moreover, even the most knowledgeable and perceptive critic may become anxious and somewhat conservative when his or her own child's psyche seems to be hanging in the balance.

The question of audience has always been a difficult one in the field, and discussions about it are usually full of apparent paradoxes. What *does* the child see in these books we are reviewing? Sendak has asserted repeatedly that the child understands what is really going on while the adult lumbers along too worried and distracted by the effect on young minds of naked boys and scary beasts to find out what the books are actually saying. And those adults who claim to have a special ability to understand how children respond—the artists and editors—frequently invoke the "child inside themselves" to explain how they create or make judgments. But this child inside us is in some ways an unconvincing creature, burdened as it is with a sense of irony and nostalgia that children do not have and that is hard to ignore. Moreover, while children may bring to the works the sense of wonder that the children's book artist presumably longs for, they cannot make critical judgments. They may like Sendak's work better than something else but they usually cannot say why.

There are some books that seem to touch us all, children and adults, in a primary way. *Charlotte's Web* comes most immediately to mind. But Sendak, in his quest for both audiences, may actually be leaving the child behind. *Higglety, Pigglety, Pop* and the selections of Grimm tales for *The Juniper Tree* suggest his interest in taking the forms and genres of children's literature into the adult world. Neither work really seems appropriate for children. And his most recent work, *Outside Over There*, despite its handling of sibling rivalry and oedipal feelings, seemingly so close to a child's experience, may also be a heavier burden than some children can be expected to bear.

The difficulties, the obscurities of *Outside Over There* seem to spring from what is essentially an allegorical sensibility, a sensibility that needs to charge its works with layer upon layer of meaning, one that is obsessive, that thrives on detail, that must cover every inch of literal and metaphorical ground. This is not, of course, a negative quality in itself. Some of the greatest artists of our culture seem to have worked from the same impulses. It does account, however, for the extravagant, secretive quality of Sendak's work and may explain why he sometimes passes the child by.

Even in art for adults, allegory has not, at least since the nineteenth century, been a particularly popular form. It has traditionally been regarded with suspicion and impatience as being too doctrinal and mechanical, in contrast to "symbolic" literature, wherein the symbol is felt to inhere in the work, to be more intrinsically related, rather than being tediously strung along throughout.[3] A traditional reading of allegory would, as Paul Alpers pointed out, produce the kind of commentary that Ruskin did for Book I of *The Faerie Queene*: "[Holiness] . . . has Truth (or Una) at its side, but presently enters the Wandering Wood, and encounters the serpent Error; that is to say, Error in her universal form, the first enemy of Reverence and Holiness."[4] But even Spenser cannot be read this way throughout.

What such a reading suggests, though, and what probably repels many avoiders of allegory, is the certainties that it implies, the sense that the writer (and the interpreter) have worked life out and can prescribe a course of action. Yet what modern critics, most notably Angus Fletcher, have been demonstrating is that even if some allegory expresses its author's faith in right actions, it is also just as emphatically showing how immensely difficult it is to fulfill them. Hence all the mistakes the heroes make along the way. Fletcher argues that most allegories, from the Christian poem of Spenser to the works of Kafka, are characterized by ambivalence and anxiety. More recently, structuralist and post-structuralist critics, concerned with the uncertainties of the critical, interpretive activity itself, have begun to find the allegorical mode particularly attractive. Thus Jonathan Culler writes:

> Allegory [as opposed to symbolism] . . . stresses the difference between levels, flaunts the gap we must leap to produce meaning, and thus displays the activity of interpretation in all its conventionality. . . . Allegory, one might say, is the mode which recognizes the impossibility of fusing the empirical and the eternal and thus demystifies the symbolic relation by stressing the separateness of the two levels, the impossibility of bringing them together except momentarily.[5]

Stephen Greenblatt's introduction to a recent collection of essays on allegory extends this idea even further:

> [Allegory's] actual effect is to acknowledge the darkness, the arbitrariness, and the void that underlie, and paradoxically make possible, all representation of realms of light, order, and presence. Insofar as the project of mimesis is the direct representation of a stable, objective reality, allegory, in attempting and always failing to present Reality, inevitably reveals the impossibility of this project.[6]

Greenblatt goes on to cite the perceptions of Joel Fineman that allegory "arises in periods of loss, periods in which a once powerful theological, political, or familial authority is threatened with effacement. Allegory arises then from the painful absence of that which it claims to recover."[7] For Fineman, Greenblatt says, "the longing for an origin whose loss is the necessary condition of that longing is the character not only of all discourse but of human existence itself."[8] This sense that reality is impossible to represent, and that the desire to try to represent it grows out of a sense of loss, sheds much light on the quality of Sendak's work. It may account for its fussiness—its cantankerousness, I might almost say—for its themes of childhood anger and struggle, and for Sendak's increasing tendency to depict the child's triumphs as fragile, partial, and sorely bought.

That Sendak sees himself as working in a tradition that seeks to reveal difficult, perhaps ultimately ineffable truths is evident from his own commentary on his work. Regarding his illustrations for the Grimm fairy tales, for example, he says, "The tales work on two levels: first, as stories; second, as the unraveling of deep psychological dramas"; further, "I wanted my pictures to tell any reader who thinks the stories are simple to go back to the beginning and read them again. I searched for what was really underneath. It was hard. There was not one story that gave its secret right away."[9] Allegory, of course, is not the only mode that speaks to us on more than one level. We can read any realistic piece of fiction and take from it not only the story but some more essential statement about life. But allegory compels us into that interpretive frame of mind. The story qua story is strange, enigmatic, distorted; it demands a reading. This may seem inappropriate for children's stories, stories whose success we would assume to lie in their simplicity. At times, as I am arguing here, Sendak does go too far. But at times the allegorical mode does work. Fairy tales, despite their spare surface, are not simple, and by and large children love them. They haunt us with their threats and promises, their taboos, their intimations of life that lie below their surface. And this is what Sendak strives for in his works.

Moreover, while we might, on first consideration, expect a children's book writer to move toward simplicity, from another point of view it makes sense that children's literature would yield multiple meanings. At the very least any children's book writer has to sustain two visions: the adult's and the child's. In some way he has to become connected to his own childhood, to his perceptions of the world of his past, from its physical scale in relation to himself, to his confusions and fears and naive interpretations of things he could not possibly understand fully. So there is always a certain amount of irony in children's books, from the adult's point of view, due to simplifications of information and necessary deletions of certain kinds of experience.

These distinctions between big and small, innocence and experience, provide an important source of layering in Sendak's work. His childhood remembrances seem more vivid and acute than those of most adults—perhaps the effect of writing for children, but possibly his reason for doing so. He depends in a very conscious way on his unconscious—his repository of childhood experiences—to supply him with material, expressing a clear preference for the kind of material the unconscious can offer him:

> My unconscious knows exactly what they are, only I don't with my thinking mind, but every day I get a little clue. "Listen, dumdum, here's a word for you. See what you can make of it." So my unconscious throws it out and I catch it: "Oh, a word, fantastic!" And then I do without for three days, and the unconscious says, "This man's too much to believe; he walks, he thinks, he sits, he doesn't do anything, he's a bore, throw him another word, otherwise he'll sit there forever and have a coronary."[10]

The obsessive devotion to the treasures of the unconscious expressed in this comic statement of anxiety is manifested in much of Sendak's work, as in his quest narratives that represent the conscious self in some relation to the unconscious. As he says, his three major picture books, the self-styled trilogy of *Where the Wild Things Are*, *In the Night Kitchen*, and *Outside Over There*, all deal with "how children master various feelings—anger, boredom, fear, frustration, jealousy—and manage to come to grips with the realities of their lives."[11] All three dreamlike fantasy journeys, and as the "fascination of what's difficult" has grown in Sendak, each has become deliberately more laden with "meaning." He told Jonathan Cott:

> This last part of my trilogy is going to be the strangest. *Wild Things* now seems to me to be a very simple book—its simplicity

is probably what made it successful, but I could never be that
simple again. *Night Kitchen* I much prefer—it reverberates on
double levels. But this third book will reverberate on triple
levels.[12]

He was right about *Outside Over There* and the result is a book that
is at times disturbingly implausible on a literal level, surrendering
some of its harmony for hidden meanings, some universal but some
highly idiosyncratic, that lie heavily on us.

Sendak's comments on his work show quite clearly his inclinations
toward allegory. To be sure, most of his works are not fully developed examples, but even the simplest of them displays aspects
of allegorical art, and looking at them with a definition of allegory
in mind makes it clear where a work like *Outside Over There* comes
from. Angus Fletcher's definition of allegory is particularly helpful
because it analyzes allegorical art in terms of its component parts—
agency, imagery, themes, action, causation, and values—and this
analysis helps us to see where the non-allegorical works, or rather
those that are not full allegories, share characteristics of the mode.

Briefly, in Fletcher's scheme, allegorical characters (he calls them
"daemonic agents") act as if possessed by daemons who "compart-
mentalize function" so that they seem pathologically single-minded.[13]
Such characters are remarkably rigid and restricted in behavior,
always tending toward becoming icons in an allegorical cosmos.[14]
Daemonic agents perceive the characters around them as aspects of
the conflicts within themselves. And "by analyzing the projections,
we determine what is going on in the mind of the highly imaginative
projector."[15] With his restricted view of the universe, the daemonic
agent reminds us that we see only what our preoccupied minds allow
us to see. On the simplest, most childish level—and children are
often remarkably like this—we have Pierre, "who only would say 'I
don't care,'" and Chicken Soup, who is what he eats: chicken soup
with rice twelve months a year. In *Chicken Soup with Rice* Sendak is
reflecting a small child's pleasure in routine and repetition. In *Pierre*
he reflects the child's negativism. Neither work reveals allegorical
dimensions, although one could spend a little time talking about
Pierre's getting swallowed by the lion. But all of these motifs—the
repetitions, the obsessiveness, the self-containment, the child-eating

lion—are used again allegorically in *Higglety, Pigglety, Pop*, a work that does demand interpretation. It is a more difficult, more serious work in which Sendak comes to terms with the death of his dog Jennie by giving her eternal life as the leading lady in the World Mother Goose Theatre where every day she gets to eat a mop made of salami.

The world of *Higglety, Pigglety, Pop* is world of enchantment, a world constructed to test Jennie's mettle. As the Red Cross Knight's universe is centered upon holiness and its enemies, Jennie's is centered upon food. Gluttony, we might say, is her abiding sin, and thus all her adventures involve eating. She even eats the plant she talks with in the opening pages. When all its leaves are gone the conversation is over. Though she has "everything"—bowls, pills, pillows—she knows there "must be more to life" than that. What she lacks is "experience," a commodity, Sendak tenderly implies, that she could never get under his hothouse care. So she goes out into the world, genuinely on a quest, though like most untried heroes not quite sure what she is looking for. But the other characters, all members of the World Mother Goose Theatre, do know what she needs, and beguiling her with food, they lead her to the house of Baby, who won't eat, and whose name nobody knows, except for her parents at Castle Yonder. Castle Yonder is clearly heaven, and Lanes points out that at the time of the writing, Sendak was also anticipating his mother's death.[16] It is not surprising then that Baby looks like Sendak's own baby pictures. Jennie, who is determined to feed Baby, winds up eating the breakfast herself and thus failing at her "experience." But she is prepared to sacrifice herself to save his life. Putting her head into the lion's mouth, she is saved at the final moment unwittingly by saying Baby's name, Mother Goose. Baby and the lion then immediately disappear to Castle Yonder and Jennie, who had everything, now finds herself in a wood with nothing. But she has gained experience. She has learned to sacrifice for someone else, to stop eating, to let herself in fact be food for a lion. She has endured—and died—and is ready to be led to the Mother Goose Theatre, at Castle Yonder, by Mother Goose herself, who was Baby/Sendak, now transformed into an orchestrator of tales. Jennie's "final reward" is to live forever in the nursery rhyme of the title.[17]

It is clear that Jennie is a daemonic agent rather than a fully rounded, mimetic character. One might well answer that she is a dog, after all; how complex can she be? But if we compare her, say, to William Steig's Dominic, we can see the difference. Dominic's doglike nature is not ignored. But he travels through a universe that is fuller and more varied, that has an existence apart from him. The world of Sendak's story, by contrast, reads like a projection of Jennie's mind. The pig wears a sandwich board that contains free sandwiches; the milkman's truck is filled with milk that Jennie drinks. Like the world of dreams, it all pertains to her; she has to figure out what it means and without her it does not exist.

The imagery in such a world is what Fletcher terms "cosmic," which is to say that every item appearing before us has its place in the cosmic hierarchy and is to be regarded as a sign. The macrocosm is reflected as well in the microcosm; nothing is too large or too small to be ignored. The protagonist traveling through such a landscape is generally in a state of anxiety because he cannot read the signs (see Sendak's statement about his unconscious) or because he is trying to ignore the import. And while the gap between the sign and the thing signified may never be fully bridged, so that one will never be completely assured that what he perceives is reality, part of the reader's pleasure, nonetheless, is in trying to decode the signs and understand the meaning of the protagonist's response to them. Names, dress, and place are all a part of this universe of signs, reflecting to an extraordinary degree the state of one's mind or soul and one's position in the cosmos.

Consider Sendak's character Rosie, the tough little girl in a grown-up's dress, hat, and feathers. She is in costume, and the word itself, Fletcher notes, is etymologically related to the word *cosmos* and the concept of rank in the hierarchy.[18] Like Jennie, but with more complexity, she is an actress, seeking adulation, seeking stardom in Sendak's night sky, needing to transcend the claustrophobic street of his childhood. She is filled with longing—"Yes, my name is Rosie. I am a star. I'm famous and wonderful and everybody loves me and wants to be me. Who can blame them?"[19] She represents a child's pain at being locked into a place that is too constricting, even if it is a source of inspiration, as the homely streets of Sendak's childhood clearly were.

Although Sendak's language and pictures accentuate Rosie's daemonic qualities, the Rosie stories are not essentially allegorical. Rosie plays her role, but when the other children go home, Sendak reveals a lost child, lonely without her audience. Max, in his wolf suit, comes closer to allegory, his wolfishness being played out in his own dream world—one that confronts him with characters just like himself and allows him to act out his aggressions in the ritualistic fashion of allegory.

Names can help to sketch allegorical portraits, and Sendak's attention to the magical nature of names is evidenced in his account of how he settled on the name of Ida for his heroine in *Outside Over There*:

> [He] agonized a good deal . . . over his heroine's name. Was it the right one? It contained Id—all to the good, because Ida was a primal child. The name was also auspicious in that it belonged to Mrs. Ida Perles, the Sendak children's second mother as they were growing up in Brooklyn. But something about the name still nagged at him. Only after the book had been delivered to Harper and Row did Sendak realize that the letters of Ida also appear, backwards, in his mother's name—Sadie. The artist was delighted. Moreover, he is certain that he had already subconsciously known this fact when he wrote the lines:

> > If Ida backwards in the rain
> > Would only turn around again.[20]

For Sendak, Ida is more authentic, has more power by virtue of having the name she does. He can believe in the name because his unconscious—which we now substitute for what used to be taken as divine revelation—has identified her so well.

Sublime and picturesque landscapes are another familiar characteristic of allegorical art—the one in its magnitude, the other in its smallness mirroring the cosmos, both reflecting a consciousness of nature as a force filled with signs, and, through their strange distortions in size, revealing an ambivalence in the creator or protagonist. Fletcher writes:

> Where the sublime aims at great size and grandeur, the picturesque aims at littleness and a sort of modesty; where the sublime is austere, the picturesque is intricate; where the sublime pro-

duces "terror," or rather, awed anxiety, the picturesque produces an almost excessive feeling of comfort.[21]

The picture book seems a particularly apt form for this kind of
distortion, being by its very nature "picturesque," its characters
usually children or animals, its subject matter veering toward the
precious, its universe often somewhat ironically portrayed, so that
even when an artist is depicting an expanse of nature, there is always
something miniature and controlled about it.

The storm and the idyllic pastoral, the two extremes of the allegorical mode, are seen most clearly in *Outside Over There*, but *In the
Night Kitchen* presents an even more interesting tableau. Its vast
night sky of buildings is also picturesque—its buildings being food
boxes in a pantry. Sendak's attraction to the picturesque is also
evident in his Nutshell Library, with its fussy, obsessive little heroes
in their tiny spaces,[22] and the boxed set elaborately decorated with
columns, a mock-enigmatic emblem of an acorn and oak leaves, and
Sendak's initials, in the decorative, riddling tradition of allegory.

The basic movement in allegory is the quest—the journey away
from the familiar to hidden external and internal truths. It includes
alternating states of progress and battle, interspersed with periods
of rest and understanding. For the allegorical hero, however, there
is almost never total peace or harmony, at least not while he is on this
earth. Ambivalence haunts him, the degree to which it is resolved
depending on how idealistic the work is. But even the most hopeful
of allegories are by their very nature filled with conflict, with characters pulled by polar desires, since it is the function of allegory to set
up an intellectual and emotional dialectic that the hero must work
through.

Sendak's simplest representation of the child's quest "to come to
grips with the realities of his life" is, as he says, *Where the Wild Things
Are*. In any early version of the story Max's mother turns into a
wolf,[23] embodying the agent-to-image change that sometimes occurs in allegory. And an early draft of the text has a passage of
commands and conflictingly alluring visual messages reminiscent of
passages in Spenser:[24] "He entered a magic garden though the sign
said do not enter and looked round the tree though the sign said

do not look. He thought this might be the place where the wild horses are."[25] But Sendak finally pared away the florid excesses and what remains is a beautifully clean visual and verbal story of Max's rebellion—his working through his hostility to his mother, being the wild thing that his wolf suit says he is, charging through the tiny space of the first pages into the vast double-page spreads where the wild things are. Eating, a favorite subject of Sendak's, and a common source of sensual pleasure in children's books, is here the vehicle through which Max reveals his aggressions. "I'll eat you up," he tells his mother and is sent to bed without his supper. One is reminded of Sendak's sequence of sketches of the baby who begins by sucking at its mother's breast and ends by contentedly swallowing her.[26] Max, in his wolfish state of mind, might be inclined to do the same. But then what would he do for his next meal?

The quest, then, for all that it is liberating and wish-fulfilling, with Max ordering everyone around, is also, as it is for Jennie, civilizing. Max may rule the wild things but they are not giving him anything to eat. They can only offer to "eat him up [they] love him so," which is in the right spirit, but the wrong solution. Max needs someone unlike himself to "love him best of all" and cook his supper, regardless of the compromise to his freedom. The story is a remarkably subtle and affectionate rendition of a child's desire for independence and dominance in conflict with his need for security and love, and we finish reading it with a sense of comic, cathartic relief.

Visually as well as textually *Where the Wild Things Are* is a wonderful work, the gray confining space of the house opening up, as the borders disappear, into the expansive, rosy fantasy world and pages of "wild rumpus," a sublime conception that is also, by virtue of its preciousness and safety, picturesque. One could call such a work simple—once it is all laid out it seems so clear—but such simplicity is deceptive. The book is inspired and rendered with remarkable balance and restraint. Surface and underlying meaning are close; that it is not a "difficult," enigmatic book is part of its charm. It is truly an allegory for a small child, one that can be apprehended in its totality, without explanation.

*In the Night Kitchen* is a more complicated, idiosyncratic work, presenting us with a more self-consciously allegorical Sendak, someone more fully exploiting the potential of the mode. Mickey's night sky/city/pantry is a surreal world conjured up by innocence with perfect logic, given the fragmentary state of a child's understanding of terms like the Milky Way. Everything in this night kitchen is comfortingly labeled, as food boxes are. Everything has a name, a place, a significance that can be read. To be sure, Sendak embeds his own private associations in the pictures: June 10, 1928, a date on a box, is, as we might have guessed, his own birthday, and other names are those of people important in his life. But what makes the work so appealing is that the images are not merely clever; Sendak can turn the giant milk bottle into a womb and have it make perfect sense psychologically. Drinking from the bottle as he floats in the milk, Mickey says, "I'm in the milk and the milk's in me. God bless milk and God bless me." It's an intriguing image that expresses a preoccupation of Sendak's—being inside and outside at the same time, being in the womb, contained, and at the same time incorporating, containing; being supremely sheltered and yet conquering. Conflicting, ambivalent desires are momentarily resolved in this image of infantile sensual pleasure. And the overriding statement of the work, focusing of Mickey's driving need to learn what goes on in the night kitchen and save the day by finding milk, is true to a child's experience.

Mickey's fantasy is more social then Max's, involving an awareness of what one could call community that Max doesn't yet have. Mickey is both showing off and doing something useful. "And that's why, thanks to Mickey, we have milk every morning." For both children, however, the struggle is purely self-centered. And for the time being, in each case, that is enough. It is not the case, however, for Ida in *Outside Over There*. The eldest and most complex of the three protagonists, her story is quite different.

Structurally the third book follows the same form as the first two, moving from the inside, Ida's room—though it's not her private bedroom but a day room that she shares with her sister—to a place of fantasy and risk, to "outside over there." The phrase represents the abstract concept of externality, otherness, as a child might state it. For while all three books bring the child from one relatively safe place to another where one tests one's prowess, this third book not only involves getting beyond one's room but also past the night places of one's own fantasy world to a place that encompasses the needs and will of other people, outside the mind itself. Of course this is still Ida's struggle with herself—conquering the goblins in herself that would do away with her sister. But Ida's quest is also social. She is older than Max and Mickey, who are hardly more than babies themselves, and she is female. One is grateful to Sendak for recognizing how early in life girls learn to feel the conflict between their desire to achieve for themselves and the demands placed on them to take care of others. Another writer might have indicated that Ida's achievement *was* in taking care of the baby, and, of course, in part it is, but while he allows approval to Ida for finally being a good sister, Sendak keeps the two roles separate.

Another sign that this quest is more complex is that Ida needs help in completing it. Max and Mickey had only to dream, becoming in their dreams figures appropriately dressed—or undressed—to express their psychic state, both conjuring up and conquering their adversaries. Ida, as Sendak says, starts out badly and only recovers by listening to her father's song—her father being the traditional guardian figure of the fairy tale, the wise part of the psyche, which helps to "turn her around" and allow her to find her strength. Another indication of the complexity of her problem is that there is no food in this work. Ida takes her pleasure and solace in her wonder horn, her music being both what distracts her from her sister and what she uses to bring the sister back. This is a world not of sensuality but of work and art.

As Fletcher and others have noted, allegory is "the art of subterfuge par excellence," an art "proper to those moments when nothing but subterfuge will work."[27] The situation in *Outside Over There* is clearly such a moment for a child. Placing Ida in charge of her baby sister while her father is away at sea and her mother sits immobile in the arbor, Sendak creates a tableau of oedipal feelings, and from beginning to end there is not an easy moment. These are the great taboos of childhood—the longings from which the dreamwork of allegory springs. The feelings to which Sendak gives shape are terrible and frightening, and the excessively careful narrative just barely veils what is going on.[28]

We can understand the rationale of the situation as simple story: papas go to sea, children help with younger siblings. That's the grown-up and moral way. Yet we still feel the unfairness of it, from Ida's point of view. There is something suspect about the parents, the profoundly passive mother so wrapped in missing papa she can hardly move, the father so unattainable and beyond reproach, and Ida stuck with the baby, big, heavy, and helpless, requiring Ida's undivided attention. Turn away for a second and the goblins come. And papa from afar—his picture hanging watchfully on the wall— knows just what's happening.

We feel for Ida not only as we feel for a child but as we feel for ourselves. She is anyone feeling abandoned and burdened, needing love, recognition, and time to herself, anyone feeling guilt at not being all she is expected to be. That Sendak manages to embody so much in her is impressive. He expresses the depth and complexity of a universal situation. But his handling of other aspects of the story is disturbing. On a simple narrative level, for example, the kidnapping of the baby by the goblins is horrifying: the terrified baby is hustled out the window while Ida "never knowing" plays her horn; on the next page we see Ida embracing the changeling "ice thing" and saying "how I love you." These are nightmare images and one keeps turning back to them, wondering how a child would understand them. By now such complaints must be an old song for Sendak. But perhaps all one can do is worry anew over each new frightening image and try to make distinctions among them. In this story, as opposed to *Wild Things*, there is no humor to lighten the burden. We are not seeing a child brazenly seeking out an adorably depicted danger; rather, a totally innocent and helpless baby is being threatened because of the neglect of her sister.

And why are the goblins babies? It seems a bit arch and coy at first, tied up as it is with Sendak's private associations about the Dionne quintuplets and the Lindbergh kidnapping. But symbolically it does make sense. It is characteristic of allegorical imagery that false creatures mimic their true counterparts. Consider Una and false Una in Book I of *The Faerie Queene* or Florimell and false Florimell, who, like the ice baby, is an effigy in snow. Ida's unconscious might well depict the goblins as babies since that is the form that troubles her. She is angry at babies. In some way the baby is to blame. Furthermore it makes the rescue more complex. Ida cannot simply pluck her sister away. Everyone looks the same. How can she tell the false from the true? It is an essential question in allegory. And since appearances are always deceiving, there is no direct way to find out. With her father's help, she must discover her own resources—her music—and let its power work for her. For the goblins the music is Dionysian; it makes them sick. But it leaves her sister safely reborn to Ida in the eggshell. This is the way with allegory. The truth can only be known through signs and rituals: the baby that doesn't dance itself into a frenzy is the human child.

Ida seems bewildered through most of the story, but on a symbolic level it all makes sense. She begins her journey to rescue her sister by putting on her mother's yellow cloak and floating backwards out the window. Why is she floating and why backwards? She is still too passive and still looking inward rather than to "outside over there," where the world and her responsibility lie. And her mother's cloak can only hinder her because she has failed in taking her mother's place. Only her father can help her now (who else, we think smugly), by revealing her own strength to her. So even though she seems in a state of shock through most of the experience, Ida is learning, simply by virtue of enduring.

When her ordeal is over, Ida passes through a wood, a picturesque setting where Mozart sits in a little house playing the harpsichord. Sendak told Selma Lanes that he played nothing but Mozart throughout the composition of this book—the horn and the kidnapping are allusions to *The Magic Flute*. So a Mozartean spirit is meant to infuse the work. Mozart is its reigning deity. And Ida, like many allegorical heroes having endured a struggle and accomplished the quest, has her moment of peace in his presence. Fletcher calls such places as this house in the wood "temples in the labyrinth." Northrop Frye earlier labeled them "houses of recognition."[29] They are a common feature of allegorical literature. But Ida doesn't go near the house; she seems, in fact, unaware of it—which is another problem in the work. Ida's perpetual isolation is oppressive. Nonetheless she is in an enchanted place. Earlier she loomed large, awkward, engulfed in the luminous lightning-colored cape, in a world full of distortions.

Now order and proportion are restored. The shepherd tends his sheep; there are butterflies. Lest we forget, however, that we are never really out of danger, there are also, as John Gardner points out, sinister, skull-shaped leaves in the foreground,[30] and the limbs of the tree next to Ida are threatening hands. But things are somewhat better when Ida returns home. Though he is still away, her father has sent a letter, her mother has perked up a bit, and she still has her horn.

The artwork for this book is a striking departure from that of the two previous picture books, though its delicate loveliness is present elsewhere in Sendak. *Outside Over There* has a sumptuous painterly quality totally different from the cartoon drawings of the other two works. The change is, of course, appropriate to this more serious, complex work, and Ida has a dignity in her troubled state that Max and Mickey don't really need. But the characteristic allegorical distortions are there. The painting is mannered and the imagery borders on the surreal in a subtler way than it does in *Night Kitchen*, where the giant milk bottle is a playful and clearly understood surrealistic sign. Mannerism and surrealism are characteristic of allegorical art, each suggesting, in its degree of distortion, the importance of certain features and objects symbolically. Fletcher describes surrealism as implying "obsessional and dream imagery, unexpected, even shocking collocations of heterogeneous objects, psychological emblems (usually Freudian), hyperdefinite draftsmanship, distortions of perspective—with all these working together to produce enigmatic combinations of materials."[31] Naturally in a children's book such qualities will be minimized, but they do characterize Sendak's art, with its compression of landscapes and exaggeration of features. Ears and eyes are larger than they should be; Ida's ankles and sturdy feet are peculiarly prominent. And even though one recognizes the proportions in live children, they here remain dis-integrated, isolated, "hyperdefinite," as Fletcher says. It is a style Sendak may have developed in reaction to the doll-like drawings of earlier illustrators, but his own drawings, particularly in this work, have their own sentimental effect, the square, solid little bodies and bewildered faces of children suggesting an awful, almost unbearable vulnerability.

And objects, too, are scaled or selected to produce slightly surreal effects. Consider the enormous sunflowers—sinister, sublime foliage—pushing their way through Ida's window. Throughout the work the figures are compressed into an extravagantly detailed, slightly miniature landscape, a landscape that seems made for slightly smaller people than those who inhabit it, but which nonetheless encompasses sea, sky, and land. It is a segmented, claustrophobic world wherein the father's boat, the mother's arbor, the enormous dog, the goblins, the proper hats (that seem, after a while, curiously important emblems of order)—all must find their place. Sendak also produces a subtle sense of disorientation by combining different styles on a page. The enormous German shepherd, for example, is drawn in a far more realistic style than the characters, so that when the baby extends her slightly cartoonish hand toward the animal, it is as if she is reaching out toward a creature of a different medium.

The language of the book is disorienting and one suspects that the lack of comedy afflicts it as well. Sendak's picture book prose style is generally characterized by shifting rhythms, movements in and out of rhyme, and much assonance and alliteration, the last being features of allegorical writing, words that sound the same not only providing pleasant aural effects but also suggesting connections between objects signified. The style is apparent in *Wild Things*:

> But the wild things cried, "Oh please don't go—
> we'll eat you up—we love you so!"
> And Max said, "No!"
> The wild things roared their terrible roars and gnashed
> their terrible teeth
> and rolled their terrible eyes and showed their terrible claws
> but Max stepped into his private boat
> and waved good-bye
> and sailed back over a year
> and in and out of weeks
> and through a day
> and into the night of his very own room
> where he found his supper waiting for him
> and it was still hot.[32]

The style is coy and petulant—like Max, and its preciousness is
bearable for that reason.

In *Night Kitchen* the techniques are refined and further exploited,
producing a text that is a kind of playful poem:

> Did you ever hear of Mickey,
> How he heard a racket in the night
> and shouted Quiet Down There
> And fell through the dark, out of his clothes
> past the moon & his mama & papa sleeping tight
> Into the light of the night kitchen?
> Where the bakers who bake till the
> dawn so we can have cake in the morn
> mixed Mickey in batter, chanting:
> Milk in the batter! Milk in the batter!
> Stir it! Scrape it! Make it! Bake it!
> And they put that batter up to bake
> a delicious Mickey-cake.[33]

The narrative moves in and out of small sections of verse, with frequent shifts of rhythm, and while at times the shifts seem capricious,
the overall effect is appealing. Again, it is fitting to Mickey.

The playfulness, however, is missing from *Outside Over There*,
leaving the work with an old, labored syntax that calls attention to
itself continually:

> When Papa was away at sea,
> And Mama in the arbor,
> Ida played her wonder horn
> to rock the baby still—
> but never watched.
> So the goblins came.
> They pushed their way in
> and pulled baby out,
> leaving another all made of ice.
> Poor Ida, never knowing, hugged the changeling
> and she murmured: "How I love you."
> The ice thing only dripped and stared,
> and Ida mad knew goblins had been there.

> "They stole my sister away!" she cried,
> "To be a nasty goblin's bride!"
> Now Ida in a hurry
> snatched her Mama's yellow rain cloak,
> tucked her horn safe in a pocket,
> and made a serious mistake.
> She climbed backwards out her window
> into outside over there.[34]

This borders on verse in a way similar to the text of the other two books, but it is awkward because of its humorlessness and the need for each word in this very abbreviated narrative to function the way the language of poetry does—when much of it simply isn't poetic. The narrative details are presented in a way that suggests an archetypal situation but that also echoes the pretend intimacy of baby talk: "Mama and Papa," "pulled baby out," "the goblins came." And there are lines that are not poetic or musical or significant in any way, lines that simply convey information but by virtue of the strange syntax and fussiness of detail seem to be trying to do more: "Now Ida in a hurry / snatched her Mama's yellow rain cloak."

Recognizing Sendak's allegorical leanings helps one to understand the quality of this writing, with its portentous subtext hinted at, its Freudian themes waiting to be apprehended by the intuitive reader. But one feels uneasiness here that goes beyond the state of mind of a heroine who is just beginning to struggle with the complex relationships of her life. One feels pressure in this work to transcend, to create a picture book more psychologically astute, more complex, more visually dazzling than anything Sendak had done yet, a picture book that adults would embrace as a fine work of art. In some ways Sendak succeeds. The book has its achingly beautiful moments. It is often richer and more risk-taking than anything else around. But it is also overworked, self-conscious, its surface meaning sometimes disturbing and absurd. One needs Sendak's own descriptions of what he has done as a running gloss. The book is also curiously static and bleak, Ida's face often frozen into a bewildered half-smile. The seriousness of her plight seems contrived, so that even while one is moved by this delicately terrifying story and the beauty of its characters, a kind of better judgment frowns on it, distancing one from the work as too melodramatic and manipulative. And there is no release. One looks, in the moment after Ida's struggle, for something to suggest relaxation. But there is nothing there, and when the book ends, its last line "And that is just what Ida did" suggesting resolution, we nevertheless still feel oppressed. Is this the way it is psychologically? Perhaps. But sometimes we all need a break—not happiness ever after, but something to hold onto. It is as great a human need as the need to tell the truth about emotions, and we—particularly children—are left at the end of this work with too much pain.

If it is true, as contemporary critics contend, that allegory grows out of longing, that it expresses the impossibility of ever fully recovering that which we have lost or of fully articulating that loss, then perhaps the sadness of this most recent book of Sendak's is inevitable. Certainly the strain one senses in the work has to do with his need to get ever nearer to some final and immensely complex statement through indirection. But one still hopes that now that the trilogy has been completed and the statement of that trilogy has come as close to being made as it perhaps will be, something more spontaneous will next emerge. For whatever reservations we may have about individual works, Sendak is certainly one of the great children's artists of our time and, given the astonishing fertility and inventiveness of his work to date, I look forward to whatever he has in store.

## Notes

1. Selma G. Lanes, *The Art of Maurice Sendak* (New York: Harry N. Abrams, Inc., 1980), p. 235.

2. "Audacious Fantasist" (review of *The Art of Maurice Sendak*), *New York Times Book Review*, November 9, 1980, p. 47.

3. See Angus Fletcher's discussion of Coleridge's distinction between symbolism and allegory in Fletcher, *Allegory: The Theory of a Symbolic Mode* (1964; rpt. Ithaca: Cornell University Press, 1970), pp. 15ff.

4. Quoted in Paul Alpers, *The Poetry of "The Faerie Queene"* (Princeton: Princeton Univ. Press, 1967), p. 4.

5. Jonathan Culler, *Structuralist Poetics: Structuralism, Linguistics, and the Study of Literature* (1975; rpt. Ithaca: Cornell University Press, 1976), pp. 229–30.

6. Preface to *Allegory and Representation: Selected Papers from the English Institute, 1979–80*, ed. Stephen J. Greenblatt (Baltimore: Johns Hopkins Univ. Press, 1981), pp. vii–viii.

7. Greenblatt, p. viii.

8. Ibid.

9. Lanes, p. 204.

10. Lanes, p. 218.

11. Lanes, p. 227.

12. Quoted in Lanes, p. 227.

13. Fletcher, p. 40. The post-structuralist critics also discuss the psychoanalytic analogues in allegory. See Greenblatt, ed., *Allegory and Representation*.

14. See, for example, Malbecco in Book III of *The Faerie Queene* who is so consumed with jealousy over his wife' infidelity with a band of satyrs that he *becomes* Jealousy:

> There dwels he ever, miserable swaine,
> Hatefull both to him selfe, and every wight:
> Where he through privy griefe, and horrour vaine,
> Is woxen so deformed, that he has quight
> Forgot he was a man, and Gealosie is hight. [III.x.60]

Hugh Maclean, ed., *Edmund Spenser's Poetry* (New York: Norton, 1968), pp. 326–27.

15. Flethcher, p. 35.

16. Lanes, p. 160. There is a picture of Sendak and his mother in Lanes, p. 11. The picture was also the basis for a drawing in the dream in *Fly by Night*.

17. Selma Lanes, p. 162, describes the lion as "representing aggression and destructiveness" and interprets Jennie's action as "nothing less than the rescue of Baby from his own rage and negative impulses"—clearly an allegorical reading.

18. Fletcher, pp. 118–19.

19. *Maurice Sendak's Really Rosie Starring the Nutshell Kids* (New York: Harper & Row, 1975).

20. Lanes, pp. 233–34.

21. Fletcher, p. 253.

22. Pierre, the hero of one of these picturesque works, is, Sendak says, named after Melville's novel, Melville being a hero of Sendak's and another artist working in the allegorical tradition. See Jonathan Cott's interview with Sendak in *Rolling Stone*, December 30, 1976, p. 59, where Sendak says, "It's the two levels of writing—one visible, one invisible—that fascinate me most about Melville. As far down as the whale goes in the water is as deep as Herman writes . . . "

23. See Lanes, p. 92.

24. See Britomart at the Castle of Busyrane in Book III of *The Faerie Queene*:

> And as she lookt about, she did behold,
> How over that same dore was likewise writ,
> *Be bold, be bold,* and every where *Be bold,*
> That much she muzed, yet could not construe it
> By any ridling skill, or commune wit.
> At last she spyde at the roomes upper end,
> Another yron dore, on which was writ,
> *Be not too bold*; whereto though she did bend
> Her earnest mind, yet wist not what it might intend. [III.xi.54]

*Edmund Spenser's Poetry*, p. 339.

25. Lanes, p. 89.

26. See Cott, p. 55.

27. Fletcher, p. 345.

28. In Joel Fineman's essay, "The Structure of Allegorical Desire," he investigates the way in which the "longing" of allegory is created in the opening lines of *The Canterbury Tales*, where the journey to Canterbury is initiated in April: "Thanne longen folk to goon on pilgrimages." He points out that the language and imagery of the opening lines contain the psychological origins of that longing: "Whan that April with his showres soote / The droughte of March hath perced to the roote . . ." In those lines, Fineman says, are embodied the primal sounds "pa" and "ma" and the image of the masculine showers piercing the feminine earth to "engender flowers." He writes:

> With the piercing of March by April, then, the allegorical structure thus enunciated has already lost its center and thereby discovered a project: to recover the loss dis-covered by the structure of language and literature. In thematic terms, this journey back to a foreclosed origin writes itself out as a pilgrimage to the sacred founding shrine, made such by murder, that is the motive of its movement. . . .
>
> Perhaps this is one reason why, as Angus Fletcher has remarked, allegory seems by its nature to be incompletable, never quite fulfilling its grand design. So too, this explains the formal affinity of allegory with obsessional neurosis, which, as Freud develops it in the case of the Wolfman, derives precisely from such a search for lost origins, epitomized in the consequences of the primal scene, which answers the child's question of where he came from with a diacritical solution that he cannot accept and that his neurosis thereupon represses and denies.

Greenblatt, ed., *Allegory and Representation*, p. 44–45. In the primal situation unfolded at the beginning of *Outside Over There*, we find the same language and similar imagery: the longing for "papa" and "mama," now separated, the father associated with water, away at sea, the mother in the arbor, and both inaccessible to Ida, who is feeling isolated and burdened.

29. See Angus Fletcher, *The Prophetic Moment: An Essay on Spenser* (Chicago: Univ. of Chicago Press, 1971), pp. 11ff., and Northrop Frye, "The Structure of Imagery in *The Faerie Queene*," in *Fables of Identity: Studies in Poetic Mythology* (New York: Harcourt, Brace & World, 1963), p. 77.

30. John Gardner, "Fun and Games and Dark Imaginings" (review of *Outside Over There*), *New York Times Book Review*, April 26, 1981, p. 65.

31. Fletcher, p. 379.

32. *Where the Wild Things Are* (New York: Harper & Row, 1963).

33. *In the Night Kitchen* (New York: Harper & Row, 1970).

34. *Outside Over There* (New York: Harper & Row, 1981).

# "For the Instruction of the Young": The Deerfield Captivity Narratives

Alexander Medlicott, Jr.

Our American Puritan ancestors wrote no books to entertain. But they did produce a body of literature that titillated the senses, aroused the passions, and frightened the readers—and they called such tales religious and moral instruction. These stories were the Indian captivity narratives, America's first significant books. Long before the War for Independence, these narratives, rivaled only by John Bunyan's *Pilgrim's Progress*, were the most widely read books in the colonies.[1]

For the most part, Indian captivity narratives were true (or nearly true) accounts of white English colonists who fell into the hands of Indians and were carried into captivity, where the majority suffered physical privation and torture, spiritual humiliation, and psychological traumas. Most of the captives, at least those who survived, returned home after being ransomed by their families and friends. A few remained in captivity, gradually adapting to Indian ways and living out their days among their captors.[2]

Much has been written about Indian captivity narratives as a literary genre. Critics have viewed them as "religious confessional[s]" expressions "of the Frontier Mind," "noisomely visceral thriller[s]," and "propaganda" against Popish influences in the colonies,[3] or more recently as mythic narratives.[4] Historians find them to be valuable as American sagas[5] and as sources of information about the Native American and his cultural milieu. But no one has discussed the Indian capativity narratives as a body of literature which appealed to youthful readers, a literature which in the late seventeenth and early eighteenth centuries catered to a large audience of young readers who longed for excitement, suspense, and terror in much the same way that youth new seek similar stimulation in horror movies, space epics, and neo-gothic romances.

The Indian captivity narratives were not consciously designed for youthful readers. Yet the authors continually appealed to their readers to see the horrors of captivity in Biblical terms that re-affirmed their dependence upon a parental God. Both captives and readers were, after all, the children of Israel; and the slaughters of innocent children are vividly portrayed. No readers of Mrs. Mary Rowlandson's ordeal could be unaffected by her graphic account of the destruction of Lancaster, Massachusetts, the subsequent savagery against its inhabitants, and the image she drew of children being torn from their parents: "The Indians laid hold of us, pulling me one way, and the children another. . . ."[6] Nor could any reader be blind to the parallels which the Reverend John Williams drew be-tween the massacre at Deerfield, Massachusetts, and the Scriptural lessons he employed in the introduction to his famed *"The Redeemed Captive Returning to Zion*: *"For I fear him* [the heathen Indian] *lest he will come and smite me, and the mother with the children.*[7] Whereas such narratives were not specifically intended for young people, they served as moral lessons for generations of adolescent readers. Both Mrs. Rowlandson's and the Reverend Mr. Williams's narra-tives (to cite two of the most famous of the genre), then, were jeremiads—extended sermons warning the colonists against their loss of faith.

In the nineteenth century, however, the focus on backsliding and sin blurs somewhat in the Indian captivity narratives. In some mea-sure, the narrative as religious tract or moral lesson lost its appeal to readers less pious than their Puritan brethren of a century or two earlier. Roy Harvey Pearce argues that the captivity narrative had gradually become a "pulp thriller"[8] rather than a factual account to document the harsh realities of frontier existence. A great many of the narratives, particularly as Americans moved West to encounter other Indian tribes and perils, were downright fraudulent; they were simply colorful, lively accounts designed to turn a dollar for their authors and to satisfy more "civilized" readers who still hungered for gory tales of life on the expanding American frontier. But the Deerfield accounts remained more than mere "pulp thrillers." The popularity of these narratives as instructional tales is evident in works such as the Reverend Titus Strong's retelling of the Reverend John Williams's ordeal, *The Deerfield Captive*, which appeared in several editions between 1832 and 1837. Strong's little book is subtitled "For the Instruction of the Young,"[9] an indication that his narrative was written for a more youthful audience than the 1707 original. As we shall see, however, both accounts of the Deerfield massacre has similar didactic intentions and employed similar literary devices.

Fascination with the Deerfield massacre continued into the twentieth century. The travail of the Reverend Mr. Williams's son Stephen, as well as others taken captive in the Deerfield raid, became the subject of two very popular books at the beginning of this century: Mary P. Wells Smith's *Boy Captive of Old Deerfield* (1904) and its sequel, *The Boy Captive in Canada* (1905).[10] *The Boy Captive of Old Deerfield* might be termed a historical novel. Although it relies heavily on the facts of the Deerfield massacre and the capture of its inhabitants, the horrors of looting, pillage, scalping, torture, forced winter marches, and long captivity became exaggerated into romance. Moreover, the narrative is no longer a thinly disguised religious tract or extended sermon. Rather, as the title suggests, it is a book aimed squarely at the youthful audience—one that would see the Indian and his captive as romantic figures, thanks in large measure to the romances of James Fenimore Cooper and the dime novels of the American West. No longer an actual threat to the white man at the turn of the century, the Native American began to emerge in literature as a figure developed from Rousseau, Cooper, and the American artists who painted the "savages" as noble beings, wise in the ways of the woods and the streams.[11] In short, the American Indian captivity narrative had passed from the realm of religious persuasion to that of popular, romantic fiction.

## II

The Deerfield saga, then, represents a paradigm of the changing emphasis on Indian capitivity narratives between 1707 and the early decades of the twentieth century. In order to see this change more clearly, we must know something of the Deerfield raid, of Rev. John Williams and his family, and of the subsequent fate of the captives. What happened at Deerfield is in part an allegorical history of Puritan New England—a tale of the soul held in bondage by agents of the devil, of the enslavement of the Israelites in a wilderness of temptation and sin, and of the miraculous salvation of God's lost children. Such episodes are, of course, the fit stuff of allegorical interpretation.

They are also the wellspring of a body of American literature that became engrossing fare for a vast reading public, especially the young. The Deerfield massacre was one of colonial New England's most dramatic moments, and lent itself to heroic retellings. And each of the four Indian captivity narratives from three separate centuries that focus on Deerfield—Rev. John William's *The Redeemed Captive Returning to Zion*, Rev. Titus Strong's *The Deerfield Captive*, and Mrs. Mary P. Wells Smith's *The Boy Captive of Old Deerfield* and *The Boy Captive in Canada*—combines its narrative flair with a focus on Christian piety and moral endurance.

The sack of Deerfield, and the subsequent capture, slaughter, and travail of its inhabitants, has now become a New England legend.[12] Nearly three centuries separate that event from our time. Yet the literature it has spawned and the continual historical interest it continues to arouse expand that one brief moment in colonial history into an event of epic scale. It all began in the winter of 1703/04, a particularly bitter one, even by New England standards. Snow had fallen steadily throughout January and February.[13] Alternating thaws and freezes has turned the snow to ice. Several days before the raid on Deerfield, it had rained; then the weather turned frigid and the snow that had drifted up against the settlement's stockade formed one long ramp—a ramp hard enough to support the weight of many men.

Before daybreak on the morning of February 29, 1703/04, two hundred Abnaki and Caughnawaga Indians, supported and led by fifty French soldiers from Canada, arrived in the meadowlands just north of Deerfield. Sensing immediately that the stockade wall was unmanned (the guards had left their posts early that night, convinced there was no danger of mischief in such weather), the French commander split his forces, sending one large band of Indians against the homes outside the stockade and the rest against the homes inside the wall. The attackers easily scurried over the snow crusted against the stockade, dropped down behind the palisades, and turned against the ten houses that surrounded the Deerfield meetinghouse. What the Indians were assigned to do they did quickly and brutally. Twenty Abnakis smashed through the door of the Williams parsonage, fanned out through the house, and quickly subdued and bound the Reverend Mr. Williams, his family, and the servants. The minister's two youngest children (six-year-old John and the baby, Jerusha, less than a month old) were killed immediately, as was Parentha, the family's Negro servant. Their bodies lay in the snow while the other settlement captives were herded into the lee of the meetinghouse. Around the terrified prisoners, Deerfield burned ferociously. Those homes not already in flames were being stripped of their contents.

Outside the stockade the settlers fared no better. In spite of sporadic resistance from a few well-fortified houses, the town of Deerfield had been all but wiped out by dawn. Of the original forty-one homes there, only twenty-four remained standing. Fifty-four townspeople sprawled dead in the snow or in the ashes of their homes. Plunder lay everywhere. The last buildings destroyed in Deerfield that morning were Rev. John Williams's home and barn. What had once been the most northern English settlement in the Connecticut Valley now lay devastated.

Shortly after daybreak on March 1, the long trek into Canada began for more than a hundred Deerfield prisoners. The horrors of what they had seen in their town were compounded on the journey north by what they were told awaited them in the "popish country" (*RC*, p. 13) of Quebec, three hundred and fifty miles away.

Less than an hour after the captive train began its march, a suckling child—considered excess baggage by the Indians—was thrown into a camp fire. That night, buoyed up by their incredible successes at Deerfield, the Indians burned at the stake the Reverend Mr. Williams's Negro servant, Frank. And the following day, Williams's wife, Eunice, weakened by the recent birth of her daughter Jerusha, plunged through the ice while fording the Green River, a few miles north of Greenfield, Massachusetts. She was wet, chilled, and unable to continue the march: "the cruel and bloodthirsty savage, who took her captive, slew her with his hatchet, at one stroke" (*RC*, p. 19). A day later, when the captives reached

The massacre at Deerfield. From *An Unredeemed Captive* by Clifton Johnson, published in 1897.

The capture of the Reverend John Williams, from *The Deerfield Captive, An Indian Story* by Titus Strong, published in 1834.

the French and Indian supply depot at the confluence of the Connecticut and West rivers (north of present-day Brattleboro, Vermont), a few of the wounded attackers and several prisoners were loaded on dogsleds and carried north on the ice of the Connecticut River. More of the weaker captives were slain.

On Sunday, five days and more than forty miles from Deerfield, the captives arrived just north of what is now the town of Bellows Falls, Vermont. There, for the first time in a week, the Indians relaxed their guard and allowed the Reverend Mr. Williams to preach to his flock. Appropriately, he chose a passage from Lamentations as his sermon text: "The Lord is righteous, for I have rebelled against his commandment: Hear, I pray you, all people, and behold my sorrow: My virgins and my young men are gone into captivity" (Lam. 1. 18). Then the captives gathered on the bank of the Connecticut at the mouth of what is now known as the Williams River and sang a psalm. After the services, however, the Indians killed a dozen women and children, weak from the cold and hunger.

By Wednesday, the captives were at the mouth of the White River of New Hampshire, forty miles north of the Williams River. Here, two more women were slain and the Williams family was separated. Ten-year-old Stephen Williams remained with his Indian captors, as did five-year-old Warham; Rev. John Williams, his two daughters, Eunice and Esther, and a son, Samuel, headed off over a route familiar to other Indian captives: up the White River, north across the foothills of the Green Mountains to Lake Champlain, then along the Richelieu River to the St. Lawrence, and eastward to Montreal, where the Reverend Mr. Williams was quickly ransomed by Phillipe de Rigaud, Marquis de Vaudril, Governor General of Canada. The other Williams captives (with the exception of daughter Eunice) were ransomed later. Esther was released to the colonies in the spring of 1705; Stephen came home in the early autumn of 1706; Samuel and Warham arrived with their father in Boston in November of the same year. Rev. John Williams returned to Deerfield to "look after his sheep in the wilderness"[14] that winter, where the town had agreed to rebuild the meetinghouse and erect a suitable home for him. A few years later he remarried.

Eunice, ten years old by the time her father, sister, and brothers were redeemed, remained in Canada. At sixteen she converted to Catholicism and married an Indian at St. Francis. For many years she continued to be the object of repeated attempts to "rescue" her from her life among the savages. Although she never returned to the colonies permanently, she did make several trips south to visit friends and relatives. When she died about 1786, she had outlived all the members of her family and every one of the captives taken in the Deerfield raid.

Captivity for Rev. John Williams was relatively easy, compared to the hardships suffered by so many English captives. Although he was continually threatened with death if he did not attend Mass and kiss the crucifix and warned repeatedly that he would never see his children alive if he refused to "stay among the French and be of their religion" (*RC*, p. 66), he was not subjected to any physical abuse. For young Stephen Williams, however, captivity was far more terrifying, as any such ordeal must have been for a ten-year-old separated from his family and friends and held in bondage by a race that he had been taught since birth were agents of the devil in his Christian world. Yet such an ordeal had all the earmarks of an experience that could not help but appeal to an adolescent audience. Such harrowing adventures supplied the realistic foundations upon which countless literary narratives of Indian captivity have been built.

After leaving his father, sisters, and brother at the White River, Stephen was forced northward at a staggering pace through the lower Cowass (now Newbury, Vermont), along the River Richelieu past Fort Anne to Chambly, just east of Montreal. From Chambly—it was now July—young Stephen pressed on to Sorel, a small settlement at the mouth of the Richelieu. Then he moved northward again to St. Francis, an Indian fort at the juncture of the St. Lawrence and St. Francis rivers. By this time, all attempts to ransom the boy had ended. He spent the rest of that summer and the autumn gathering firewood for the Indian encampment. From what he wrote of his captivity years later, Stephen Williams had abandoned all hope of ever returning to the colonies, for "I was as it were at the brink of eternity." Only God, he wrote, "stayed the hands of those that took up their weapons to slay me with."[15]

Finally, after sixteen months among the Indians—months of constant movement, harrassment, and fear—Stephen Williams was ransomed for forty crowns. On May 11, 1706, he and his father were reunited at the town of Chateauriche for the first time since they had prayed together on the banks of the White and Connecticut rivers, almost two years earlier. By the time Stephen had reached Boston after "a tedious voyage"[16] of forty days aboard an English brigantine, twenty months had passed since that night in Deerfield.

Such was the ordeal suffered by one of the families taken at Deerfield, similar to many such adventures experienced by the New England colonists. It was the Williams's trial, however, that was soon shared by hundreds of New England readers through the pages of Williams's *The Redeemed Captive Returning to Zion* and the several significant retellings of the tale in the centuries after the Deerfield raid.

## III

*The Redeemed Captive Returning to Zion*, first published in 1707, is the most authoritative account of the Deerfield massacre and its aftermath. Although it lacks the brisk pace and the terseness of Mrs. Rowlandson's seventeenth century account of the Lancaster raid, it chronicles a far longer captivity than hers with the same sense of allegorical vision that most early examples of this genre employ. Perhaps it is Mrs. Rowlandson's three months' captivity that accounts for the crispness of her account; the Reverend John Williams's captivity lasted for almost two years, and thus the immediacy and suspense conveyed in her narrative are missing from his.

At the very outset of *The Redeemed Captive*, Williams establishes the tone and the aim of his book: it is a somber work. Its aim is didactic:

> The history I am going to write, proves, that days of fasting and prayer, without reformation, will not avail to turn away the anger of God from a professing people; and yet witnesseth, how very advantageous, gracious supplications are, to prepare particular Christians, patiently to suffer the will of God, in very trying public calamities. [*RC*, p. 7]

What happened between the destruction of Deerfield and the Reverend Mr. Williams's redemption is detailed precisely and sprinkled with appropriate parallels drawn between his ordeal in the New England forests and French Canadian settlements and that of the wandering tribes of Israel. A few days after Deerfield was taken, for example, the captives were allowed to rest at the Williams River, where Williams preached his sermon from Lamentations. Shortly after this, when the pastor had time to consider his plight, he once again signaled his resolve to endure by summoning up the words from two psalms and a passage from Nehemiah, passages that recalled the suffering of the Israelites:

> *I shall not die, but live: And declare the works of the Lord.* Psalm xlii.
> II. *Why art thou cast down, O my soul? And why art thou disquieted within me? Hope thou in God; for I shall praise him, who is the health of my countenance, and my God.* Nehem. i. 8, 9. [RC, pp. 27–28]

Those segments taken from *The Redeemed Captive* which deal with the Reverend Mr. Williams's long imprisonment among the French in Canada are less graphic than his account of the early days of his captivity, and thus the pace of his narrative is uneven. But the main thrust of this latter part of *The Redeemed Captive* is clearly intended to reveal how the English hostages fared among those of the "Romish faith" (*RC*, p. 83), for soon after the captives had begun their long trek from Deerfield they were separated and parcelled out to various Indians from a number of French-Canadian villages. The struggle for life under an Indian hatchet is the stuff of dramatic and terrifying literature; the struggle of the soul under intimidating "Romanists" (*RC*, p. 119) became for Williams as dramatic and terrifying as the physical ordeal which the English colonists suffered in those bleak hours and days after the Deerfield raid.

The ordeal suffered by Samuel Williams, the minister's fifteen-year-old son, is a case in point. When the Deerfield captives were separated from one another at the White River in late February, young Samuel was taken to a small French village several hundred miles west of Montreal, where his father and a number of other captives were being held. There Samuel was alternately abused and cajoled by his captors in an attempt to get the boy to adopt their "Romish faith." At one point they threatened to return him to his Indian masters (far harsher in their treatment of captives than where were the French themselves), and at another time he was whipped by a device made from "three branches, with about twelve great knots tied in it" (*RC*, p. 90). Then he was bade to make "the sign of the cross" (*RC*, p. 91). When he failed to do that, even though he "shed many tears" (*RC*, p. 91), and would not submit to a French school and its language, he was forced to kneel and "so kept . . . for an hour and a half" (*RC*, p. 91).

While such brainwashing ordeals seem less dramatic than the slaughter at Deerfield and the awful march through the snow and the cold, contemporary readers of Rev. John Williams's narrative must have shuddered at his tales of the body and soul in double jeopardy: on the one hand stood the Indians, ever ready to turn their savage wrath against their captives; on the other hovered the equally terrifying specter of the loss of faith in an alien wilderness, miles from what Williams called "God's sanctuary" (*RC*, p.13) in the New England colonies. To a youthful reader, the pain described in such ordeals must have struck home. Children in the American colonies, nurtured as they were on the Calvinistic theory of infant damnation (dramatized in Michael Wigglesworth's *Day of Doom*), could easily identify with youthful Samuel Williams's fears: eternal damnation in hell for a loss of faith, and the endless agony of life among the devil's emissaries in the forests of French Canada. Such narratives as *The Redeemed Captive* might well have served the parents of recalcitrant children both as instructional books and as warnings: unchristian behavior would send a child to hell. Or to the Indians! It is little wonder, then, that the children in the New England colonies found the Indian captivity narratives so deliciously appealing—appealing in the same way that many children in any age enjoy such tales of terror and suspense.

The Reverend Titus Strong's nineteenth century version of the Deerfield massacre adheres closely to the facts surrounding the destruction of the town and the murder and captivity of its inhabitants. But because it is a secondhand (and third person) account of the incident, it loses much of the verisimilitude of the original. It does, of course, like its predecessor, function as an extended sermon on the nature of evil and a warning against such sins as moral slackness, wavering faith, and false pride.[17] These were the sins that both the Rev. Mr. Williams and the Reverend Mr. Strong imply led to the destruction of Deerfield. Strong is blatant about his intent in the book. It is, as part of the subtitle reads, "intended for the instruction and improvement of children and youth," a document written with a "moral and religious tendency" which is perfectly suited for "Sunday as well as other schools" (*DC*, p. 5).

At the very outset of *The Deerfield Captive*, the author calls the attention of his "young readers" (*DC*, p. 6) to other books which deal with the French and Indian Wars, books which he hopes they have read "with attention and profit" (*DC*, p. 10) for those who would take away that what was rightfully theirs:

> In a great measure [it was the English settlers'] own fault, that the Indians were led to wage war against them. They had seated themselves in a country which the latter supposed entirely to themselves; and in consequence of a few imprudent acts, which carried the appearance of injustice and cruelty, there was a general disposition and desire among the tribes to obtain revenge by exterminating the intruders.
>
> It was a great mistake with the white people who first settled in New England, to suppose that like the ancient Jews who invaded the land of Canaan, they acted by divine authority, and had a right to drive out the inhabitants and inherit their possessions.
>
> And we need not wonder that the Indians, when they found themselves wronged and deceived; deprived of their hunting grounds, and banished from the banks of their pleasant streams, would be filled with madness, and determine, at once, to destroy their oppressors. [*DC*, pp. 10–12].

Although Strong balances such justification in his narrative with accounts of Indian barbarity and the pagan nature or their lives, he concludes that the Indians "were rather to be pitied than to be blamed" (*DC*, p. 15).[18]

In chapter 4 of *The Deerfield Captive*, he focuses on the raid and

The murder of Eunice Williams, from Titus Strong's *Deerfield Captive*.

those taken captive there, interrupting his account from time to time for pious instruction, warnings, and pithy moral lessons, including his admonition against the "many books which are intended to convey instruction by fictitious narratives" (*DC*, p. 30). Nor does he lose too many chances to turn his own narrative into a sermon. For example, shortly after the murder of Eunice Williams at the Green River (which he claims happened in full view of her surviving children and husband), the Reverend Mr. Strong notes:

> But what shall we think of the children who are now in the hands of the cruel Indians? They had seen their dear mother killed in a moment, and they knew that their father was wholly unable to help them.—In the midst of a dreary wilderness; with painted savages for their conductors, and not knowing whither they were to be carried, how must their young hearts have been

filled with the most dreadful apprehensions and alarms!

We will venture to hope that they were good children, and that, in this day of trouble, they did not forget the pious instructions which they had received from their parents. [*DC*, pp. 36–37]

And to draw parallels between this history of a family's captivity and the lives of Rev. Titus Strong's contemporaries, he relates the same tale of young Samuel Williams being whipped by his captors for failing to convert to Catholicism, as taken from the original account:

It may be that some of my young friends who read this story are at school, away from their parents. How different is their condition from that in which this poor boy was placed! They are permitted to read their Bibles and to worship GOD in spirit and in truth. And how diligent ought they to be in improving their opportunities! Let them consider what their feelings would be if they were subject to such trials as the poor captive children endured in Canada, and remember that it is owing to the goodness of GOD that they are so highly favored in a land of liberty, with all the means of moral and religious instruction. [*DC*, p. 63]

Finally, in keeping with a long-standing tradition of didacticism in colonial American literature, the Reverend Mr. Strong ties up the loose ends of his narrative with an all-encompassing moral lesson:

When you read this story, I hope, my young friends, that you will not forget to thank GOD for giving you kind parents and a good home. Read about the sufferings of others and remember you own enjoyments. And as you know not what may be your lot hereafter, endeavor, now in your youth, to fortify your minds with the principles of virtue and religion, so that whatever may happen to you, you will be able to put your trust in GOD, and to hold fast the blessings of a good conscience. [*RC*, pp. 67–68]

Mrs. Mary P. Wells Smith's early twentieth-century renderings of the Deerfield saga, aimed directly at a youthful audience, are a blend of fact and fiction. The historical facts of the raid and its aftermath are essentially accurate, but her narrative of Stephen Williams in Canadian captivity is heavily romanticized.

*The Boy Captive of Old Deerfield* contains a great many vestiges of the literary Puritan world. In the preface of this book, Mrs. Smith admonishes her readers to remember the moral fiber of their ancestors, reminding them of the "contrast between the lives of children in the Connecticut valley today and those of their ancestors two centuries ago" (*BC*, p. vii). She alludes also to the "demand for heroism, self-denial, and devotion on those living in it." If "the children of today would serve their time faithfully," she continues, "and leave this world a little better because they were born into it, they will need something of the same steadfastness and unwavering religious faith which enabled Stephen Williams and other young captives to endure the most incredible hardships which befell them" (*BC*, p. viii).

What follows is an attempt to sketch the raw outlines of history, but the work is marred by stilted dialogue, stereotypical characters, and too much attention to extraneous detail. For all those shortcomings, however, it is a book filled with enough incidents of courage, hairbreadth escapes, moments of suspense, and vignettes of loyalty and affection to seduce an adult reader as cunningly as a more youthful reader would be seduced by a novel of James Fenimore Cooper, William Gilmore Simms, or Owen Wister. And just below the surface of the reality of captivity and the romance of frontier life in *The Boy Captive* lies a vein of piety which puts the book firmly into the tradition of the religious and moral instruction manuals which informed earlier examples of this genre. Most important, however, Smith's Deerfield captivity series was designed as adventure stories written specifically for young boys and girls. Whatever Mrs. Smith might have said about morals and faith, she was first a writer of historical fiction who directed her work at an audience she knew would respond to thrilling tales of their Puritan ancestors.

As the novel moves forward and he is taken deeper into French-Canadian captivity, Stephen Williams displays more and more of those traditional frontier traits which endear him to us. He is self-sacrificing, brave, hardy, resourceful, and compassionate. And when the ordeal of the forced march and captivity seems to overwhelm him and his fellow captives, Stephen's stoicism and innate strength of character place him firmly in the American frontier spirit—a spirit that Mrs. Smith suggests every young reader should try to emulate. Part of this spirit, of course, is man's devotion to God. Nowhere in the novel does Mrs. Smith lose the opportunity to preach, usually through the words and thoughts of her young protagonist. In moments of great anguish, for example, Stephen speaks more like his father in the pulpit than he does like a ten-year-old from a tiny New England village: "'I must not forget now what father had always told me,' thought the boy. 'God is here. He can see me now, just as plainly as if I were at home in my own bed in Deerfield'"(*BC*, p. 163). Although he cannot "help crying a little at this thought," he "bravely repress[es] his grief" (*BC*, p. 163).

Moments like these reveal one of the major weaknesses of *The Boy Captive*: it is filled with dialogue more fitted to romantic fiction than to a realistic account of a New England town. But Mrs. Smith is not guilty of turning Stephen Williams into her sole spokesman for colonial values and piety. Everyone in the novel speaks the same way. Her account of the death of Eunice Williams offers a typical example. Her strength sapped by all that she has endured, Mrs. Williams is slain by her captor on the banks of the Green River. The Reverend Mr. Williams is told of the murder by a deacon of his church. The minister's response is stilted romanticizing and sounds remarkably like Prince Hamlet's first soliloquy, in which he speaks of his father's tender love for Queen Gertrude:

> Mr. Williams burst into tears. For the time, his agony seemed unbearable. That his beloved wife, whom he had cherished so tenderly, whom he would gladly have shielded lest even a rough breath of wind blow on her too rudely, should be slain thus remorselessly while alone among her enemies, her body left a prey to wild beasts! [*BC*, p. 109]

His Indian captor responds to this show of emotion with words that smack of a blend of Cooper's Maquas and the Apaches and Cheyennes of the dime Western novel:

> [The Indian] gazed on [Williams's] grief with infinite disgust and contempt.
>
> "The English are not better than squaws," he said. "Even an Indian papoose would be ashamed to weep like the pale-face father." And binding on Mr. Williams's pack again, he drove him along. [*BC*, p. 109]

The Reverend John Williams's reply to this incident is vintage Puritan sermonizing:

> "O God, I pray thee, suffer not my faith to fail me in this hour of sore need. She is at rest, released from her sufferings and fears. . . . My faith staggers under this weight of anguish. Strengthen me, I pray thee, for the sake of my poor children, and all these afflicted ones, who look to me as their guide and helper. [*BC*, pp. 109–10]

Another weakness in *The Boy Captive* lies in Mrs. Smith's propensity to give names to all the Indians in the novel and to refer to Stephen Williams by a name she imagined his captors might have called him. Thus "Walahowey," "Kewakcum," "Mummumcott," "Oioteet," "Suckkeecoo," and "Teokunhko" are some of the names given to the ferocious Indians who sacked Deerfield—every name a figment of Mrs. Smith's imagination. And "Cosannip" is the name she chooses to have the Indians call Stephen Williams throughout the novel. There is, of course, no authentic historical evidence behind these names, but because Mrs. Smith was writing for a special audience of young people, the names fall comfortably on the ear and ring as true as Cooper's "Chingachgook" and William Gilmore Simm's "Sanutee."

The long-lasting appeal of *The Boy Captive*, however, lies in Mrs. Smith's focus on young Stephen Williams as an identifiable lad from America's romantic past. In her eyes he *is* American youth: a highly stylized and romanticized youth with all the appeal of a Norman Rockwell illustration or a poster of the American Boy Scout. Prior to his capture by the Indians, for example, Stephen's life in Deerfield is depicted as a model of Christian piety and social grace. But rather than paint her hero as a goody-goody, Mrs. Smith allows him a few youthful pranks and an occasional display of rebellion. In most matters relating to his colonial family and town Stephen Williams is Everyboy.

For all these minor flaws, *The Boy Captive of Old Deerfield* found a large and appreciative audience when it first appeared in 1904, and the book has now gone through more than ten editions, is still in print, and sells briskly. And well it should, for among those early twentieth-century narratives of America's colonial period, and among those tales of Indian captivity, few can compare with it. Moreover, its rather nice blend of historical fact and historical fiction, coupled with the fascination that so many readers find in tales of Indian capture, bondage, and escape, makes *The Boy Captive of Old Deerfield* a remarkably contemporary book.[19]

Although it did not appear in as many editions as did *The Boy Captive of Old Deerfield*, Mrs. Smith's sequel, *The Boy Captive in Canada*, is in some ways a better book. What it lacks is the high drama of the former, which contains all the ingredients basic to Indian captivity narratives: the raid; the capture, pillage, and destruction of the town; the slaughter of its defenders; the long march into captivity. Hundreds of other American captivity narratives are built on these same elements. *Canada*, on the other hand, is appealing because of the information it contains—information on the lore of the wilderness and on Indian life and customs. *Canada* is a book of facts, a "how-to" book. Young readers can learn the techniques employed by the Indians to fish in summer and winter, jack a deer at night, build a dugout canoe, chip arrowheads from slabs of flint, stay warm in the winter, avoid mosquitoes in the summer, and turn animal hides into clothing, bow strings, and thongs. Readers can also learn how the Indians gambled (and why they did), played games, engaged in their own religious ceremonies, and spent their idle time in the Canadian wilderness.

*Canada* is also a narrative of a boy's painful growth from youth to maturity. The "rites of passage" theme is, of course, focused primarily on Stephen Williams, but Mrs. Smith emphasizes the same theme in her portrayal of the young Indian boys who are Stephen's captors, teachers and companions. As Mrs. Smith tells it, Stephen's long ordeal in bondage gives him ample opportunity to evaluate the natural, primitive life he is forced to lead and the none-too-subtle blandishments of his Indian masters and the Jesuit priests who hover about him, ever ready to ensnare his soul for the Catholic Church. Throughout his captivity, Stephen seems to be preparing himself for his future life among his own people. Even though Mrs. Smith dramatizes his torments, frustrations, dreams of home and freedom, and the horror at the anguish of his fellow prisoners, *Canada* is a novel of romantic visions and passages rich in praise of life in what every Puritan writer described as "the howling wilderness." Such an education as Stephen receives, "daily harder and more unendurable" (*BCC*, p. 179) to bear, fitted the young man for the long and vigorous life he led after his return to the colonies. Indeed, Stephen Williams's sixty-six-year tenure as pastor at Longmeadow, Massachusetts, was among the lengthiest recorded in the annals of the Connecticut Valley Congregational Church.

It is hard to categorize *Canada* as a compassionate novel, for it contains too many incidents of physical cruelty and psychological trauma. But Mrs. Smith portrays many of the French and Indians in a more favorable light here than she did in *The Boy Captive of Old Deerfield*. A number of French women, soldiers, and Quebec merchants, for example, speak out against the kind of warfare being waged by the Indians against the English settlements to the south. "It is terrible, what the Indian allies do" among the colonial villages, says a French soldier at one of the forts where Stephen Williams is held in bondage. His wife replies, "It will bring a curse on New France!" (*BCC*, pp. 91–92). And when Stephen and his father are finally reunited at Quebec, the Reverend Mr. Williams tells his son of a compassionate Jesuit who "abhorred the course of his government in sending the heathen down to commit ravages against the English people, and said it was more like committing murders than managing a war" (*BCC*, pp. 235–36). Even Mrs. Smith's young Indians, taught since birth to exhibit no emotion, openly express their remorse and humanity when "Cosannip" says goodbye to his captors when he is ransomed.

All the weaknesses found in *The Boy Captive of Old Deerfield* are evident in *The Boy Captive in Canada*. Young Stephen speaks like a mature adult. Mrs. Smith's Indians speak like racial stereotypes. "Deer plenty here," says an Indian hunter. "Venison taste heap good" (*BCC*, p. 35). Ignorance and superstition are everywhere rampant in her portrayal of the Indians, and "Sagamore George," a name Mrs. Smith assigns to Stephen's most brutal captor, winds up in a French jail after his bout with the perennial nemesis of all caricatured Indians, firewater.

These flaws, however, don't seriously detract from the novel. Its pace is lively; the scraps of cultural, historical, and social lore sprinkled throughout give it a richness not so evident in *The Boy Captive of Old Deerfield*. Stephen William's long captivity, often as dreary as it is frightening, is suspenseful, and the young captive's reunion with his sister and father is delivered in passages of genuine emotion and artistic skill. And Mrs. Smith's intent—to portray a young boy coming to maturity while in the grasp of a feared and hated enemy, and to emphasize that such maturity is due in large measure to the youth's Christian fortitude—makes this novel a more successful literary statement of growth.

A French soldier, watching the arrival of Stephen Williams at Quebec after almost two years among the Indians, speaks for Mrs. Smith when he says, "Voila, le pauvre Anglois! Un autre captif de Guerfiel. . . ." (*BCC*, p. 216). Poor Englishman indeed. But throughout his suffering and loneliness, Stephen Williams emerges as the stalwart lad of American literary romanticism—and as the appealing protagonist of two remarkably readable tales of the New England frontier.

Thus, for a period of time longer than America has been a nation, the dramatic story of Deerfield and its destruction has served as a model for an enduring series of Indian captivity narratives. While the first Deerfield captivity narrative was written primarily to allegorize men's lives in the howling wilderness, it served as well as a literary document to instruct the young in the wondrous, and often irrational, ways of their Puritan God. In succeeding generations, however, the purely religious intent found the Reverend John William's account was replaced by a message more appropriate to the adolescent audience it sought to instruct and to entertain. By the twentieth century, the Deerfield saga attracted readers nurtured on a body of romantic literature which strove to keep alive the history and the heritage of America's past, rather than to employ it as an extended allegory of God's chosen people laboring in the vineyards of a New Jerusalem. What originally began as a New England pastor's graphic account of the destruction of his town and flock gradually became a thrilling, and highly instructive, yarn to be read by those already thrilled with the romances of America's frontier writers. Morever, the Indian captivity narratives reached an even larger audience by appealing as much to youthful readers as they did to adults, and by moving away from sober moral counsel to downright entertainment. Our American Puritan ancestors would not have approved.

## Notes

1. In the last two decades of the seventeenth century, and in the first two of the eighteenth, the most widely read books in the American colonies were Mrs. Mary Rowlandsons's *The Soveraignty & Goodness of God, Together with the Faithfulness of His Promises Displayed: Being a Narrative of the Captivity and Restauration of Mrs. Mary Rowlandson* (c. 1662), Jonathan Dickinson's *Journals: or God's Protecting Providence* (1699), and the Reverend John Williams's *The Redeemed Captive Returning to Zion* (1707). See James D. Hart, *The Popular Book* (Berkeley and Los Angeles: University of California Press, 1963), pp. 41–42, 302.

2. Alexander Medlicott, Jr., "Return to This Land of Light: A Plea to an Unredeemed Captive," *New England Quarterly*, 38 (1966), 206–16.

3. Roy Harvey Pearce, "The Significance of the Captivity Narrative," *American Literature*, 19 (1947), 1, 20.

4. Richard Van Der Beets, "The Indian Captivity Narrative as Ritual," *American Literature*, 43 (1972), 548–62.

5. Phillips D. Carleton, "The Indian Captivity," *American Literature*, 15 (1943), 180.

6. *The Captivity & Deliverance of Mr. John Williams, Pastor of Deerfield, and Mrs. Rowlandson of Lancaster, who were taken, together with their families and neighbors, by the French and Indians, and carried to Canada. Written by Themselves* (Brookfield, MA, 1811), p. 6 (misnumbered as p. 9).

7. John Williams, *The Redeemed Captive Returning to Zion, or The Captivity and Deliverance of Rev. John Williams of Deerfield*, 8th ed. (1707; rpt. Springfield, MA: The H. R. Huntting Co., 1908), p. 7. Subsequent references are to this edition and appear parenthetically in the text as *RC*.

8. Pearce, p. 20.

9. The Reverend Titus Strong, *The Deerfield Captive, an Indian Story: being a Narrative of Facts, for the Instruction of the Young*, 2nd ed. (Greenfield, MA, 1834). Subsequent references are to this edition and appear parenthetically in the text as *DC*.

10. Mary P. Wells Smith, *The Boy Captive of Old Deerfield* (Boston: Little, Brown, and Company, 1904), and *The Boy Captive in Canada* (Little, Brown, and Company, 1905). These editions are referred to as "The Old Deerfield Series" and were two of four novels written by Mrs. Smith on the town and its inhabitants. Subsequent references are to these editions and appear parenthetically in the text as *BC* and *BCC*.

11. The idea that the Indians were no longer a threat to the white man is best summed up in the words of Moss Coit Tyler, the nineteenth-century American historian: "To us, of course, the American Indian is no longer a mysterious or even an interesting personage—he is simply a fierce dull biped standing in our way." (*A History of American Literature: 1607–1765* [New York: G. P. Putnam's Sons, 1893], p. 10).

12. The history of the Deerfield massacre is found in a number of sources. Among

the most authoritative are: C. Alice Baker, *True Stories of New England Captives* (Greenfield, MA: E. A. Hall & Co., 1897); George Sheldon, *A History of Deerfield*, 2 vols. (Greenfield, MA: E. A. Hall & Co., 1895, vol. 1; and Emma Lewis Coleman, *New England Captives Carried to Canada*, 2 vols. (Portland, ME, 1925).

13. The dates are, of course, according to the Julian Calendar or Old Style.

14. John Langdon Sibley, *Biographical Sketches of Graduates of Harvard University*, (Cambridge: Harvard Univ. Press, 1885), 3, 257.

15. George Sheldon, ed., *What Befell Stephen Williams in his Captivity* (Greenfield, MA: E. A. Hall & Co., 1889), p. 12.

16. Ibid.

17. The Reverend Titus Strong (1787–1855) was minister of the St. James Episcopal Church in Greenfield, Massachusetts, for forty-one years. In his time he was known as a poet of some stature and as the author of "several popular school books." He was given honorary degrees by Dartmouth and Williams colleges. See Francis M. Thompson, *History of Greenfield*, 2 vols. (Greenfield, MA: T. Morey & Son, 1904), 1, 488–90; 2 1194–95; and the *Greenfield Gazette*, February 1, 1892, pp. 17 and 19.

18. It is interesting that all the captivity narratives that focus on Deerfield contain similar attitudes toward the Indians. From *The Redeemed Captive* to *The Boy Captive in Canada*, the Native American is portrayed as ruthless, cunning, and vicious. However "noble" he might have been in the late nineteenth-century and early twentieth-century romances, his image as it appears in the Deerfield story is uniformly that of dark or satanic romance: a grinning, painted savage, bent on pillage, greed, torture, and the fulfillment of his own animal desires. Only Rev. Titus Strong offers some sympathy for and understanding of the Indians and their way of life. But one comes away from even his account with visions of Indian bestiality most firmly in mind.

19. Tales of white children living among the Indians continue to attract twentieth-century writers. Two popular novels that have become children's classics are *The Hidden Valley* by Laura Benet and *The Light in the Forest* by Conrad Richter. And Deerfield and its history continue to fascinate writers and readers. *The Cold Journey*, by Grace Zaring Stone (first published in 1934 and subsequently republished in five paperback editions, the most recent in 1970), is a historical novel which uses the name "Redfield" as a fictional counterpart for Deerfield. Although it takes liberties with the facts of the Deerfield raid and the fate of its survivors, its major premise is based on authentic history. Lewis Lupton's *Captured: An Historical Romance of New England* was first published in an English paperback (London, 1965). It too takes liberties with authenticated Deerfield history, but it is a lively entertainment written (as two of the three prefaces suggest) for "younger, young folk" (p. 10). And like the Rev. Strong's account, Lupton's book was written for obvious didactic reasons. "We . . . believe," he writes, "that this simple tale of a Puritan Pastor carried off into captivity with his flock of New Englanders by Indian savages presents these same values in such a picturesque and vivid manner that it will gain the interest of many people who do not at present regard the Christian faith as relevant to our times" (p. 6).

# Hans Brinker: *Sunny World, Angry Waters*

Jerome Griswold

Holland, a life on skates, and the boy who stuck his finger in the dyke—adults grow starry-eyed when they remember their first acquaintance with these in the pages of *Hans Brinker; or, The Silver Skates*. Published shortly after Christmas in 1865, Mary Mapes Dodge's novel became an immediate success; in the following year only Dickens's *Our Mutual Friend* sold as well. And it continues to sell well, with over one hundred editions available in six languages. One proof of its popularity is the way the Dutch have embraced the book—even to the point of creating a student bar in Amsterdam full of silver skates—as if it had been written by one of their own rather than by an American woman who, at that point, had never traveled to Europe.

Dodge traded upon a long history of American fascination with the Dutch and an Anglo-Saxon notion of Holland as a place of temptation. When the Puritans left England and stayed in Holland prior to their departure for America, William Bradford urged a hurried departure since Puritan children were being "drawn away by evil examples into extravagant and dangerous courses, getting the reins off their necks and departing from their parents."[1] Later, their customs of dancing and kissing gave the Dutch in New York a scandalous reputation among their Puritan neighbors to the north. Later still, Washington Irving would celebrate their eccentricities and mock the Puritan work ethic with his portrait of that great slouch Rip Van Winkle. Finally, in 1823, Clement Moore set visions of sugar plums dancing in American children's heads with "A Visit from St. Nicholas," adding Dutch customs of Santa and gift-giving to what had otherwise been the solemn religious celebration of Christmas. Sixty years after the publication of *Hans Brinker*, Fitzgerald added another chapter to this American fascination by ending *The Great Gatsby* with a sad envy of the wonder only possible in Dutch sailor's eyes.

*Hans Brinker* has a twofold plot. Dodge explained in her preface that "this little work aims to combine the instructive features of a

47

book of travels with the interest of a domestic tale." It was not to be
simply Cummins's *The Lamplighter* of the decade before, that kind of
domestic tale written for girls which some parents condemned as the
juvenile versions of today's Harlequin romances; it would have facts.
But neither was it simply the "wearisome spinning out of facts," as
Dodge has described Goodrich's geography lessons for children that
masqueraded as the travelogue *Peter Parley's Travels Abroad*; it would
have a touching story. In this way Dodge proposed a hybrid of the
two best selling strains of children's books of her time and appealed
to parent and child alike with the promise that her novel would both
teach and delight.

Modern-day children would just as soon forgo the teaching. Perhaps half the novel is a file-card collection of facts about Holland
that Dodge culled from Dutch friends, encyclopedias, and almanacs.
This information—from anecdotes about Dutch history and customs to the exact number of stops in the organ at St. Bavon's
(sixty-four) or windmills to be seen from a tower in Leyden (ninety-
eight)—is scarcely palatable even though Dodge has smuggled it into
a travelogue in which Peter Van Holp takes a company of well-to-do
boys on a skating expedition to Haarlem, Leyden, The Hague, and
back. The boys use the occasion of the trip and the presence of a
foreigner (the English schoolboy, Ben Dobbs) to give such long and
detailed accounts—for example, of Dutch wars in the 1600s—that
any reader must wince in disbelief at their prodigious memories. But
the continued popularity of the book probably rests on the ability of
children to overlook Dodge's minutiae and didacticism; they simply
skim over those history and geography lessons to get at the heart of
the book, which is the story of the Brinkers.

The other half of the novel, then, is the domestic tale about the
Brinker family: how Raff Brinker was injured by a fall from the
dyke and changed from a loving father into a senseless idiot;[2] how
Hans and Gretel and their mother care for the invalid and live a life
of poverty; how Hans persuades the famous Dr. Boekman to help
this family of "rag-pickers" and finally cure his father; and how this
cure results in the recovery of the Brinkers' missing savings, a
reunion between Dr. Boekman and his estranged son, and a splendid future for Hans and everyone else.

What is remarkable about the title character is that he is so unremarkable; Hans Brinker is milk-and-water compared to, say, Little Lord Fauntleroy or Tom Sawyer. One reviewer in *Scribner's Monthly* (February 1874) found this the charm of the book: the "author has no Ideal Child in her mind, . . . not even an ideal Real Child—that precious creature who is the bane of much of the finer sort of juvenile literature of our day." What does distinguish Hans is his unfailing cheerfulness; and, in this regard, *Hans Brinker* would establish a tradition in American children's books that would reach its apogee in the unremitting cheerfulness of *Pollyanna*. After a fruitless morning of looking for work to feed his needy family, without a morsel in the house, Hans still holds up his chin and whistles as he resolutely heads out the door to mend matters.

This incident fairly describes the particular emotional tone of the novel and the personality Hans inherited from his creator. Like many others in American juvenile literature, Mary Mapes Dodge was a scribbling widow. Her husband, William Dodge, committed suicide in 1859 after a bout of melancholy, drowning himself in the Atlantic and leaving his two sons fatherless. Mrs. Dodge's response, apparently, was to tuck up her skirt and roll up her sleeves and put all that behind her with a briskness which concealed her wounds. She returned to her father's house, began writing magazine articles, and then turned out *Hans Brinker*—a novel involving a mother that townspeople call "Widow Brinker" and two children who lost their father during an oceanic storm but later recovered him.

Dodge's other novels were forgettable but this did not diminish her influence upon American literature. After stints on other juvenile magazines, Dodge became in 1873 the editor of *St. Nicholas* and remained there until her death in 1905. The list of people she befriended and persuaded to write for the magazine reads like a *Who's Who*, including Louisa May Alcott, Frances Hodgson Burnett, Jack London, Mark Twain, Rudyard Kipling, Robert Louis Stevenson, William Cullen Bryant, Henry Wadsworth Longfellow, Helen Hunt Jackson, Frank Stockton, Lucretia P. Hale, Susan Coolidge, Howard Pyle, Joel Chandler Harris, Edna St. Vincent Millay, and Kate Douglas Wiggin.

There are a number of things about *St. Nicholas* that reveal Dodge's personality and how it shaped the emotional tone of *Hans Brinker*. First there is the magazine's title. Dodge revered Christmas. Her first publication was "A Song of St. Nicholas" and her subsequent work, especially in *St. Nicholas*, was full of talk of Santa and Christmas. *Hans Brinker* is no exception: the events of the novel occur during the holiday season; stories about and songs to St. Nicholas abound; an extended glimpse of a Dutch family's Christmas is provided; and a lengthy discussion of the difference between Dutch and American ways of celebrating begins with a reference to Clement Moore's poem: "We all know how, before the Christmas tree began to flourish in the home life of our country, a certain 'right jolly old elf,' with 'eight tiny reindeer,' used to drive his sleigh-load of toys up to our house-tops."[3]

Part of the emotional tone of *Hans Brinker* is the holiday feeling. School is out and every child is on skates. Their flying on the ice induces a vacation mood not unlike that of the river life in *Huckleberry Finn*. But there is one difference. Dodge could never abide the wholesome frivolity of Twain's character trailing his bare feet in the water; she condemns one of her characters because "she was never in earnest. . . . A pleasant heart, a pleasant manner—these only last for an hour" (p. 85). Beneath the good cheer, then, must be an earnestness.

Part of Dodge's personality was a kind of no-nonsense matter-of-factness. This was perhaps most evident, a biographer notes, in the editorial policies she adopted at *St. Nicholas*:

> Two things to which Lizzie stuck firmly and forever were goodness and reality—even her fairies were good and real, and nothing deep, esoteric or subtle passed her test—an iron-bound policy based on personal conviction against . . . allegory and the suggested. She wanted her tales to convey to stalwart and intelligent young Americans, stalwart and intelligent facts— she fed them oatmeal deliberately, and if a fairy popped into the cereal, she must be a real fairy and not a symbol. It was Europeans who indulged in the subterranean meaning: the hidden underlying the visible; the delicate handling and subtlety such as that of Lang and Anderson and Kingsley, or the macabre and terrifying . . . of Brothers Grimm.[4]

And indeed, though she became a good friend of George Mac-
Donald, she never solicited or published anything by him because
his work was deep rather than straightforward.

Dodge was a logical positivist when it came to enchantment. This,
too, shapes the emotional tone of *Hans Brinker*. Fairies are people
like Peter Van Holp's sister and Annie Bouman who earn that
epithet simply because they are charming. Hans and Gretel Brinker
are the down-to-earth namesakes of their Grimm ancestors; and
when Gretel is called the Goosegirl, it is not because the children
have seen her resemblance to the character in the fairy tale but
because she tends geese. Holland serves Dodge in the same way. In
her eyes, the great virtue of the country was that it was a real place
yet as fascinating as any land of enchantment: "Holland is one of
the greatest countries under the sun. It should be called Odd-land
or Contrary-land, for in nearly everything it is different from other
parts of the world" (p. 14). Because the lowlands are surrounded by
dykes, ships can be seen floating higher than the rooftops, gardens
are kept on canal boats, houses are built on stilts, and windmills are
everywhere. This netherland offered Dodge something as close to a
fairyland as she could come within her realistic guidelines.

Dodge also apparently felt an imperative for a robust healthy-
mindedness. Describing the ideal juvenile magazine before the
premier of *St. Nicholas*, she would use such words as *stronger, truer,
bolder, uncompromising, cheer, freshness, heartiness, life* and *joy*. At one
point in *Hans Brinker* the Dutch poet Jacob Cats comes off better in a
comparison with Shakespeare (who, it is conceded, wrote very good
plays): "Cats sees no daggers in the air, he has no white woman
falling in love with dusky moors; no young fools sighing to be a lady's
glove, no crazy princes mistaking respectable old gentlemen for rats.
No, no. He writes only sense" (p. 57). Dodge was a literary version of
Teddy Roosevelt, who would have told Bartleby the Scrivener to do
calisthenics and put the melancholy Hamlet in jogging shoes; her
sunny work in *Hans Brinker* is robust and healthy-minded, all pink
cheeks and skating.

The atmosphere of her novel, then, is one of peremptory cheerfulness. When, for example, Peter Van Holp leads his company of
boys on their skating expedition from their homes in Broek to The

Hague, they get only half way before they discover that Peter has lost
the purse containing their funds for the trip. When the boys grow
sullen and finally surly, Peter proposes they make "the best of a bad
business and go back pleasantly, like men" and the boys cheer; Peter
proposes that "we may as well make up our mind there's no place like
Broek, after all" and the boys cheer; Peter proposes they put on their
skates and head home, and the boys leave with faces "nearly as
bright" as those they had a half-hour before (p. 78).

It is as if no trouble can descend without the author sweeping
in with a rosy glow on her cheeks and her sleeves rolled up, seizing
the child on the brink of a blue funk, and hurrying him along
with a snatch from the tune "Pack Up Your Troubles in Your Old
Kit Bag." This seems to explain the briskness of the novel, the
constant motion of children and the streaking of skaters, the tran-
sience of events and the hurry of errands, and the contest of the
silver skates "For the Fleetest." But troubles swept away can also be
troubles swept under the rug. Despite the novel's gregariousness,
the fact that this is a wounded and defensive *joie de vivre* is evident
in darker ways— in a suspicion of moodiness, an emphasis upon
watchfulness, and a preoccupation with the danger of broken dykes.

## II

The most famous anecdote in *Hans Brinker* is the story of the boy
who stuck his finger in the dyke. That boy, incidentally, is not Hans;
the story of "The Hero of Haarlem" is something Dodge inserted
into her novel as an account of Holland being read by English
schoolchildren while her Dutch characters are exploring the country and its customs. The story is also not a piece of Dutch folklore;
Dodge herself invented it.[5] But the fact that this story is so widely
remembered, and that it almost seems to have taken on a life of its
own, suggests its importance. This opinion is shared by the Dutch
characters of the book when one says, "That little boy represents the
spirit of the whole country." And, indeed, the story provides clues to
understanding the larger story of the novel.

The actual tale of "The Hero of Haarlem" is easily told. It is about
a sunny-haired boy whose father works on the dykes as a sluicer. The

boy knows the importance of "strong dykes or barriers" without which the surrounding country would be inundated, how "constant watchfulness is required" to keep the ocean in its place, how "a moment's neglect of the sluicer's duty may bring ruin and death to all" (p. 101). One day he sets out to deliver cakes to a blind man and on his return he glances out at the angry waters beyond the dykes. The day grows darker, he feels lonely and remembers nursery tales about orphans lost in the woods, and then he spots the leak. Into the hole goes his chubby finger: "The angry waters must stay back now! Haarlem shall not be drowned while *I* am here!" (p. 103). During the night he fights off cold and sleepiness and controls his emotions and in the morning the little hero is found and the dyke repaired.

This story is but one example of the importance of dykes in the novel. Among the thousand things of life in Holland—tulips or windmills or wooden shoes—Dodge is most preoccupied with these barriers or boundaries. She also leaves the impression that her Dutch share this preoccupation and that every second thought of theirs concerns the safety of the dykes; as a nation, they seem to live in a mild but constant paranoia: "Holland is often in a state of alarm. The greatest care is taken to prevent accidents. Engineers and workmen are stationed all along [the dykes] in threatened places and a close watch is kept up night and day" (p. 21). Finally, Dodge suggests that "leaks" come in various forms when she says the boy who sticks his finger in the dyke "represents the spirit of the whole country. Not a leak can show itself anywhere, either in politics, honor, or public safety, that a million fingers are not ready to stop it at any cost" (p. 104).

*Hans Brinker* is a novel full of threats and varied forms of protection. "Leaks" and "floods" come in different shapes, as well as the need for "dykes." But, as Robert Frost said, "Before I built a wall I'd ask to know / What I was walling in or walling out."

Among all other things, the danger Dodge seems to fear on the other side of the dykes is the flood of emotions, what Freud called the "oceanic," the loss of ego when overwhelmed by the wildness of feelings. Emotions are suspect in this novel. One of the most revealing statements in the book occurs when Hans turns away as Gretel starts to cry: "He had a true Dutch horror of tears, or emotion of

any kind" (p. 30). The message of Dodge's *Hans Brinker* is: control
your feelings.

One example involves music, because music has the power to
evoke a flood of emotions that can threaten the dykes of self-control.
When Peter Van Holp and his party of boys are on their expedition,
they happen to stop at St. Bavon's just as the celebrated organ of that
church begins to play:

> Louder it grew until it became like the din and roar of some
> mighty tempest, or like the ocean surging on the shore. . . .
> [The boys'] eyes grew dim and their souls dizzy . . . with no wish
> but to hear forever those beautiful sounds—when suddenly
> Van Holp's sleeve was pulled impatiently and a gruff voice
> beside him asked: "How long are you going to stay here,
> captain—blinking at the ceiling like a sick rabbit?" [pp. 91–92]

This is the psychic version of coitus interruptus. Whenever emotions
come dangerously close to floodstage, Dodge finds the need and
occasion to bring them under control, to shore up the dykes against
ruin, to keep the oceanic within bounds. Her battery of facts about
Holland serves her well in this fervid assertion of the reality princi-
ple; immediately after the boys nearly lose themselves in the ecstasy
of the organ music, Dodge dampens the mood by shoveling in such
facts as the height and width of the organ and the number of pipes,
stops, and keyboards.

This suspicion of emotions includes a similar apprehension about
another state when the dykes of self-control are weak. Sleep seems
dangerous in this novel. Early in the book Hans's mother tells a story
about three sons who depart from their father and stay at an inn
where they fall asleep and are murdered by the landlord. Some
pages later Peter and his traveling companions stay at the Red Lion
Inn and while they sleep a knife-bearing robber enters their room.
On the same trip, one of the boys ( Jacob Poot) grows cold and tired
and falls asleep outdoors; everyone endeavors to wake him because
they know sleeping in the snow leads to death. Something similar
happens to Gretel. When Dr. Boekman begins to operate on Raff
Brinker, Gretel goes outside, becomes hysterical, and then drops
off to sleep; fortunately, her friend Hilda van Gleck sees the

child crumpled in the snow and energetically forces Gretel to wake up. Wakefulness and watchfulness are, consequently, praiseworthy postures. This is what is commendable about Dame Brinker as she keeps a sleepless vigil over her invalid husband in the fear that the man may go berserk or drift from sleep to death. It is what is commendable about the boy who fights off sleepiness and self-pity to keep his finger in the dyke. The dykes must be manned against the oceanic, those things which threaten to swamp the ego.

Dr. Boekman also exhibits emotional control. He was wounded when his son Laurens abandoned him after a misunderstanding. To protect his feelings so they cannot be hurt again, Dr. Boekman adopted a defensive posture and earned the reputation of being "the crossest man in Holland" (p. 82). The control of feelings is so important to him that before he operates on Raff Brinker, he insists that the females leave the house (because of their inclination to cry or faint), and he dispassionately discusses the success of a colleague's operation, ignoring the fact that the patient died.

But above all other emotions, anger must controlled. It is mentioned in the story of the boy who puts his finger in the dyke when the boy begins to muse: "He thought of his father's brave gates and feld glad of their strength for, thought he, 'if *they* gave way, where would his father and mother be? These pretty fields would be all covered with the angry waters—father always calls them the *angry* waters; I suppose he thinks they are mad at him for keeping them out so long'" (p. 102). If this passage is interpreted psychologically, the boy's question is: without the strong gates or dykes of the father, without the protective father of childhood, where would his family be? The answer is: drowned in the angry water, drowned in the waters the father thinks are mad at him. Without the protective father, the family is in danger of being drowned by madness-at-the-father.

This is the secret of the novel and the key to the Brinkers' name. After his accident, Raff Brinker (who was once a brave and strong dyke keeper) is no longer the protective father; in fact, he is a threatening father, since he occasionally goes berserk. On one occasion, for example, he turns into a hysteric madman who tries to push his wife into the fire while his children helplessly look on. This

Thomas Nast's illustration for the first edition of *Hans Brinker; or, the Silver Skates*, published in 1865.

has created a dangerous situation where the family unit might easily be destroyed by a tidal wave of madness-at-the-father. But the Brinkers resist this. Though they live on the brink of a dangerous situation, they man the dykes against this emotion. There is, however, an occasional leak; in a moment of freethinking reverie Gretel acknowledges that there is something else beneath her surface affection for her father. She wonders

> whether it was very wicked to care more for one parent than for the other—and sure, yes, quite sure that she dreaded her father, while she clung to her mother with a love that was almost idolatry. "Hans loves the father so well," she thought,

"why cannot I? . . . If this sickness [of the father] lasts we shall never skate any more . . . Hans and I will not see the race," and Gretel's eyes that had been dry before, grew full of tears. "Never cry, child," said her mother soothingly . . . Gretel sobbed now. "Oh, mother, . . . you do not know at all—I am very, very bad and wicked!" . . . Gretel looked up . . . and said in a trembling voice: "The father tried to burn you—he did—I saw him, and he was *laughing!*" "Hush, child!" The mother's words came suddenly and sharply. [pp. 87–89]

Raff Brinker stands in the way and, despite her mother's urging her to control her emotions, Gretel's anger against her father sometimes leaks through. All the other children of the novel have lives full, Dodge says repeatedly, of fun and frolic; but Gretel's life is poor and unhappy because, unlike her neighbors, she comes from a "broken home." For all the other children, the Silver Skates to be won at the great race are like visions of sugar plums. For Gretel they are "treasures passing hopelessly out of her reach" (p. 84) as her father's illness grows worse.

There is only one exception in the host of juvenile dreamers: "the vision of the Silver Skates failed to appear" to Hans Brinker (p. 84). Like Gretel's, Hans's life is different from the lives of the other children of the novel; while Peter Van Holp and his company of boys skate off on their expedition, Hans is busy locating a doctor, trying to find work, and discovering ways to provide food because his father is ill. Unlike his sister, though, Hans does not give in to anger and resentment toward his father. He mans the dykes and controls his emotions. In the darkest times, he maintains his cheerful and even disposition. He does not even long for the Silver Skates, much less see his father as an obstacle to winning them. Like the boy who saves the dyke, Hans is self-sacrificing, Duty's child. In the absence of the protective father, he becomes the protector and the child savior. Hans sees to the recovery of his father, the reconstitution of the family, and the restoration of their savings. Even more than the hero of Haarlem, Hans Brinker can be seen as the representative of a country ever on guard against leaks.

Hans, then, is a particular kind of hero. Compared to Huck Finn,

Little Lord Fauntleroy, or Rebecca of Sunnybrook Farm, he is dull
and ordinary. But these are his virtues in Dodge's novel. The fact
that he is undramatic is proof that he can control his emotions. He
not only has no feelings of resentment, but he must also turn away
when he sees his sister about to cry and is stunned when his mother
affectionately uses the familiar form and addresses him as "thee."
Hans controls his feelings. He is a strong individual who creates his
ego out of the ocean of id and maintains this "Holland" against the
threats of uncontrolled passions.

There may well be biographical roots in this endorsement of Hans
Brinker. Perhaps after the suicide of her husband, Dodge, too, felt a
"madness-at-the-father," and anger that her husband had left her a
widow and her two sons without a father. Perhaps she discovered
that the undramatic and rigorously maintained cheerfulness and
even temper of Hans Brinker was best. Or perhaps the fact that her
husband drowned himself in the ocean after being overcome by
melancholy led her to see the importance of dykes against emotions.

Whatever the case, it should be noted that this creates a contradic-
tory novel. While the book advocates the control of emotions, Dodge
uses every conceivable trick of the sentimental novel to create a
tear-jerker. The clearest example of this duplicity occurs in the story
of the hero of Haarlem, which, it must be remembered, is being read
by children in their school. In the passages Dodge puts in brackets
the classroom readers are urged to control their emotions, while the
story they read employs every possible trick to set them blubbering:

> ["Now, Henry," said the teacher, nodding to the next little
> reader.]
>
> "Suddenly the boy looked around in dismay. . . . It was grow-
> ing dark, he was still some distance from home, and in a lonely
> ravine . . . and with a beating heart recalled many a nursery tale
> of children belated in dreary forests. . . . He looked up and saw
> a small hole in the dyke. . . . His chubby finger was thrust in
> almost before he knew it. . . .
>
> "But the night was falling rapidly; chill vapors filled air.
> Our little hero began to tremble with cold and dread. He
> shouted loudly; he screamed 'Come here! Come here!' but no
> one came. The cold grew intense, a numbness, commencing in

the tired little finger, crept over his hand and arm, and soon his whole body was filled with pain. He shouted again, 'Will no one come? Mother! Mother!' . . . He tried to whistle, perhaps some straggling boy might heed the signal; but his teeth chattered so, it was impossible. Then he called on God for help; and the answer came, through a holy resolution—'I will stay here 'til morning.'"

["Now, Jenny Dobbs," said the teacher. Jenny's eyes were glistening, but she took a long breath and commenced:]

"How can we know the sufferings of that long and fearful watch—what falterings of purpose, what childish terrors came over the boy as he thought of the warm little bed at home, of his parents, his brothers and sisters, then looked into the cold, dreary night! . . . He was not sure of living. What did this strange buzzing mean? and then the knives that seemed to be pricking him from head to foot? . . .

["Jenny Dobbs," said the teacher, rather impatiently, "if you cannot control your feelings so as to read distinctly, we will wait until you recover yourself."] [pp. 102–03]

The voice of the teacher who chides the emotional child-reader is that of Mary Mapes Dodge. But Dodge is also the author of the tale the child reads, a story which attempts to evoke the child's emotion. In a sense, this is what Dodge does throughout the novel; she creates emotional situations and then urges control. When Raff Brinker undergoes a perilous operation and is brought back to his senses and family, she asks that no tears fall upon the page; when Dr. Boekman is reunited at long last with his estranged son Laurens, that no lump form in the throat; when Gretel finally gets her wish and enters the great race and wins the Silver Skates, that no heart flutter; and when Hans shivers in the cold and wonders where to get work or food, that no reader feel pangs of pity. This, of course, is close to impossible. But in this way Dodge creates an incredible tension. She institutes a taboo and, at the very same time, supplies elaborate occasions to sin. She provides abundant temptations to test her readers' resolve and seduces them to abandon it, thereby creating the juvenile version of the romance novel. Contemplated adultery, Denis de Rougemont says in *Love in the Western World*,[6] is the heart of the romance because it creates that kind of exhilarating tension seen in the legend of Tristan and Iseult, where the two lovers lie down with a sword between them as a symbol of the boundary/taboo they must not but long to cross. In *Hans Brinker*, Dodge teases for tears but at the same time condemns tears as leaks, as emotional adultery that jeopardizes not a marriage, but a family.

## Notes

1. William Bradford, *Of Plymouth Plantation, 1620–1647*, ed. Samuel Eliot Morison (New York: Knopf, 1959), p. 25.

2. Raff Brinker's actual condition defies medical description. It might be referred to as amnesia or the Rip Van Winkle syndrome, since for ten years he remained alive but with a diminished mental capacity and loss of memory. This amnesia, incidentally, provides a welcome relief to readers already suffering from the prodigious memories of Dodge's juvenile historians in their unusually long chronicles of Dutch events.

3. Mary Mapes Dodge, *Hans Brinker; or, The Silver Skates* (1865, rpt. New York: Airmont, 1966). In lieu of footnotes, subsequent references appear parenthetically in the text.

4. Catherine Morris Wright, *Lady of the Silver Skates* (Jameston, RI: Clingstone Press, 1979), p. 158.

5. Ibid., p. 32.

6. Denis de Rougemont, *Love in the Western World*, trans. Montgomery Belgion (Greenwich: Fawcett, 1966), pp. 15–58 and passim.

# "Men Sell Not Such in any Town:"
## Christina Rossetti's Goblin Fruit of Fairy Tale

Jeanie Watson

Although *Goblin Market* has long enjoyed a reputation as one of the finest of children's poems[1] and has repeatedly been labeled a fairy tale, in line with Christina Rossetti's own insistence on this point, there has been no serious, extensive consideration of *Goblin Market* as a children's poem drawing upon the themes and forms of traditional children's literature. This is true because, in large part, readers from the beginning to the present have had difficulty concentrating on anything other than the framework of Christian allegory—a more "adult" genre—which is so apparent in the poem. This over-riding critical attention to the allegorical moral, while it has produced a number of instructive and illuminating readings, has been less than entirely satisfactory. It is the contention of this essay that only by viewing *Goblin Market* as a tale for children, a tale which is structurally based on the interweaving of the predominant nineteenth-century strands of children's literature—the fairy tale and the moral tale—can the poem's true moral, for children and adults, be understood. Further, it is the interplay between moral tale and fairy tale that allows *Goblin Market's* thematic statement to be utterly subversive and yet ultimately moral.

I

In 1898, Mackenzie Bell, Christina Rossetti's early biographer, quotes Christina's surviving brother as having written: "I have more than once heard C[hristina] aver that the poem has not any profound or ulterior meaning—it is just a fairy story: yet one can discern that it implies at any rate this much—that to succumb to a temptation makes one a victim to that same continuous temptation; that the remedy does not always lie with oneself; and that a stronger and more righteous will may prove of avail to restore one's lost estate."[2] The ambivalent reaction to the dual elements of fairy tale and

61

allegory are neatly summarized by Bell's commentary on a contemporary critic:

> James Ashcroft Noble, in a penetrating essay called "The Burden of Christina Rossetti," . . . says that "*Goblin Market* may be read and enjoyed merely as a charming fairy-fantasy, and as such it is delightful and satisfying; but behind the simple story of two children and the goblin fruit-sellers is a little spiritual drama of love's vicarious redemption, in which the child redeemer goes into the wilderness to be tempted of the devil, that by her painful conquest she may succour and save the sister who has been vanquished and all but slain. The luscious juices of the goblin fruit, bitter and deadly when sucked by selfish greed, become bitter and medicinal when spilt in unselfish conflict."
> This is admirably and eloquently put, but it may be questioned whether the critic has not perhaps somewhat overstated the case for didacticism in the poem. [pp. 206–07]

With only a few dissenting voices,[3] the moral of *Goblin Market* has, then, from the beginning been seen primarily within the framework of the Christian allegory of temptation, fall, and redemption. The goblin fruits become the forbidden fruit of Genesis and Revelation, the fruit of illicit sensuality. Knowing she should not, Laura trafficks with the goblin men, buys their fruit with a golden curl and a single tear. Having once eaten of the fruit, she is no longer a maiden and can no longer hear the goblins' cry, "Come buy, come buy" (l.4).[4] She is saved from death only by the redemptive act of her sister Lizzie. Laura's commentary at the end that "there is no friend like a sister" becomes a tribute to Lizzie's saving love.

The moral is very clearly stated and seems to fit the allegorical redemption:

> For there is no friend like a sister
> In calm or stormy weather;
> To cheer one on the tedious way,
> To fetch one if one goes astray,
> To lift one if one totters down,
> To strengthen whilst one stands. [ll. 562–67]

It *should* be a neat and satisfactory ending, but it is not. Indeed, far from being satisfactory, the allegorical moral makes many readers very uncomfortable, although they cannot readily explain their lack of ease. Eleanor Walter Thomas, a Rossetti biographer, writes about an early critic who sounds frustrated, almost angry: "The critic, F. A. Rudd, wrote paragraph after paragraph in solemn condemnation of the fantastic *Goblin Market* as immoral: he could find not a syllable in the poem to show that yielding to evil as incarnate in the goblins was at all wrong in itself. What is the moral? he weightily inquires. 'Not resist the devil and he will flee from you, but cheat the devil and he won't catch you. Now all these sayings and silences are gravely wrong and false to a writer's true functions.'"[5] Similarly, other readers simply do not believe that the poem says what the allegory says it says. They argue that rather than condemning physical passion, the story of Laura and Lizzie celebrates that passion: "Temptation, in both its human and theological sense, is the thematic core of *Goblin Market*. . . . *Goblin Market* celebrates by condemning sensuous passion."[6] In the same vein, Ellen Golub says: "Rossetti seems to condemn such [sexual] passion, but in her condemnation she offers much description of it. Eros being very much present, it is the seduction of girls by goblins which engages reader attention."[7]

Those who are able to accept the moral at face value either have the courage of an appalling lack of sensibility (for example, "The most charming scene of all is that of the sisters, grown to woman's estate, telling their own children of their terrific adventure" [Meigs, p. 291]), or they read the lines as an accommodation to the prevailing status of women, and women writers in particular, in Victorian times, the very necessity of that accommodation calling forth a proud and defiant independence. Jerome J. McGann argues that the goblins represent the Victorian marketplace, "institutionalized patterns of social destructiveness operating in nineteenth-century England" that promise women fulfillment of their desires through love and marriage, promises which are illusionary and by which women are betrayed.[8] But, continues McGann, "the poem is unusual in Christina Rossetti's canon in that it has developed a convincing positive symbol for an alternative, uncorrupted mode of social relations—the love of sisters" (p. 250). Gilbert and Gubar also see

Rossetti as making a virtue of necessity: "Christina Rossetti and, to a lesser extent, Elizabeth Barrett Browning build their art on a willing acceptance of passionate or demure destitution. They . . . are the nineteenth-century women singers of renunciation as necessity's highest and noblest virtue."[9] Gilbert and Gubar discuss the important connection which *Goblin Market* sets up between "the unnatural but honey-sweet fruit of art" and the "luscious fruit of self-gratifying sensual pleasure" (p. 570), and they rightly assert that "the fruit of 'Goblin Market' has fed on the desirous substrata of the psyche, the childishly self-gratifying fantasies of the imagination." But, they conclude, since "young ladies like Laura, Maude, and Christina Rossetti should not loiter in the glen of imagination, which is the haunt of goblin men like Keats and Tennyson," they must learn "the lesson of renunciation" and feed on "bitter repressive wisdom, the wisdom of necessity's virtue, in order to be redeemed" (p. 573).

As insightful as many of these readings of *Goblin Market* are, they still do not banish our discomfort over the ending of the poem. That this is so is because, finally, Christina Rossetti does not want us to be comfortable. It may well be that Victorian institutions necessitate a positive sisterly alliance in a male-less world. And it may be that women's sexuality and creative impulses are systematically and severely repressed. But Rossetti does not believe that it should be so. To be redeemed in this kind of world is to be damned. *Goblin Market* is an extremely subversive poem which, while acknowledging the "wisdom of necessity's virtue," refuses to accept it, insisting instead on the right to dearly bought goblin fruit. This stance is made possible through Rossetti's choice of form for the poem: the interplay of fairy tale and moral tale. This interplay subverts the accepted moral into the immoral and makes imaginative knowledge the only righteousness acceptable.

## II

Mary F. Thwaite, in her history of children's books, *From Primer to Pleasure in Reading*, lauds *Goblin Market* by saying: "With Christina Rossetti . . . the children's muse found the crystal springs of true poetry. There had been nothing of the quality of her lyrics for the young since *Songs of Innocence*. Finest of all is her fairy poem *Goblin Market*. . . . Both the theme and the style are fascinating, expressed with a lilt and pace new in children's verse" (p. 135). Although the poem may appear to be something new, its form is firmly rooted in two traditional genres of children's literature. *Goblin Market* is, as Christina Rossetti repeatedly insisted, a fairy tale. But the poem is also a moral tale. Both genres have had a long history in children's literature, and both were popular in Rossetti's time. That she was familiar with the whole range of moral tales and fairy tales is clear from her own and others' accounts of her youthful reading.[10] However, the forms are essentially antithetical, one being used for didactic purposes to teach children proper spiritual and social conduct, the other being secular or amoral, or even immoral, in its lesson.

Moral tales of the mid-nineteenth century, some of which emphasized a virtuous life founded on right conduct and some of which were unabashedly religious in their didacticism, had their source in the emblem books, Christian allegories, and stories of saints and martyrs of earlier centuries. The subsequent evolution of the moral tale occurred in response to social and philosophical changes, stimulated by the theories of John Locke, who held that books for children should be pleasant and entertaining to read. Morality and right conduct were seen as more important than knowledge, and reason as preferable to imagination. "Fairies and fairy lore, 'goblins and spirits'; with other superstitions, he [Locke] regarded as belonging to the useless trumpery. Imagination and enthusiasm were to be avoided—as were unintelligible ideas about God, the Supreme Being whom children should be taught to love and reverence. The sober light of reason and common-sense was to illumine the child's life" (Thwaite, p. 34).[11]

The strictures against fairy tales, which had caused them to be available for many years primarily only in chapbooks, had, by the end of the eighteenth century, been eased by the tales being transformed—albeit through truncation and softening—into models for moral instruction. The fairy tale, thus bowdlerized, became domesticated and acceptable. "The moralizing of fairy tales (when they were admitted by the creators of juvenile literature at this period) was recognized as a cunning method of utilizing for good the youthful predilection for the fabulous" (Thwaite, p. 72). Still, reputable English editions of the Perrault tales were published in the last half of the eighteenth century, and *German Popular Stories*, or *Grimm's Fairy Tales*, was published in English in two volumes (1823–26). Therefore, by mid-nineteenth century, legitimate fairy tales were readily available.

In *Goblin Market*, Christina Rossetti combines the social and religious forms of the nineteenth-century moral tale, making the religious allegory seem to serve the social function of warning against any illicit desire or action outside the boundaries accepted by society. At the same time, the context for this moral tale is the goblin fairy tale, precisely the imaginative, out-of-bounds kind of story that had aroused so much suspicion.[12] Rossetti uses these two popular, but embattled, forms for her own purposes, simultaneously diffusing and intensifying the true moral of her poem by making it a poem for children.

The musical lilt and fast-paced narrative of *Goblin Market*, the short, easily read lines and the concrete, sensory imagery of color, taste, sound, and texture all argue for the poem's special appeal to children, as do also the fantastic goblin creatures and the fairy "haunted glen" (l. 552). But it is not only on the level of the Victorian child as audience that *Goblin Market* is a tale for children. Within the poem itself, the story of Laura and Lizzie's encounter with the goblins is the story told the children, time after enraptured time, by the maiden turned mother. The tale that Laura lived becomes the tale her children—and we—hear. There is a shift in critical perspective when we listen as a child to the poem. What seduces us into wanting to hear the story again and again is not the moral tale warning but the same thing that enthralls the children and seduced Laura: the goblin fruit of a fairy tale. The overt text of the moral tale makes the story "acceptable"; the subtext of the fairy tale presents Rossetti's moral. And we believe the fairy tale.

### III

*Goblin Market's* Laura and Lizzie live in the safe and orderly daytime world of the moral tale in which one event follows another in predictable, simple fashion:

> Early in the morning
> When the first cock crowed his warning,
> Neat like bees, as sweet and busy,
> Laura rose with Lizzie:
> Fetched in honey, milked the cows,
> Aired and set to rights the house,
> Kneaded cakes of whitest wheat,
> Cakes for dainty mouths to eat,
> Next churned butter, whipped up cream,
> Fed their poultry, sat and sewed;
> Talked as modest maidens should:   [ll. 199–209]

In this domestic scene, work, common sense, and right conduct prevail, and the moral tale assures us that this, indeed, is the way things ought to be. The maidens' orderly lives are lived within boundaries, a life of milk and honey, cakes and cream, wholesome food of innocence and righteousness. They are, in fact, as Rossetti makes clear through her verbal allusions, following the moral precept of Isaac Watts's well-known poem "Against Idleness and Mischief," published in 1715 as one of his *Divine Songs for Children*:

> How doth the little busy bee
>   Improve each shining hour,
> And gather honey all the day
>   From every opening flower![13]

The admonition to be as neat as the bee is followed by the warning that Satan will find mischief for idle hands. Presumably, as long as one is industrious, one is safe. However, Laura has always been busy as a bee, and still she has eaten goblin fruit. In addition, it is after her eating of the fruit that the passage comparing the sisters to bees occurs. It is not until Laura realizes that she cannot have more goblin fruit that

> She no more swept the house,
> Tended the fowls or cows,
> Fetched honey, kneaded cakes of wheat,
> Brought water from the brook:
> But sat down listless in the chimney-nook
> And would not eat. [ll. 293–98]

If Laura cannot have the goblin fruit, she will not eat the cake and honey either.

There is other evidence as well that the overt didacticism of the moral tale is at variance the acutal message of the poem, that the fairy tale, in other words, is subverting the moral tale. By not doing her chores, Laura leaves herself open to the punishment warned against in country superstition for those who do not keep their houses clean and tidy—to be pinched by the fairies. Although a visit by the goblins is precisely what Laura desires, they do not come to her. It is, instead, Lizzie who is pinched "black as ink," having offered the goblins the payment of a "silver penny" (ll. 427, 324)— the traditional reward left in the shoe of the neat housekeeper. The moral tale sequence of cause and effect and the usual admonitory system of punishments do not seem to hold in the expected way. We are in the out-of-bounds world of fairy tale rather than the orderly world of the moral tale.

Wariness of *Goblin Market's* moral tale message increases when we recall another instance from the earlier moral tale tradition of the bee's being used for moral instruction. In 1686, John Bunyan published *A Book for Boys and Girls; or Country Rhimes for Children*. This book, known in the mid-nineteenth-century as *Divine Emblems; Or Temporal Things Spiritualized*, has as one of its figures the bee:

Upon the Bee
The Bee goes out and Honey home doth bring;
And some who seek that Honey find a sting.
Now wouldst thou have the Honey and be free
From stinging; in the first place kill the Bee.

Comparison
This Bee an Emblem truly is of sin
Whose sweet unto a many death hath been.
Now wouldst have Sweet from sin, and yet not dye,
Do thou it in the first place mortifie.[14]

In his poem on the busy bee, Watts had domesticated the bee, turning it into an example of industry and order. Rossetti, through the force of her fairy tale, undercuts this meaning and goes back to Bunyan's earlier identification of the bee with sin. Bunyan advises those who wish the honey without the sting to first kill the bee. The fruits of the goblin men are "like honey to the throat / But poison in the blood" (ll. 554–55). The words are spoken by Laura at the end of *Goblin Market,* and like the speaker in Bunyan's poem, she has wished to divide the honey from the sting. The moral of Rossetti's poem is that one who would have the sweet "and yet not dye" must "in the first place mortifie" the neat and busy little bee of the moral tale. Goblin gifts often bring a curse with them;[15] in this case, the curse is the painful death of the view which the moral tale embodies.

In *Goblin Market,* the bounded and orderly world of cottage and domesticity is juxtaposed to the "haunted glen" of "wicked quaint fruit–merchant men" (ll. 552–53). Traditionally, goblins were "evil and malicious spirits, usually small and grotesque in appearance,"[16] who were known "to tempt mortals to their undoing" (Thwaite, p. 135). The temptation in *Goblin Market* is to leave the world of moral tale and enter the world of fairy tale. Katherine Briggs notes in *The Faeries in English Tradition and Literature* that "the plot of [*Goblin Market*] is a variant of three main fairy themes: the danger of peeping at the fairies, the TABOO against eating FAIRY FOOD, and the rescue from Fairyland" (p. 193). Christina Rossetti's original title for the poem was *A Peep at the Fairies,* indicating perhaps that the poem is her own dangerous peep at the fairies, despite the injunctions against such a look.

True fairy tales often bear little resemblance to light, delightful fantasies; in fact, they are stories of abandonment, betrayal, violence, and irrationality. To enter the world of fairy tales is to enter a world different from the world of order and reason and common sense which we inhabit in our daytime lives; there are ordering principles in fairy tales, but they operate the boundaries of ordinary life. As Bettelheim argues, "The 'truth' of fairy stories is the truth of our imagination, not that of moral causality."[17] Fairy tales are "spiritual explorations" and hence "the most life-like," revealing "human life as seen, or felt, or divined from the inside."[18] The world of fairy tale is a world of knowledge, knowledge not accessible within the limits of the real world. The real world limits us to the known; it is safe, rational, capable of empirical proof. The fairy tale world is the "long, long ago" world of infinite possibility, existent now only in

and through the imagination. Entering into the realm of possibility
is dangerous—for possibility includes both vision and nightmare—
but necessary for wholeness. The risk of imagination is most assuredly
a temptation, the risk of chaos for the possibility of knowledge which
is truth, truth which is beauty.

The temptation of fairy tale is immediate and urgent in *Goblin
Market*. Maidens are urged to eat the luscious fruits of the natural
world, which are also, paradoxically and magically, the fruits of
imaginative creativity. The fairy tale world is inhabited by creatures
of the imagination, born out of the human psyche. Here, natural
and supernatural meet. Here, there is a suspension of disbelief.
Here is the place where the oxymoronic exists. In the fairy tale
world, one risks going beyond the boundaries of empirical rationality to experience more fundamental and intuitive truths. The fairy
tale world is tempting because it promises knowledge and because
we sense the underlying truth of that knowledge. "Subjected to the
rational teachings of others, the child only buries his 'true knowledge' deeper in his soul and it remains untouched by rationality"
(Bettelheim, p. 46). It is this "true knowledge" that *Goblin Market*
tempts us to, away from the rational teachings which limit and
restrict the imagination. The cry of the goblin men is almost hyp-
notic in its rich catalogue of fruits so numerous as to be virtually
unending. The kinds and quantities and combinations of taste and
color are unlimited, appealing to the senses and to the possibilities of
imagination. The fruits are all ripe to the bursting point and "All
ripe together / In summer weather" (ll. 15–16); they are "full and
fine," ready to "fill" the mouth (ll. 21, 28), very like "Joy's grape" of
Keats's *Ode to Melancholy*:

> Joy, whose hand is ever at his lips
> Bidding adieu; and aching Pleasure nigh,
>    Turning to Poison while the bee-mouth sips: [ll. 22–24][19]

Intensity of experience, whether sensual or imaginative, requires
the reconciliation of opposites, Melancholy and Delight. Joy that
dwells with Beauty is achieved only through the sacramental bursting of the grape. "Honey to the throat" and "Poison in the blood" are
necessary accompaniments.

The "mossy glen" (l. 87) where maidens may hear the cry of goblin men is a haunted, fairy place with "brookside rushes" (l. 33), fertile and rich and erotic in its connotations. It is a place as much feminine as masculine. In addition, as Gilbert and Gubar point out, the glen "represents a chasm in the mind, analogous to that enchanted romantic chasm" (p. 570) of Coleridge's *Kubla Khan*, a "holy and enchanted" place, "haunted / By woman wailing for her demon lover!"[20] Coleridge's chasm is itself the fertile ground of the androgynous creative imagination. The goblin men, who presumably also eat the fruit they sell, are similar to Coleridge's poet of whom one should beware and around whom one should weave a circle thrice since "he on honeydew hath fed, / And drunk the milk of Paradise" (ll. 53–54). So Lizzie says, "We must not look at goblin men" (l. 42). The goblin men may be seen as androgynous creatures, unlike the men—or the women—of the town. Rossetti's liking for animals, especially unusual or bizarre ones,[21] should keep us from assuming that she intends us to see the appearance of the goblin men in a negative way. Rather, their form combines the parts of the masculine–rational–mind and feminine–animal passion–emotion traditional dichotomy. It is they who are the possessors of the sensuous fruits of the imagination, but they also desire that maidens buy the fruit. "We must not buy their fruits," says Laura. "Who knows upon what soil they fed / Their hungry thirsty roots?" (ll. 43–45). Since the fruit shapes are full and round, erotically masculine and feminine, the soil would seem to be the androgynous ground of creative imagination.

A number of critics have noted in passing the resemblance between Christina Rossetti's poetry and that of Coleridge.[22] *The Rime of the Ancient Mariner*, in both its similarities and dissimilarities, seems a particularly instructive gloss for *Goblin Market* since the same concerns are at issue in both poems. To begin with, the *Rime* and *Goblin Market* are both, broadly speaking, fairy tales. Both are journey stories, quests for the fruits of knowledge. The Mariner leaves the safe harbor of the rational and the known to enter, through an act of "irrationality," the world of fairy tale, that is, the world of the supernatural. Out-of-bounds and separated from the support provided by the dependable order of the natural world, community

with his fellows, and a domesticated religious structure, he suffers
the nightmare time of life-in-death. Finally, through an intuitive act
of imagination and love, he perceives the beauty of the water snakes
and the spell breaks. If one participates fully in the imaginative
world, then that world is perceived in its wholeness and perceived as
beautiful. Lack of participation shifts the perception so that the
beautiful becomes ugly and destructive. In his spiritual alienation,
the Mariner is repulsed by the crawling, slimy water snakes. Recon-
ciled with, and by, the wholeness of love, he says, "No tongue / Their
beauty might declare" (ll. 282–83). At last, he is spirited back to the
safety of the land where he is compelled to tell his story to those who
are receptive to its meaning.

Laura leaves the cottage and goes to the haunted glen. Despite all
the warnings, she moves outside the limits of safety to buy with the
coin of her body and the anguish of experience the fruits which
cannot be had in any other way: "(Men sell not such in any town)"
(l. 101). The goblin men invite maidens to "sit down and feast with
us, / Be welcome guest with us" (ll. 380–81), and as long as the
maidens do feast, the merchants' voices coo like doves and sound
"kind and full of loves" (l. 79). It is only when Lizzie tries to give
them back the silver fairy penny, in accordance with the moral tale,
that the goblins revenge themselves on her. The punishing "rape"
in which the goblin men try to force Lizzie to eat the fruit is a
nightmare vision not unlike the "viper's thoughts" of the "dark
dream" (ll. 94–95) summoned by the imaginative storm of Coleridge's
*Dejection: An Ode.*

Laura, like the Mariner, becomes a storyteller, and the overt
moral at the end of *Goblin Market* is strikingly similar to the moral at
the end of the *Rime*:

> He prayeth best, who loveth best
> All things both great and small;
> For the dear God who loveth us,
> He made and loveth all. [ll. 614–17]

Both morals, childishly sing-songey in cadence and almost simple-
minded in tone, sound disconcertingly inadequate to the reader as
summary statements for the turmoil that has preceded them. In

both cases, we as readers are supposed to understand more than the speaker. What the Mariner says is true, but truer than he can explain. What Laura says is true, but not true enough; her vision is insufficient and, therefore, true to the moral tale but not to the fairy tale. The Mariner is changed by his experience. His tale is a "ghastly" one, and his glittering eye holds the listener. Because his moral is true to the fairy tale, the listener, the Wedding-Guest, is also changed:

> He went like one that hath been stunned,
> And is of sense forlorn:
> A sadder and a wiser man,
> He rose the morrow morn. [ll. 622–25]

Laura and Lizzie repudiate the fruits of knowledge. They are neither sadder nor wiser the following morning. For a terrifying experience of grace, they substitute a formulaic religiosity. We believe the Mariner's moral, but we do not believe in the efficacy of Laura's. What we *do* believe in *Goblin Market* is the truth of the fairy tale. Laura and Lizzie are saved to their damnation, and we and Christina Rossetti know it, even if they do not. The whole poem then becomes a moral poem of a different kind, one in which the immoral moral triumphs.

To see with the eye of imagination is to be outside the safe confines of conventional life; it calls for perception and participation in whole vision. The institutions and cultural attitudes of Victorian society make goblin fruit forbidden to maidens—and almost kindly so: one taste of the fruit cuts them off from expected female domesticity, and yet they are not allowed full and continued feasting. "Must your light like mine be hidden / Your young life like mine be wasted," Laura asks Lizzie. The light of imagination must be hidden, and thus life is wasted. Girls like Jeanie, who eat the goblins' fruit and wear the crown of flowers, pine away in "noonlight" (l. 153), lost equally to the glen and to the town. Lizzie's intervention keeps Laura from Jeanie's fate, but the "salvation" scene is strangely ambiguous. Laura, admonished by Lizzie to "Hug me, kiss me, suck my juices" (l. 468), "Kissed and kissed and kissed her." And again, "She kissed and kissed her with a hungry mouth" (ll. 486, 492) in an orgy of hunger for goblin fruit. But at the same time that she writhes "as one possessed," leaping and singing in a frenzy of Dionysian ecstasy,[23] she "loathed the feast" and "gorged on bitterness without a name" (ll. 495–96, 510). Does the bitterness come from having eaten the fruit or from having to be saved from her desire for its taste? Similarly, who is speaking the lines, "Ah fool, to choose such part / Of soul-consuming care!" (ll. 511–12)—Laura or the narrator? And where, exactly, is the foolishness? There is a tone of longing even at the point of rejection. Laura has desired that which is forbidden her, though it should be hers by right. Perhaps what we hear in her voice is frustrated anger.

What is clear to the reader at the end of the poem is that the progression from innocence to experience and back to original innocence is no progression at all; it is at best, sad—we are the ones sadder and wiser—and at worst, immoral. Had Keats's Madeline in *The Eve of St. Agnes*[24] remained

> Blissfully havened both from joy and pain;
> ...........................................................
> Blinded alike from sunshine and from rain,
> As though a rose should shut, and be a bud again, [ll. 240, 242–43]

she would have been lost. For a rose to become a bud again is no more natural than to regain one's innocence; therefore, Laura's salvation becomes ironic:

> Sense failed in the mortal strife:
> Like the watch-tower of a town
> Which an earthquake shatters down,
> Like a lightning-stricken mast,
> Like a wind up-rooted tree
> Spun about,
> Like a foam-topped waterspout
> Cast down headlong in the sea,
> She fell at last;
> Pleasure past and anguish past,
> Is it death or is it life? [ll. 513–23]

The Mariner falls "down in a swound" (392); when his "living life returned" (l. 394), he prays, "O let me be awake, my God! / Or let me sleep alway" (ll. 470–71). He awakes to speak of the unity of life. Laura, her sense having failed, chooses "Life out of death" and falls at last, past the possibilities of both pleasure and anguish, "Blinded alike from sunshine and from rain." She has become a bud again.

Fairy tales have traditionally been able to triumph over the morals attached to them. The moral tags may or may not fit the story; they may be cynical or comforting; they may disappear altogether.[25] But, as Christina Rossetti knows, the power of the story remains, impervious to attack, reaching out like Laura's own yearning after goblin fruit:

> Like a rush-imbedded swan,
> Like a lily from the beck,
> Like a moonlit poplar branch,
> Like a vessel at the launch
> When its last restraint is gone. [ll. 82–86]

The power of the fairy tale remains as long as the story is told, passed down from generation to generation, whatever the intent of the teller. Thus,

> Laura would call the little ones
> And tell them of her early prime,
> Those pleasant days long gone
> Of not-returning time:
> Would talk about the haunted glen,
> The wicked quaint fruit-merchant men,
> Their fruits like honey to the throat
> But poison in the blood
> (Men sell not such in any town). [ll. 548–56]

The children listen—as do we—fascinated and intrigued by the story of the goblin men and their fruit. And Christina Rossetti, by letting her female character tell a fairy tale which delights and entertains as the children join "hands to little hands" (l. 560) to form a magic circle, affirms the truth of imagination and knowledge over conventional moral conduct. Maidens have the right to buy the fruit of Goblin Market.

## Notes

1. The following is typical commentary found in histories of children's literature: "In the midst of what was, for the most part, merely pleasant verse for children, Christina Rossetti (1830–1894) provided them with one real, one can even say, one great poem in 'Goblin Market' (1862)," in Cornelia Meigs, et al., *A Critical History of Children's Literature* (New York: The Macmillan Co., 1953), p. 290. See also Mary F. Thwaite, *From Primer to Pleasure in Reading* (Boston: Horn Book, 1963), p. 135.

2. Mackenzie Bell, *Christina Rossetti: A Biographical and Critical Study* (1898; rpt. New York: Haskell House Publishers, 1971), p. 206.

3. Delores Rosenblum, in "Christina Rossetti: The Inward Pose," in Sandra M. Gilbert and Susan Gubar, eds., *Shakespeare's Sisters: Feminist Essays on Women Poets* (Bloomington: Indiana University Press, 1979), says, "The poem really has less to do with temptation than with the consequences of indulgence" (p. 95).

4. Christina Rossetti, *The Complete Poems*, ed. R. W. Crump, 3 vols. (Baton Rouge: Louisiana State University Press, 1979), 1:11–26. References to *Goblin Market* will be taken from this edition.

5. Eleanor Walter Thomas, *Christina Georgina Rossetti* (New York: Columbia University Press, 1931), p. 60.

6. Lona Mosk Packer, *Christina Rossetti* (Berkeley: The University of California Press, 1963), p. 142.

7. Ellen Golub, "Untying Goblin Apron Strings: A Psychoanalytic Reading of 'Goblin Market,'" *Literature and Psychology*, 25 (1975), 158.

8. Jerome J. McGann, "Christina Rossetti's Poems: A New Edition and a Revaluation," *Victorian Studies*, 23 (1979–80), 237–54.

9. Sandra M. Gilbert and Susan Gubar, *The Madwoman in the Attic: The Woman Writer and the Nineteenth-Century Literary Imagination* (New Haven: Yale University Press, 1979), p. 564.

10. Packer, pp. 13–14, discusses Rossetti's early reading, as does B. Ifor Evans, "The Sources of Christina Rossetti's 'Goblin Market,'" *Modern Language Review*, 28 (1933), 156–65. See also Thomas, pp. 151–52.

11. For a full treatment of John Locke's influence on children's literature, see Samuel F. Pickering, Jr., *John Locke and Children's Books in Eighteenth-Century England* (Knoxville: The University of Tennessee Press, 1981).

12. For accounts of this controversy see F. J. Harvey Darton, *Children's Books in England: Five Centuries of Social Life* (1939; rpt. Cambridge: Cambridge University Press, 1970), pp. 218 ff.; Paul Hazard, *Books, Children and Men* (Boston: The Horn Book, 1944); Michael Rotzin, "The Fairy Tale in England, 1800–1870," *Journal of Popular Culture*, 4 (Summer 1970), 130–54; Anita Moss, "Varieties of Literary Fairy Tale," *Children's Literature Association Quarterly*, 7, No. 4 (Summer 1982), 15–17.

13. Patricia Demers and Gordon Moyles, eds., *From Instruction to Delight: An Anthology of Children's Literature* (Toronto: Oxford University Press, 1982), p. 68.

14. *John Bunyan: The Poems*, ed. Graham Midgley (Oxford: Clarenden Press, 1980), which is vol. 6 of *The Miscellaneous Works of Paul Bunyan*, gen. ed. Roger Sharrock.

15. Katherine Briggs, *The Fairies in English Tradition and Literature* (Chicago: University of Chicago Press, 1967), p. 59.

16. Katherine Briggs, *An Encyclopedia of Fairies* (New York: Pantheon Books, 1976), p. 194.

17. Bruno Bettelheim, *The Uses of Enchantment* (New York: Alfred A. Knopf, 1976), p. 117.

18. Quoted by Bettelheim, p. 24, from G. K. Chesterton, *Orthodoxy* (London: John Lane, 1909) and from C. S. Lewis, *The Allegory of Love* (Oxford: Oxford University Press, 1936).

19. John Keats, *The Poems*, ed. Jack Stillinger (Cambridge: The Belknap Press, Harvard University, 1978). Quotations from Keats's poetry will be taken from this edition.

20. Samuel Taylor Coleridge, *Complete Poetical Works*, ed., E. H. Coleridge, 2 vols. (Oxford, 1912). Quotations from Coleridge's poetry will be taken from this edition.

21. See, for example, Packer, who observes: "We have seen that in *From House to Home*, written only six months before *Goblin Market*, such small animals form part of the speaker's earthly paradise" (p. 143).

22. See, for example, Zaturenska, p. 79; Packer, pp. 129, 132, 135, 198. D. M. Stuart, in *Christina Rossetti* (London: Macmillan and Co., 1930), says explicitly: "One of the earliest admirers of 'Goblin Market' was Mrs. Caroline Norton, who compared it to 'The Ancient Mariner.' It has, indeed, certain vague affinities with more than one of Coleridge's dream poems" (p. 54).

23. Carolyn G. Heilbrun's quotation from critic Thomas Rosenmeyer's discussion of *The Bacchae* of Euripides is interestingly appropriate: "Dionysus appears to be neither woman nor man; or, better, he represents himself as woman-in-man, or man-in-woman, the unlimited personality. . . . To follow him or to comprehend him we must ourselves give up our precariously controlled, socially desirable limitations," in *Toward a Recognition of Androgyny* (New York: Colophon Books, 1974), p. xi.

24. "It was in Hone's three-volume popular miscellany (1825) that Christina at nine discovered Keats. . . . She, and not Gabriel or Holman Hunt, was the first 'Pre-Raphaelite' to appreciate Keats. The poem which caught her fancy . . . was *The Eve of St. Agnes*" (Packer, p. 14). Barbara Foss, in "Christina Rossetti and St. Agnes' Eve," *Victorian Poetry*, 14 (1976), 33–46, discusses Rossetti's awareness of the passive role of Victorian woman and the frustration of always having to wait in inactivity. Rossetti's lines in *From the Antique*:

> It's a weary life, it is, she said:—
> Doubly blank in a woman's lot:
> I wish and I wish I were a man:
> Or, better than any being, were not: [ll. 1–4]

echo Tennyson's "Mariana" in the weariness and wish for death that often accompanies the unimaginative passivity of "a woman's lot." It is little wonder that the goblin fruits are so tempting and being forbidden to feast on them so frustrating.

25. For example, in Perrault's *Little Red Riding Hood*, the girl learns that "young lasses . . . do very wrong to listen to strangers" (Charles Perrault, *Perrault's Complete Fairy Tales*, trans. A. E. Johnson et al. [New York: Dodd, Mead & Company, 1961], p. 77). What Red Cap learns in the Grimms' tale is to obey her mother. The moral at the end of *Puss in Boots* adjuring young people to value "industry, knowledge, and a clever mind" (Perrault, p. 25) is totally at variance with the success through deception taught by the tale itself. *Moralités* have now all but disappeared in the hands of today's publishers of fairy tales.

# *Tailpiece:* The Tale of Two Bad Mice

Suzanne Rahn

The last years of the nineteenth century and first of the twentieth were years of considerable political ferment in England, culminating in the General Election of 1906, which gave the Labour party an unprecedented fifty-three seats in Parliament. "You'll have a revolt of your slaves if you're not careful," said E. Nesbit's Queen of Babylon in *The Story of the Amulet,* and she was not alone in her prediction. *The Story of the Amulet* (1906) is very much a product of those days of turmoil, and so, in part and from an opposite political standpoint, is Kenneth Grahame's *Wind in the Willows* (1908), in whose final chapters a lower-class mob of stoats and weasels invades the stately home, Toad Hall, and must be forcibly driven out again.[1] That even a shy, sheltered, comfortably middle-class children's author like Beatrix Potter might be affected by this atmosphere is suggested by her *Tale of Two Bad Mice,* published in 1904.

The story begins with the description of a "very beautiful doll's house; it was red brick with white windows, and it had real muslin curtains and a front door and a chimney."[2] The house is inhabited by two dolls, Lucinda and Jane (the Cook). One day, when Lucinda and Jane are out for a drive, two mice—Tom Thumb and his wife, Hunca Munca—[3]venture into the doll's-house. They help themselves to the "lovely dinner" laid out in the dining room, but when they discover that the food is only painted plaster, "there was no end to the rage and disappointment of Tom Thumb and Hunca Munca" (p. 30). They smash the food and "set to work to do all the mischief they could," especially Tom:

> He took Jane's clothes out of the chest of drawers in her bedroom, and he threw them out of the top floor window.
> But Hunca Munca had a frugal mind. After pulling half the

Illustrations in this article are reproduced from *The Tale of Two Bad Mice* by Beatrix Potter and *A History of the Writings of Beatrix Potter* by Leslie Linder, © by Frederick Warne & Co., Inc.

feathers out of Lucinda's bolster, she remembered that she herself was in want of a feather bed. [p. 37]

The two mice manage to carry off the bolster, a cradle, some clothes, and several other items before the dolls return to view the scene of destruction. Retribution seems imminent:

> The little girl that the doll's-house belonged to, said,—"I will get a doll dressed like a policeman!"
> But the nurse said,—"I will set a mouse-trap!" [pp. 53–54]

But the story ends, rather surprisingly, with the two mice voluntarily paying for the damage they have done; they stuff a crooked sixpence into one of the dolls' stockings on Christmas Eve,

> And very early every morning—before anybody is awake— Hunca Munca comes with her dust-pan and her broom to sweep the Dollies' house!" [p. 59]

*Two Bad Mice* has always been popular with children. It is a good story; it has suspense and humor and vigorous action and character interest as well, for the bland and ineffectual dolls are a perfect foil for the daring, impulsive, and resourceful mice. It satisfies the young child's strong and complementary needs for adventure and for security, the adventure of disrupting one's world and the security of putting things back just as they were. (It is rather like *Peter Rabbit* in that respect, except that Peter's naughtiness is the outdoor variety—running away, getting lost, trespassing—and the naughtiness of the two mice is the indoor variety, getting into things and playing with them and breaking them.) Finally, as protagonists mice have a particular appeal. As Margaret Blount reminds us:

> Stories about them outnumber those about any other kind of animal: perhaps it is easier to imagine them members of their own hidden social systems and to think that when out of sight they might be a part of a miniature mirror world. Their fur and appearance help them to win our love, their apparently timorous and desperate courage, our sympathy; and they are easy to "dress."[4]

Moreover, they are exactly the right size to explore a doll's house, so that we experience the double enchantment in *Two Bad Mice* of one miniature world superimposed upon another.

But we can also see *The Tale of Two Bad Mice* as something other than a charming nursery story, for like *The Story of the Amulet* and *The Wind in the Willows* it reflects the tensions of its age. The doll's-house itself is a perfect emblem of upper-middle-class smugness and prosperity. Its handsome red brick façade and real muslin curtains conceal not life but a hollow imitation of it. The two dolls, Lucinda who "never ordered meals" and a Cook who "never did any cooking" (p. 10), preserve a set of class distinctions that have become meaningless (we see later, on p. 57, that they share the same bed). In this world even food no longer nourishes but is valued only for its impressive appearance:

> There were two red lobsters and a ham, a fish, a pudding, and some pears and oranges.
> They would not come off the plates, but they were extremely beautiful. [p. 13]

Taking advantage, like the stoats and weasels of *The Wind in the Willows,* of the absence of the rightful owners, a hungry mob (if we may call two mice a mob) from the lower levels of society invades the doll's-house. When they recognize the false values (symbolized by the inedible plaster ham) of the doll's-house for what they are, they are enraged and set out to destroy them, but they are distracted by the material wealth around them and turn to looting instead. Perhaps they are even a little corrupted by their exposure to luxury, for they steal not only useful things such as the bolster but also a birdcage and a bookcase which (significantly) will not fit into their mouse-hole (p. 41). The ineffectiveness of the police in dealing with such major civil disorders is shown in the illustration of the "doll dressed like a policeman" on p. 52; Hunca Munca is holding up one of her babies to look (perhaps jeer) at him, with no sign of trepidation, while two other mice peer in the doll's-house windows behind his back. The mouse-trap is another matter—something more like martial law—and the illustration of it (p. 55) shows Tom Thumb pointing it out very carefully to his children.

"Tom Thumb paid for everything he broke." Note the two dolls in bed together; in this picture they are portrayed as children and the mice as parents, filling their stockings on Christmas Eve.

Up to this turn of the story, we might assume Beatrix Potter to be in sympathy with the revolutionary uprising she has depicted; certainly she is in sympathy with the mice rather than with the passive and uninteresting dolls. The ending, however, reveals a political stance unmistakably Conservative. No only is the property damage paid for, but Hunca Munca becomes a servant to the very dolls she had robbed. The former social order is not only restored but reinforced.

Such a conclusion would go well in harness with what we know of Beatrix Potter's political convictions. According to her biographer

"I will get a doll dressed like a policeman!"

"But the nurse said,—'I will set a mouse-trap!'"

Margaret Lane, Beatrix Potter "by temperament and upbringing was an unshakable Conservative."[5] Entries in the private journal she kept from 1881 to 1897 show her eager to follow her father's lead in denouncing Gladstone (the Liberal Prime Minister at this time), the supporters of Home Rule for Ireland, and the leaders of the unemployed rioters of 1885.[6] Her day-by-day entries at the time of these riots show clearly that middle-class people like the Potters were frightened not so much by the actual violence of the riots as by the greater violence they might portend. "Why, they ought to be hung at once like dogs," she wrote of the four leaders of the riots who stood trial in February 1886. "I consider they are the most dangerous kind of criminals in existence. A murderer affects but a small circle, they, if unchecked, will cause wholesale slaughter, and ruin society."[7] Although Beatrix Potter was no longer keeping a journal in 1904, we can see from these entries that the possibility of lower-class uprisings on a large scale was familiar to her in her teens. Her only personal foray into politics was made not too long after *Two Bad Mice*, in the General Election of 1910, when she campaigned vigorously against the Liberal policy of Free Trade which had robbed her of her American royalties.[8]

A certain degree of political consciousness, then, was part of Beatrix Potter's outlook and may well have had some influence on her work. Another piece of evidence shows that she did think of her characters in class terms and, specifically, that she mentally categorized her two mouse-protagonists as lower-class, which in the text of the story itself is left somewhat in doubt. She used to amuse her child-friends by sending them miniature letters, supposedly to and from characters in her own books. A surviving letter from Lucinda to Hunca Munca dating from after the events in the story, together with Hunca Munca's reply, makes clear the relative class positions of these two characters. Lucinda refers to herself only in the third person and does not address Hunca Munca directly, while Hunca Munca not only uses the first person but addresses Lucinda with an obsequious "Honoured Madam":

Mrs Tom Thumb, Mouse Hole.
 Miss Lucinda Doll will be obliged if Hunca Munca will come half an hour earlier than usual on Tuesday morning, as Tom

Kitten is expected to sweep the kitchen chimney at 6 o'clock.
Lucinda wishes Hunca Munca to come not later than 5.45 a.m.

Miss Lucinda Doll, Doll's House.
Honoured Madam,
   I have received your note for which I thank you kindly,
informing me that T. Kitten will arrive to sweep the chimney at
6. I will come punctually at 7. Thanking you for past favours I
am, honoured Madam, your obedient humble Servant,
                                                Hunca Munca[9]

Beneath their polished surface, however, these little letters tell a
different story. Hunca Munca is *not* coming at 5:45, as requested,
but at 7:00; without wasting time in argument or self-justification,
she lets Lucinda know that things will be arranged to suit her
convenience, not Lucinda's. Seen from this perspective her "Honoured Madam" and "obedient humble Servant" are only the frosting
of convention, while "Thanking you for past favours" may well
remind us (and Lucinda) that the dress Hunca Munca wears when
she comes to sweep (see p. 58), and even her dustpan and broom,
originally belonged to Lucinda and Jane (Tom Thumb is shown in
flight with the broom on p. 44). Nominally a servant, Hunca Munca
retains not only her self-respect but the upper hand.

   In fact, *Two Bad Mice* as a whole does not reflect what we know to
have been Beatrix Potter's political opinions with any degree of
consistency. If the rampage of the two mice represents a lower-class
uprising like the riots that damaged shops and houses in 1885, it is
an uprising which we are invited to enjoy and even approve. There is
a kind of triumph, as of truth over falsehood, in Tom Thumb's destruction of the plaster ham. There is satisfaction in seeing Hunca
Munca, with her "frugal mind," salvaging what she wants from the
doll's-house like Robinson Crusoe and making such good use of it.
And while the mice do pay for what they have stolen or destroyed,
they clearly choose freely to do so and are not coerced by the threat
of traps or policemen. They make their own terms with the doll's-
house world.

   Viewing *Two Bad Mice* from a strictly political perspective does not
seem to make the best possible sense of it, after all. Another, more

personal element was involved in the creation of this story, and we need to understand what part this played before we can resolve the pattern of the whole.

The text of *The Tale of Two Bad Mice* was written near the end of 1903 and the book completed in the summer of 1904.[10] It was Beatrix Potter's fifth book for Frederick Warne and Company, and by now she had grown used to working closely with the youngest of the three Warne brothers, Norman, a sensitive and tactful editor. In spite of the growing disapproval of Beatrix's parents, this fruitful partnership was already ripening from friendship into love, and in the summer of 1905 Beatrix accepted Norman's proposal of marriage—an engagement that ended tragically with his death a few months later from pernicious anemia. *The Tale of Two Bad Mice,* unlike any other of Beatrix Potter's books, deserves to be considered in relation to this biographical background, for it was in large part a collaboration between her and a man she was learning to love. "It was during the preparation of *The Tale of Two Bad Mice,*" states Leslie Linder, "that Beatrix Potter and Norman Warne came to know each other well. They co-operated in a way that had not been possible during the writing of earlier books."[11]

It was Norman who built a mouse house for the real Tom Thumb and Hunca Munca, Beatrix Potter's pet mice, with a glass front so that Beatrix could observe the mice and sketch them for her illustrations. ("I have had so very much pleasure with that box, I am never tired of watching them run up and down." wrote Beatrix.) It was Norman who provided Lucinda and Jane. ("Thank you so very much for the queer little dollies; they are just exactly what I wanted.") It was Norman who bought the indispensable plaster food. ("I received the parcel from Hamley's this morning; the things will all do beautifully; the ham's appearance is enough to cause indigestion. I am getting almost more treasures than I can squeeze into one small book.") Most important of all, it was Norman who built the doll's-house.

It had been designed for his niece Winifred, and Beatrix had seen and admired it when he was still working on it in his basement workshop; perhaps, indeed, it was at that point that the idea for a story combining his doll's-house and her pet mice first took form in her mind. In February 1904, with the illustrations under way, she planned to use the finished house as a model. Unfortunately, it had already been installed in Winifred's nursery at Surbiton, and Mrs. Potter apparently refused to let Beatrix make a visit there; she must have suspected by then that her daughter was enjoying something more than a business relationship with Norman, and she objected strongly to Beatrix's marrying anyone "in trade."[12] "People who only see her casually do not know how disagreeable she can be when she takes dislikes," wrote Beatrix to Norman with unusual bluntness. In the end, Norman photographed the doll's-house inside and out, and the final illustrations were done from his photographs. "They are very good," wrote Beatrix, thanking him. "I do not see why you should be so depressed about the front door! I was going to make mine white and I will alter the top a little." Her gently teasing, affectionate tone is good evidence of the intimacy steadily growing between them as they worked together on the book.

With this background in mind, it is interesting to conjecture what personal meaning may have been incorporated into *The Tale of Two Bad Mice*. Tom Thumb and Hunca Munca are the only married couple among Beatrix Potter's many animal protagonists; is it possible that to Beatrix they represented Norman Warne and herself? If so, the book can be understood as a kind of symbolic projection, not of her present uncomfortable situation but of a future she might have begun to hope for.

The doll's-house, in this interpretation, would stand for the genteel upper-middle-class existence, all surface and no substance, which Beatrix had been born into and stifled by all her life, so well described by Margaret Lane in *The Tale of Beatrix Potter*:

> At the same hour every morning Mr. and Mrs. Rupert Potter came down to the dining-room for breakfast, a meal consumed in silence. Between ten and eleven Mr. Potter left for his club. At one o'clock a tray furnished with a small cutlet and a helping of rice pudding went up to the nursery by the back stairs, and as the clock struck two the carriage was at the door and Mrs. Potter, small and inflexibly upright and dressed in black, came down the whitened steps and got into it, and was driven away.[13]

Norman Warne took several photographs of his doll's-house for Beatrix Potter to use in her illustrations of *The Tale of Two Bad Mice*. The little girl is his niece Winifred, for whom the house was made.

Norman was dissatisfied with the front door of his doll's-house, and Beatrix promised that she would paint hers white and "alter the top a little." Her alteration makes the house appear taller and more elegant.

For Beatrix Potter, as for Ibsen, the doll's-house is a place where stereotyped roles, like those of Lucinda and Jane, disguise the basic fact that dolls have nothing to do. There is even a hint, in one of her letters to Norman, that she consciously identified the doll's-house with a way of life that was uncongenial to her: "The inside view is amusing—the kind of house where one cannot sit down without upsetting something, I know the sort. I prefer a more severe style."[14] (She was eventually to prefer a farmhouse.) It would not be surprising if whatever hostility she felt toward her repressive, unloving parents, exacerbated by their frigid disapproval of her friendship with Norman, were expressed symbolically in the violent invasion of a doll's-house as prim as their own home.

The invasion itself consists of three stages—the abortive dinner party, the rampage of destruction, and the looting of the house—each of which represents a successive stage of sophistication. The mice at first assume that the doll's-house food is real food; their rage at having been cheated makes them resolve to destroy everything within reach. But reason prevails; they realize that some things in the house are useful after all and proceed to steal all they can before the dolls return. These stages might show Beatrix Potter herself, progressing from disillusionment (the sociable Warne household was, as Margaret Lane puts it, "a revelation" to her)[15] to an embittered rejection of everything in her old life, and thence to the more mature realization that she does not really wish to reject *everything*; there are a few odds and ends worth keeping after all. And if she does rebel and marry Norman without her parents' permission, what could her parents actually say or do to prevent it? The dolls' reaction to the scene of destruction suggests that they would be too dumbfounded to do anything:

> What a sight met the eyes of Jane and Lucinda! Lucinda sat upon the upset kitchen stove and stared; and Jane leant against the kitchen dresser and smiled—but neither of them made any remark. [p. 46]

In the next pages Beatrix goes farther still into this imaginary future, revealing (as is often the case with her) more in pictures than in words. The text on p. 49 says only, "The book-case and the

Hunca Munca as a mother.

bird-cage were rescued from under the coal-box—but Hunca
Munca has got the cradle, and some of Lucinda's clothes." The
illustration facing it on p. 48 is an exquisite evocation of mother-
hood. Hunca Munca, wearing one of Lucinda's blue dresses, sits in a
chair with a baby in her lap—a baby that is somehow both mouse-
baby and human-baby, staring out at us wide-eyed, making a starfish
of one hand (paw) and sucking a finger of the other. Beside her, in
the cradle, three or four other babies nestle under a pink eiderdown,
with their tails dangling out at the foot. These irresistible mouse-
children appear in the three following pictures as well. On p. 51

Hunca Munca shows them the "useful pots and pans" from the doll's-house, on p. 52 she holds up the smallest to squeak at the policeman, and on p. 55 she and her husband instruct their children about the mouse-trap, Hunca Munca still holding the smallest baby in her arms. In all these pictures Hunca Munca is dressed, as if to acknowledge the dignity of her new role. The children are so important in these pictures that we might wonder at their not being mentioned in the text. But the text, of course, was finished before Beatrix Potter even began work on the pictures. It seems that as the book developed, and as it became more of a collaboration with Norman Warne, it also became more and more a hopeful imagining of what their lifelong collaboration might be.

The final pages make sound emotional sense after this. As a Victorian daughter—and, although she did eventually win a life of her own, she remained a dutiful daughter to the end of her days—Beatrix would always have felt a little guilty at having defied her parents' wishes. So, as Hunca Munca, she returns regularly to the doll's-house and makes symbolic reparation for the disruption she has caused there. The final mood is one of reconciliation between mouse-hole and doll's-house.

Which interpretation of *The Tale of Two Bad Mice* is the better one—the political or the biographical? A complete appreciation of the book must, I think, include both. Drawing upon her vivid memories of the riots of 1885, Beatrix Potter recreated in symbolic form the class conflict of her time, expressing what the middle classes feared and the outcome they hoped for—peaceful preservation of the social structure. And yet, her personal circumstances in 1903 had subtly altered her point of view; she herself had been made to feel oppressed and impatient with those in power over her. And so Tom Thumb and Hunca Munca are not punished but keep the loot and make their own terms of payment. At the same time, working on this book with a man she was beginning to love and thwarted in this relationship by her parents' small-minded disapproval, Beatrix Potter created a story which expresses both her inner rebellion against them and their stultifying way of life and her hope for a fulfilled and happy future. All this—and more, of course—is interwoven in *The Tale of Two Bad Mice*.

## Notes

1. See Peter Green's extensive analysis in *Kenneth Grahame: A Biography* (Cleveland: World Publishing, 1959), pp. 242–47. See also Jules Zanger's "Goblins, Morlocks, and Weasels: Classic Fantasy and the Industrial Revolution," *Children's Literature in Education*, 8, No. 4 (Winter 1977): 154–62, which analyzes from this standpoint *The Wind in the Willows*, *The Princess and the Goblin*, and *The Time Machine*. Zanger gives a good picture of the historical background, though he takes no account of strong differences in viewpoint among the three works discussed.

2. Beatrix Potter, *The Tale of Two Bad Mice* (New York: Frederick Warne, 1904), p. 9. All further quotations from this book will be from this edition.

3. The names were those of Beatrix Potter's own pet mice. Hunca Munca is also the name of Tom Thumb's princess in Henry Fielding's burlesque drama *Tom Thumb the Great* (1731).

4. Margaret Blount, *Animal Land: The Creatures of Children's Fiction* (New York: William Morrow, 1975), p. 152.

5. Margaret Lane, *The Tale of Beatrix Potter: A Biography*, rev. ed. (London and New York: Frederick Warne, 1968), p. 104.

6. See Beatrix Potter, *The Journal of Beatrix Potter from 1881 to 1897*, transcribed by Leslie Linder (London and New York: Frederick Warne, 1966), pp. 116 and 124 for typical remarks on Gladstone; p. 165 for a diatribe on the Home Rulers; p. 176 for an outburst against the leaders of the riots.

7. Potter, *Journal*, p. 176.

8. See Lane, *Tale*, pp. 103–06.

9. Quoted in Margaret Lane, *The Magic Years of Beatrix Potter* (London and New York: Frederick Warne, 1978), p. 128. It is interesting to learn from this letter that Tom Kitten, of *The Tale of Tom Kitten* and *The Tale of Samuel Whiskers, or The Roly-Poly Pudding*, has also been placed in the servant class.

10. See Leslie Linder, *A History of the Writings of Beatrix Potter, including Unpublished Work* (London and New York: Frederick Warne, 1971), pp. 149 and 153.

11. Linder, p. 154. Detailed accounts of the creation of *Two Bad Mice* appear in three separate sources, all of which make use of much the same material, chiefly Beatrix Potter's letters to Norman Warne: Margaret Lane's *Tale of Beatrix Potter* and *The Magic Years of Beatrix Potter* and Leslie Linder's *History of the Writings of Beatrix Potter*, pp. 149–55. The third, which is the most precise as regards chronology, has been my main source for the facts and quotations in the following paragraphs.

12. See Lane, *Tale*, p. 74, and *Magic Years*, pp. 125–26.

13. Lane, *Tale*, p. 14. The early scenes of the filmed ballet, *The Tales of Beatrix Potter*, followed this account very closely and were quite successful in conveying the atmosphere of the Potter household.

14. Quoted in Linder, p. 152.

15. Lane, *Tale*, p. 75.

# The Literary Transformation of a Sluggard

Mary-Agnes Taylor

I cannot claim that I learned to read from *Dick and Jane*; I can, however, say that I remember quite well the first time that I was able to decipher *Baby Ray*. I can also remember that our class was not allowed to linger with such innocent reading matter. Rather quickly we moved to more substantial tales such as those found in a collection of Aesop's fables. From the very beginning we were made to understand that the selections were somewhat akin to our Sunday School lessons. But in spite of such exalted status, there was one story which particularly troubled my child mind: how could those miserly ants be so unkind to the grasshopper? Traditionally, from the fifteenth century to the present, adults have supported a utilitarian version of poetic justice: the frugal ant enjoys the fruits of his labor, while the shiftless grasshopper suffers the consequences of his indolence. However, happily for me, a few wise poets in the nineteenth and twentieth centuries have transformed the much maligned singer by giving value to his calling.

The first printed offering of the tale for English-speaking children came from William Caxton in 1484. Written in late middle English, the version is not comprehensible to the modern child. There is, however, a faithful adaptation that has been written by John J. McKendry for a publication by the Metropolitan Museum of Art. It reads:

> A grasshopper in the wintertime went and demanded of the ant some of her corn for to eat. And then the ant said to the grasshopper, "What hast thou done all the summer last past?" And the grasshopper answered, "I have sung." And after said the ant to her, "Of my corn shalt thou none have, and if thou hast sung all summer, dance now in the winter."

The epilogue, printed in red ink, leaves no doubt about the moral:

> There is one time for to do some labor and work, and one time for to have rest, for he that worketh not nor does no good shall have oft at his teeth great cold, and lack at his need.[1]

German woodcut from *Aesop's Life and Fables* (Anton Sorg, Augsburg, about 1479 [first edition Johann Zainer, Ulm, ca. 1476–77]).

The Caxton cadence clearly reflects the rhythms of fifteenth century biblical translations. The initial "And" beginning new sentences; the "hast," the "shalt," and the "thou"; and the reverse word orders all follow those patterns. Furthermore, the epilogue is an obvious paraphrase from the third chapter of Ecclesiastes. Actually, Caxton's strong deprecation of idleness was not limited to his rendition of the fables. Many of the preface sheets of his voluminous output in other translations carried warnings about the evils of sloth. And he lived by his word, accomplishing most of his work with no skilled help. By example, Caxton has a personification of the fabled ant, and he held no truck with idle singers of song.

Although Caxton, by virtue of his early translations, holds a

coveted "first" in the history of Western children's literature, he
cannot, in a literary context, compete in charm with that seventeenth-
century gentleman commonly referred to as *Le Fablier*—Jean de La
Fontaine. In a critical analysis of La Fontaine's fables, Howard Hugo
suggests that association of the pieces with children's literature
"is more apparent than real," having grown primarily from La
Fontaine's dedication of the first several books to the six-year-old
son of Louis XIV. The appeal of the fables, he reminds us, goes far
beyond the nursery, "perpetuating and renewing the classical tradition" for the whole of mankind. In a manner characteristic of the
period of neoclassicism, La Fontaine employs a completely imper-
sonal voice, revealing the fundamental natures of his subjects in a
public rather than a private context.[2] His jocular, but objective,
spirit is preserved in Marianne Moore's translation of "The Grasshopper and the Ant."

> Until fall, a grasshopper
>    Chose to chirr;
> With starvation as foe,
> When northeasters would blow,
> And not even a gnat's residue
> Or caterpillar's to chew,
> She chirred recurrent chant
> Of want beside an ant,
> Begging it to rescue her
> With some seeds it could spare
> Till the following year's fall.
> "By August you shall have them all,
> Interest and principal."
> Share one's seeds? Now what is worse
> For any ant to do?
> Ours asked, "When fair, what brought you through?"
> —"I sang for those who might pass by chance,—
> Night and day, an't you please."
> —"Sang, you say? You have put me at ease.
> A singer! Excellent. Now dance."[3]

Here the fable ends without benefit of epilogue. La Fontaine's fable needs none. His mid-poem voice as third-party commentator has already performed the function of that traditional postscript. Initially, the grasshopper offers the ant a business proposition: she seeks a loan, not charity. But the third-party voice intrudes. "Share one's seeds? Now what is worse / For any ant to do?" La Fontaine's ant—whom he intimately calls "ours"—confirms the attitude behind the word "worse" by maintaining the established role of the self-righteous judge who chastises the singer. The refusal is managed with a chilling clarity of conscience. "Sang, you say? You have put me at ease. / A singer! Excellent. Now dance." The singer of songs remains a minstrel without champion.

Except for the third-party rhetorical question, it is difficult to find evidence that would classify La Fontaine as either ant or grasshopper in his sympathies. He leaves no clues such as those planted by Caxton. Nor is he the naturally clear-cut case of the Oliver Goldsmith and Thomas Bewick team.

Bewick, from the time of his impoverished childhood to the time of a solvent old age, exhibited antlike qualities. On the other hand, Goldsmith lived his entire life as an improvident grasshopper. Some brief biographical glimpses of the two lead to interesting speculation.

During a childhood spent on his father's modest Northumberland farm, Thomas Bewick developed two characteristics that were to shape his future: a love of drawing and a love of nature. His earliest works—mainly portraits of hunters, horses and hounds—adorned the walls of the homes of his rustic neighbors. Later, during an apprenticeship served from 1767 to 1774 at Newcastle, he received a number of commissions for woodcuts for children's books. Two of these—*New Lottery-Book of Birds and Beasts* and *Moral Instructions of a Father to His Son*—were tentative efforts that would become more sophisticated editions variously associated with Goldsmith.

As a young man, Oliver Goldsmith traveled over Europe on foot. In Flanders, Switzerland, and France he often played his flute for bed and board. Early exposure to an Irish schoolmaster, who preferred to teach tales and song rather then mathematics and letters, gave Goldsmith an inexhaustible supply of folklore. But the Italians did not care for Irish mirth, so Goldsmith there found himself at the gates of convents begging alms for food. Later, back in London, he

Wood engraving by Thomas Bewick for *Select Fables of Aesop and Others*, Newcastle, 1784.

Wood engraving by Thomas Bewick for *Fables of Aesop*, Newcastle, 1818. The rustic, rural scene of the earlier illustration is replaced by a "comfortable mansion" with lush grounds.

turned to writing as a last resort. After publishing the epic *Traveller* in 1776, his fortunes, but not his wasteful ways, changed. Bewick became his illustrator for *Traveller*, and thus the two were brought together for other publications, among which was Bewick's *Aesopus, Select Fables of Aesop and Others*, for which Goldsmith wrote an introduction that included a biography of Aesop and an essay on the moral and aesthetic values of fable. Although some scholars had already begun to question the actual existence of Aesop, that possibility did not bother Goldsmith. His biography is filled with apocryphal details about Aesop's life and death.

How much of the rest of the text in *Select Fables* was actually composed by Goldsmith and how much by Bewick is a matter of question. According to the *Dictionary of National Biography*, both *Select Fables* and *Tommy Trip's History of Beasts and Birds* were "traditionally supposed to have been by Goldsmith, but the tradition is incapable of proof."[4] The *DNB* does state, however, that *Select Fables* grew from the earlier *Moral Instructions of a Father to His Son*, and likewise that *Tommy Trip's History* was a reworking of *New-Lottery Birds and Beasts*. Some thirty years later, Bewick would again attempt yet another set of fables. If one compares the text of Bewick's third attempt—*Fables of Aesop* (1818)—with *Select Fables* (1784), enough differences emerge to lend credence to the belief that Goldsmith did indeed compose the melodramatic rhymes in *Select Fables*.

Modern editors have eschewed the Bewick fables and denounced them as some of the worst that ever were written for children. Not satisfied with the traditional epilogue to the fable of the grasshopper and the ant, Bewick, in his *Select Fables*, added a prologue that creates a ponderous overkill:

> O now, while health and vigour still remain.
> Toil, toil, my lads, to purchase honest gain!
> Shun idleness! shun pleasure's tempting snare!
> A youth of revels breeds an age of care.

The fable itself is handled in a traditional way, in neoclassical verse balancing terms and values. Like Caxton, in the epilogue the author borrows from the Bible; but instead of choosing from Ecclesiastes, he chooses from Proverbs (6:6) to support his advice that

*Action and industry is the business of a wise and a good man, and
nothing is so much to be despised as slothfulness.* Go to the Ant, thou
sluggard, *says the Royal Preacher,* consider her ways and be wise;
*which in a few words sums up the moral of this fable.*[5]

Although the moral in *Fables of Aesop* (1818) remains the same as that
in *Select Fables* (1784), both the format and the style of writing are
changed radically. The prologue is omitted, and the fable is recorded in a cumbersome single paragraph of only four sentences,
which wind ponderously through a verbal maze. The opening scene
depicts a "commonwealth of Ants" gathered in their "comfortable
mansion" as they are approached by a lone grasshopper. One ant
becomes spokesman for the group. Thus, in this particular version,
the grasshopper suffers censure not only from an individual ant, but
from a whole community of ants to expand the disapproval of the
manner in which he has spent the summer.

Instead of an epilogue, Bewick attached an "Application" in this
later edition, in which the prose remains as stilted as that in the fable.
The appendage is fully as long as the primary text. In an extended
metaphor, Bewick equates summer with youth and winter with old
age. He began *Fables* after a long illness during his mid-sixties, a
circumstance that no doubt contributed to the heavy tone. He
preaches that youth and manhood are the times when one must lay
"in such a stock as may suffice for helpless old age," but, he warns,
there are many

rational creatures, who squander away in a profuse prodigality,
whatever they get in their younger days, as if the infirmity of
age would require no supplies to support it, or at least would
find themselves administered to in some miraculous way.

The second sentence—there are only two—restates the "admirable
lesson" learned from the fable. The last part of this sentence I find of
particular interest:

for it should always be remembered, that "a youth of revels
breeds an age of care," and that temperence in youth lays the
foundation of health and comfort for old age.[6]

A question comes to mind. Why has "a youth of revels breeds an age of care" been placed in quotation marks? Certainly it is true that Bewick constantly borrowed from his own earlier works, and that many of his books for children represent a sequence of reworked materials. In light of this practice, it seems unlikely that he would, in an isolated case, put quotes around a phrase taken from an earlier work if that work had been his. The evidence is faint, but it does lend support to the belief that the rhymed verses in *Select Fables* are indeed the work of Goldsmith, and that Bewick, being the thoroughly honest man that he was, acknowledges it as such.

Caxton, La Fontaine, Bewick and Goldsmith are but a few of the many writers who have presented the grasshopper as a worthless character, but there have been some others who were not willing to vilify the long-legged singer. Somewhat parallel scenarios have been created by John Keats and John Ciardi. James Joyce has written an ironic adult parable that condemns the ant, while Leo Lionni, without chastising ants, has recast the grasshopper as a child reader's hero.

Keats's sonnet, titled "On the Grasshopper and Cricket," does not actually mention the ant, but habitual pairing admits allusion to the ant as a foil. Keats opens with the pronouncement that "The poetry of earth is never dead." This generalization is particularized in the octave through the observation that even when "all the birds are faint with the hot sun," a voice will be heard: it is the voice of the grasshopper. The sestet restates the opening line of the octave and then explains how the song is perpetuated:

> The poetry of earth is ceasing never:
> On a lone winter evening, when the frost
> Has wrought a silence, from the stove there shrills
> The Cricket's song, in warmth increasing ever,
> And seems to one in drowsiness half lost,
> The Grasshopper's among some grassy hills.[7]

The grasshopper's voice may be silenced by winter, but not song itself, for "from the stove there shrills / The Cricket's song" to effect a continuity, which is emphasized by the use of present tense and absolutes in the lines "The poetry of earth is never dead" and "The poetry of earth is ceasing never." Keats's respect for the singer contrasts sharply with that of Bewick's; and, in keeping with romantic sensibilities, it is his grasshopper-poet, not a pragmatist-ant, who reigns supreme regardless of season.

Ciardi, in a much longer verse, takes us full round literally to meet the grasshopper again next spring. He titles his rhymed melodrama *John J. Plenty and Fiddler Dan*. John J. was an ant workaholic. The summer birds sang as he packed his larder tighter and tighter. But a great sadness befell him—his beloved sister eloped with a grasshopper named Fiddler Dan. So magnetic were the fiddler's tunes that

> . . . all summer stirred to hear
> The voice of the music. Far and near
> The grasses swayed, and the sun and shade
> Danced to the love and music played.
>
> Dan played on for the world to turn,
> While his little wife lay on a fringe of fern.

John J. missed none of this. But he did pause long enough to warn that when winter came, the lovers could expect no help from him. Ciardi's winter, like that described by Keats, "wrought a silence" which assured John J. that the lovers were dead. He became so paranoid about the sufficiency of his larder that he ate only sparingly. Weakened by the self-imposed fast, he emerged in the spring. So surprised was he to hear the familiar sounds of Dan's fiddle that he fell on his face in the mud. Ciardi says he does not know where the fiddler and his wife hid during the winter. But he does "really know," just as Keats did, that you can

> . . . *Say what you like as you trudge along,*
> *The world won't turn without a song.*
> And—*Fiddlers grow thin and their hands turn blue*
> *When winter comes, but they pull through.*
> There's this about music—and, oh, it's true!—
> *It never stays stopped.*[8]

Both Ciardi and Keats write in relatively simple, positive vein to affirm the eternal worth of the grasshopper, but James Joyce attacks the entire theme of the fable itself through a highly complex and satirical parable. His ploy is imbedded in *Finnegans Wake* as Shaun tells his brother Shem the "feeble" of the "Ondt" and the "Gracehoper." Whereas these three puns reveal the gist of the parable, they can in no way do justice to the depth and the sweep of the multiple puns and foreign-language references which are detailed in William Tindall's *A Reader's Guide to Finnegans Wake*. Tindall quotes his own earlier work on Joyce, noting that "the pun is mightier than the word."[9]

*Feeble*, we can see at once, attacks the total weakness of the parent fable's argument. *Ondt* is a Danish word meaning evil and thus doubly casts the original character. *Gracehoper* is likewise cast, being simultaneously the original sluggard and the poet in whom we observe grace and take hope. Shaun is the Ondt—the economically and sexually powerful man of the world. Shem is the Gracehoper—the poet who, according to Shaun, is the offensive and ineffectual one. As Shaun relates the fable to his brother, instructing him in the worldly successes of the Ondt, it appears on the literal level that Joyce is praising the Ondt. But the whole tale is an extended example of the Irishman's superb verbal irony, for Joyce is unmistakably a grasshopper. He has the Gracehoper sing a mock apology to the Ondt for having offended him:

> I pick up your reproof, the horsegift of a friend,
> For the prize of your save is the price of my spend.
> . . . . . . . . . . . . . . . . . . . . . . . . . . . . . . . . . . . . . . . .
> Your feats end enormous, your volumes immense,
> (May the Graces I hoped for sing your Ondship sense!)
> Your genus its worldwide, your spacest sublime!
> But Holy Salmartin, why can't you beat time![10]

The Ondt responds in an epilogue which follows the apology. To pious folks his commentary may seem sacrilegeous because their eyes read, "In the name of the former and of the latter and of their holocaust. Allmen," while their ears hear, "In the name of the Father and of the Son and of the Holy Ghost. Amen."[11]

A possible objection in all of the fables discussed so far is that either the ant or the grasshopper is drawn as totally anti-heroic. One is rejected at the expense of the other. Their fixed incompatibility is synthesized by Joyce's Gracehoper: "The prize of your save is the price of my spend." Leo Lionni, however, in *Frederick* manages to present the two types in a harmonious way without belittling either. To do so, he resorts to a fundamental technique used by fablers of old. Just as they presented their humans in a disguised form— usually in feathers or fur—he takes Aesop's traditionally paired insects and recasts them as a family of mice.

From the beginning a warm tone is set: "Not far from the barn and in the granary, a chatty family of field mice had their home." "Chatty," "family," and "home" suggest compatibility—a pleasant bond. But the situation is not without conflict. The farmer had moved away, the granary was empty, and winter was approaching. The wise mice began to gather supplies. "They all worked day and night. All except Frederick." The story has scarcely begun, but the grasshopper syndrome is already apparent. The four working siblings asked Frederick why he did not work. Frederick replied, "I do work, . . . I gather sun rays for the cold winter days." Again they questioned his inactivity. He responded that he was gathering colors because winter was gray. A third time they reproached him more sternly. "Are you dreaming, Frederick?" His denial came quickly. "Oh no, I am gathering words." Lionni has set us up for the compleat artist, one who later starts his magic through the recall of sunlight and painted flowers. However, the other mice clamored for more than pictures; they wanted words. To accommodate them Frederick climbed up on a huge stone, a stage high above the others, and affecting a timid voice from the mount he asked,

> Who scatters snowflakes: Who melts the ice?
> Who spoils the weather? Who makes it nice?
> Who grows the four-leaf clovers in June?
> Who dims the daylight? Who lights the moon?
>
> Four little field mice who live in the sky.
> Four little field mice . . . like you and I.
>
> One is the Springmouse who turns on the showers.
> Then comes the Summer who paints the flowers.

The Fallmouse is next with walnuts and wheat.
And Winter is last with little cold feet.

Aren't we lucky the seasons are four?
Think of a year with one less . . . or one more!

When he finished, the others responded in gleeful surprise, "But Frederick, . . . you are a poet!" The vindicated bard "blushed, took a bow, and said shyly, 'I know it.'"[12]

In closing, one more epilogue is offered to make two points—one in the context of metaphor, and the other in a context of morality. Through early exposure to the Aesop collection, all of us have come to know some dog in the manger, some wolf in sheep's clothing, some joker who cries wolf. We know the loser who pleads sour grapes, and we know that it is almost impossible to find a brave soul to bell the cat. But we do not label anyone as lazy as a grasshopper, as worthless as a singer of songs. Admittedly, our society has never given poets unanimous support, but a few philosophers have always hailed them as the real seers of truth. To continue to cast the poets as worthless grasshoppers is to give credence to a misconception. Even though Keats, Ciardi, Joyce, and Lionni may all have been indulging in self-defense, they have at the same time defended the grasshopper, changing him from sluggard to bard. And in this time of poetry revival for children, I say unto you, "Go thou and do likewise."

## Notes

1. *Aesop, Five Centuries of Illustrated Fables*, selected by John J. McKendry (New York: Metropolitan Museum of Art, 1964), p. 14.

2. Howard E. Hugo, introduction to "Masterpieces of Neoclassicism," *World Masterpieces*, 3rd ed. (New York: Norton, 1973), 2, 9.

3. From *The Fables of La Fontaine*, trans. Marianne Moore, copyright 1954 by Marianne Moore, copyright © renewed 1982 by Lawrence E. Brinn and Louise Crane; reprinted by permission of Viking Penguin Inc.

4. *Dictionary of National Biography*, s.v. "Goldsmith, Oliver."

5. Thomas Bewick, *Treasury of Aesop's Fables illustrated by Thomas Bewick Together with the Life of Aesop, by Oliver Goldsmith* (New York: Avenel Books, Crown, 1973), pp. 56–57; rpt. from part 3 of *Aesopus, Select Fables of Aesop and Others* (Newcastle: J. Saint, 1784), commonly referred to as *Select Fables*.

6. Thomas Bewick, *Fables of Aesop*, ed. Michael Marqusee (New York: Paddington Press, 1975), pp. 307–08.

7. John Keats, *Selected Poems and Letters*, ed. Douglas Bush (New York: Houghton Mifflin, Riverside Edition, 1959), p. 19.

8. John Ciardi, *John J. Plenty and Fiddler Dan* (New York: Lippincott, 1963), unpaged.

9. William York Tindall, *A Reader's Guide to Finnegans Wake* (New York: Farrar, Straus, and Giroux, 1969), p. 7.

10. James Joyce, *Finnegans Wake* (1939; rpt. New York: Viking Compass, 1959), pp. 418–19.

11. Ibid., p. 419.

12. Leo Lionni, *Frederick* (New York: Pantheon, 1967), unpaged.

# The Narnia Books of C. S. Lewis:
## Fantastic or Wonderful?

Dennis B. Quinn

C. S. Lewis maintained that good literature for children must be good literature by adult standards, although not every good book is necessarily good for children. The current adult enthusiasm for fantasy, both popular and critical, has led to a rather uncritical acceptance of it, together with a certain recklessness concerning its nature and history. The editors of the *The Good Book Guide to Children's Books* (Penguin, 1983) declare that "the crowning glory of children's books is fantasy." Before we all plunge helter-skelter into the enchanted forest of fantasy, however, I should like to offer a few cautionary words about the genre itself and about one of its most popular practitioners, C. S. Lewis.[1]

The word *fantasy* has meant many things in the history of English. A survey of the various *Oxford English Dictionary* entries, however, reveals two basic meanings. In its earliest uses fantasy meant pretty much what it had meant in Greek and Latin—a mental picture or the faculty of forming such pictures. In short, fantasy was nearly synonymous with imagination. Very early on, however, the word took on some negative coloration. A classical Greek derivative of fantasy meant an apparition; and from that idea it is an easy step to something with no extramental reality or to something illusory, hallucinatory, extravagant, capricious, or even insane. On the whole, one may say that from Plato to Dryden fantasy meant either a mental image or appearance or (often with a negative implication) something unreal. In more recent times, while the word *imagination* has replaced fantasy in its neutral sense, the association of fantasy with unreality has persisted, though with lessening disapproval.

As a name for a genre of literature, the term *fantasy* was used at least as early as Addison's *Spectator* paper number 419. Although not entirely disapproving, Addison obviously regards it as a minor species of fiction, and he uses the word to mean pretty much what it had always meant—something unreal, something belonging entirely to the imagination and deriving ultimately from superstition. To Addison and Dryden, *A Midsummer Night's Dream* and the Arthurian stories were fantastic.

In 1927 E. M. Forster used *fantasy* to describe a wide range of serious literature from *Tristram Shandy* to *Moby-Dick* and Joyce's *Ulysses*. He defined this species of literature as one that asks the reader to accept the supernatural as playing some role, whether implicitly or explicitly:

> It implies the supernatural, but need not express it. Often it does express it, and were that type of classification helpful, we could make a list of the devices which writers of a fantastic turn have used—such as the introduction of a god, ghost, angel, monkey, monster, midget, witch into ordinary life; or the intro-duction of ordinary men into no man's land, the future, the past, the interior of the earth, the fourth dimension; or divings into and dividings of personality; or finally the device of parody or adaptation.[2]

Thus Forster admits fantasy as a respectable (if not central and hardly essential) aspect of the novel, and I believe his definition is widely accepted today. I find it both inconsistent and unacceptably broad. Monkeys and midgets are not supernatural nor are dividings of personality or parody; and if the supernatural is the *sine qua non*, then *Alice's Adventures in Wonderland* is not fantasy and *Hamlet* is.

Still more recently J. R. R. Tolkien carried the emancipation of fantasy a step further by defining it as a subcreation that has an inner consistency of its own and hence a sort of reality independent of the real world; moreover, he claims for fantasy a status equal if not superior to other literary modes. This definition retains the old association of fantasy with unreality (though this issue is rather evaded), but it adds the highest approval and prestige. I can accept the definition but not the evaluation. In doing so I believe I am following the central tradition of Western literature, both in theory and in practice. It might be assumed, then, that I must classify such forms as the traditional folk or fairy tale as fantasy; but I am not among those moderns who consign all ghosts and gods to unreality, and certainly traditional authors whose works contain representations of the strange and supernatural did not deny the reality of such phenomena. Such matters were considered real and wonderful but not unreal and fantastic. It is upon this distinction that I shall base my critique of fantasy in general and Lewis in particular.

The distinction between the wonderful and the fantastic may be observed perfectly in the conversation between Theseus and Hippolyta near the end of *A Midsummer Night's Dream*. In his famous speech Theseus comments disparagingly on the story that the young lovers have told about their adventures with the fairies in the woods. Hippolyta says that the story is strange, and Theseus replies:

> More strange than true. I never may believe
> These antique fables, nor these fairy toys.
> Lovers and madmen have such seething brains,
> Such shaping fantasies, that apprehend
> More than cool reason ever comprehends.
> The lunatic, the lover, and the poet
> Are of imagination all compact.
> . . . . . . . . . . . . . . . . . . . . . . . . . . . . . . . .
> Such tricks hath strong imagination,
> That if it would but apprehend some joy,
> It comprehends some bringer of that joy.
> Or in the night, imagining some fear
> How easily is a bush supposed a bear! [V. ii. 2–8, 18–22]

Fantasy and "strong imagination," says Theseus, lead us into a realm of unreality. This most poetical denunciation of poetry is very familiar, but Hippolyta's none too submissive reply is often forgotten:

> But all the story of the night told over
> And all their minds transfigured so together,
> More witnesseth than fancy's images,
> And grows to something of great constancy;
> But howsoever, strange and admirable. [V. i. 23–27]

The consistency of the lovers' stories, argues the Amazonian queen, strongly suggests that they are more than mere images created by "fancy," something that appears to be solid but at the same time "strange and admirable." The term *admirable* here, of course, is synonymous with *wonderful* in Shakespeare's vocabulary. Hippolyta is simply asserting a well-known distinction: the fantastic is unreal, while the wonderful is real but strange, mysterious, unexplained; and on this occasion the lady has the last word.

This distinction has very deep roots indeed, which are too extensive to explore here. But from Plato and Aristotle, wonder was seen as the emotion common to the poet and the philosopher, an idea developed and elaborated ever since by the greatest minds and hearts in the Western tradition.[3] Wonder arises from encountering an effect whose cause is unknown, that is, a strange or mysterious thing, but a real thing that might be understood. The mysterious need not be supernatural, for there are mysteries in nature—phenomena we do not understand, such as love and death, or even material objects—birds, stars, a grain of sand.

It is my intention in what follows to apply the distinction between the wonderful and the fantastic to Lewis's *Chronicles of Narnia*. Before discussing that work, however, it is necessary to identify the literary context in which Lewis wrote. I prefer to call it the neoplatonic tradition in order to distinguish Plato himself from his later interpreters. Lewis describes this tradition in its literary aspect in his book, *English Literature in the Sixteenth Century* (1954). There he argues (correctly, I think) that whereas Aristotelian principles required the direct imitation of nature, the neoplatonic ideal demanded an imitation of an image in the artist's mind. This image originates from the artist's vision of an invisible truth, an idea in the Platonic sense. Lewis quotes Plotinus:

> "If anyone disparages the arts on the ground that they imitate Nature . . . we must remind him that natural objects are themselves only imitations, and that the arts do not simply imitate what they see but re-ascend to those principles from which Nature herself is derived. . . ." Art and Nature thus [says Lewis] become rival copies of the same supersensuous original, and there is no reason why Art should not sometimes be the better of the two. Such a theory leaves the artist free to exceed the limits of Nature.[4]

It is upon this distinction between Aristotelian and neoplatonic theories of literature that Lewis bases his own distinction between "drab" and "golden" poetry, the latter being the category containing Spenser, Sidney, and Ariosto. Although Lewis insisted that he did not intend the terms *golden* and *drab* as evaluative, it is clear that he himself preferred Spenser and the other golden poets. *The Allegory of Love* proposed one of the best modern defenses of Spenser, including a defense of the neoplatonic literary theory behind Spenser.[5] It is my contention that this theory tends to produce fantastic literature, a genre that implicitly or explicitly denies or diminishes the reality of the sensible world and substitutes for it a world that exists only in the mind.[6]

Before considering Lewis himself it may be useful to consider *The Faerie Queene*, perhaps the greatest poem of fantasy. The English romantics greatly admired the sixteenth-century lover of romance for precisely the qualities I have identified with fantasy. In his lecture on Chaucer and Spenser, Hazlitt had this to say:

> In Spenser, we wander in another world, among ideal beings. The poet takes and lays us in the lap of a lovelier nature, by the sound of softer streams, among greener hills and fairer valleys. He paints nature, not as we find it, but as we expected to find it; and fulfills the delightful promise of youth. He waves his wand of enchantment—and at once embodies airy beings, and throws a delicious veil over all actual objects. The two worlds of reality and of fiction are posed on the wings of his imagination. His ideas, indeed, seem more distinct than his perceptions. He is the painter of abstractions, and describes them with dazzling minuteness.[7]

Coleridge speaks in much the same vein:

> You will take especial note of the marvellous independence and true imaginative absence of all particular space or time in the *Faery Queene*. It is in the domains neither of history nor geography; it is ignorant of all artificial boundary, all material obstacles; it is truly in the land of Faery, that is, of mental space. The poet has placed you in a dream, a charmed sleep, and you

neither wish, nor have the power, to inquire where you are, or how you got there.[8]

Allowing for romantic exaggeration and the prejudices of the age in these evaluations, I think there is no denying them some measure of truth, even in the face of modern criticism. Reacting against the romantics' emphasis on the dreamlike quality of Spenser, critics of the early part of this century attempted to justify *The Faerie Queene* by tracing its allegorical meanings. More recent scholars, and Lewis chief among them, found the rather mechanical interpretations of the preceding generation damaging to the poetic effects of Spenser. A. C. Hamilton, for example, has called for a literal reading of *The Faerie Queene* as an image. He does not, however, altogether reject the romantic reading of Spenser; it "was not wrong, only incomplete."[9] What he claims to do is to create a synthesis of the divergent approaches. Far from repudiating the judgment of Coleridge, Hamilton reaffirms it.[10]

Even more important, he also reaffirms the neoplatonic theory that Lewis claims to be the foundation for the poem: "According to this tradition, the artist does not imitate external Nature but rather its reality which he perceives in his own mind. While the Aristotelian tradition, by placing reality within and through nature, required the artist to imitate the phenomenal world, neo-Platonism led artists to scorn fidelity to fact."[11]

What I contend is that this neoplatonic theory tends to produce fantasy, a world of the mind, cut off from factual phenomena; and when this theory is applied to allegory, the effects of fantasy are exaggerated to the detriment of the form. It is not to my purpose here to spell out in detail these effects on the great Spenser poem. I should wish to insist, however, that after we have conceded that the poem is not always allegorical and that the human characters are sometimes brilliantly realized, nevertheless the abstract idea (which is the neoplatonic model) is an ever-present element and sometimes a dominating one in Spenser. This is not the case with Dante, whose literary theory is more Aristotelian. Even the most human persons in Spenser are to some degree personified abstractions, whereas almost all of Dante's characters are historical personages—as Dorothy L. Sayers observed.[12] Hamilton tries to argue away these differences, but one only need imagine what a difference it would make to *The Faerie Queene* if (as Sayers suggested) Spenser had introduced Queen Elizabeth herself as a character rather than Belphoebe. Similarly, what a difference it would make to *The Divine Comedy* if the action took place in imaginary places symbolizing hell, purgatory, and heaven rather than in those very real places as imagined by Dante!

I do not think that Lewis himself would dispute this distinction among kinds of allegory nor my placing of the Narnia books in the same category as *The Faerie Queene*. In his essay on science fiction, Lewis describes a subclass of the genre (obviously a subclass he admired greatly) as one in which "the marvellous is in the grain of the whole work. We are, throughout, in another world"—Hazlitt's very phrase! Stories of this kind, says Lewis, are not comments on life but are "actual additions to life." Among examples he gives of this type of literature is *The Faerie Queene* but no more "realistic" allegory such as *Pilgrim's Progress* or *The Divine Comedy*. I think there is no doubt that Narnia intends to be precisely and entirely "another world."[13]

In concluding this theoretical discussion, I should like to quote an eminent modern authority in the history of philosophy, Etienne Gilson, in support of the general distinction here developed:

> [There are] two irreducible mental attitudes from which flow two absolutely irreconcilable interpretations of the universe. Aristotle's universe, born of a mind that seeks the sufficient reason for things in the things themselves, detaches and separates the world from God. Plato's universe . . . inserts between God and things ideas as a middle term: it is the universe of images, the world wherein things are at once copies and symbols, with no autonomous nature belonging to themselves, essentially dependent, relative, leading thought to seek beyond things and even above itself for the reason of what they are.[14]

Lest it be thought I have exaggerated Lewis's neoplatonism, let me begin my commentary on the *Chronicles of Narnia* with a very clear example. The end of the last book in the series asserts that neither Narnia nor what it represents, England, is real. Narnia "was only a shadow or a copy of the real Narnia . . . just as our own world,

England and all, is only a shadow or a copy of something in Aslan's real world."[15] And Aslan himself explains that "England and all" were only "shadow-lands" and now that they have all died, "the dream is over" and real life begins. It is not Platonic, of course, merely to say that there is a heaven or hell and that they are real, or even to say that life in final union with God is a higher level of reality. What is Platonic is the denial of the reality of this world, God's created universe. The philosophical and theological consequences of such views are considerable, but it is their literary implications that I intend to explore here.

I must confess at this point that I have never liked the Narnia stories, even though I had a strong prejudice in their favor because of my admiration for Lewis as a literary scholar and as a Christian apologist. Consequently, although I gave the Narnia books to my children, I never could engage myself in them. When I began to teach children's literature, I compelled myself to read these books. Still not liking them, I tried to understand why. I concluded that they lack high merit simply as fictive art. That is, halfway through volume one, I said to myself, "I'll bet Edgar Rice Burroughs tells a story better than Lewis does." I tested my theory by picking up *Tarzan of the Apes*, a book I had not read since childhood. I found that picking up the book was easy but putting it down was another matter. In fact, after tearing through the first two volumes, I had to force myself to stop for fear of becoming a Tarzan addict.

I chose Burroughs deliberately because he was more or less a "hack" writer with no pretension to high literary quality. The story-teller's gift, however, is not always accompanied by the other literary qualities. Henry James, for example, greatly admired the books of Frances Hodgson Burnett—I think because she had ordinary fictive gifts that James lacked. Burroughs is by no means to be despised, and one reason is that he can tell a story as Aristotle understood a story—that is, as an action, a motion with a beginning, middle, and end. Platonists do not hold action in high esteem as a rule, and as a result their stories are rather static, rather languorous, loose and rambling. Spenser has been much criticized for this failing, and even Lewis had to admit some truth in such comments.[16]

Action in fiction is no longer generally popular, especially among intellectuals and literary critics. E. M. Forster denied that a plot (which for Aristotle is identical with the story) is an action, because happiness does not lie in action, as Aristotle thought, but in the "secret life," which cannot be manifested in action. Whether Forster was a neoplatonist or not, that is a Platonic idea. Classic children's stories, such as the *Arabian Nights* and tales of the Brothers Grimm and of Aesop, are preeminently stories of action. By action I do not mean anything so vulgar as mere violence and derring-do—although a certain amount of such vulgarity is desirable. To initiate an action in the Aristotelian sense, however, merely requires that someone set out to do something.

If we look at Lewis's second Narnia book, *Prince Caspian*, we see that as in many a story, including *Tarzan*, the child protagonists find themselves, through no wish or fault of their own, in a strange land. They are taken up by the gnomes as Tarzan is taken up by the apes. One could extend the list of similarities, but the differences are more striking. Whereas Tarzan sets off on the quest for his own identity and destiny, the children of Narnia find themselves caught up in a story that is already written. They are like characters in a play who do not quite understand their roles. Their main task is to see how they fit into preexistent design. There is a great cosmic war in progress between good and evil, and a part has been allotted to the children. They are free to participate or not, but it is clear that they are only participants. Some great power, Aslan and all he represents, has made up the story. In contrast, Tarzan makes his own story by deliberate choices and acts; everything hinges on his courage, determination, and intelligence. He does come to embody a certain struggle of animal cruelty and violence—the law of the jungle—versus the refinements of civilization, including domesticity, but the immediate struggle against this or that adversary, especially the archvillain, Rokoff, is always foremost.

Whatever interest there is in the Narnia books, it does not lie in the story. *Prince Caspian* begins with a bang when the children are whisked out of a railroad station into Narnia, but chapters 1 and 2 deal with the children's own rediscovery of where they are, with considerable reminiscence of their past lives as kings and queens in Narnia. (Much of this, I should add, is a none-too-skillful recapitulation for the benefit of readers who have not read the first volume of the series.) In chapter 3 the children rescue a dwarf, and in the next four chapters he tells about Prince Caspian: how he escaped from his wicked uncle and rediscovered the old suppressed Narnia of the talking beasts and trees; and how he prepared to restore the old kingdom. The children now understand why they have been summoned back to Narnia. We are halfway through the book, and only now do we discover what the central action is. The main villain of the book, the usurping uncle, has had but a brief appearance, and he is not very impressive. A great deal of the first seven chapters has been a recapitulation of past history and development of the various characteristics of old Narnia, with fairly long introductions to the gnomes, various types of animals, giants, dryads, and so on. Aslan (rather inevitably something of a *deus ex machina*) is introduced in chapters 9 and 10, and in chapters 11 and 12 the children are united with Prince Caspian. Peter then musters the forces of Narnia in chapter 13, and in chapter 14 he defeats the wicked uncle in single combat and his armies are routed by the forces of old Narnia.

There are incidents along the way, of course, and various obstacles are overcome, but it is the assembling of the creatures of Narnia that interests Lewis most, the creation of a vision of the Golden Age where all is restored to original innocence and peace. There is much pageantry and processional of the sort that is common in Spenser's *Faerie Queene*. The Dryads and Hamadryads and satyrs all come out to dance; Bacchus and his devotees appear and are described in some detail. What we have primarily in Lewis are spectacles and scenes and images that convey ideas, not an action in which the heroes set out to defeat an evil foe.[17]

In fantasy the meaning of things does not inhere in the story because mere human acts are only shadows or images, but in the great storytellers human deeds are the very realization of meaning. Deeds embody meaning, but in a mysterious way. The heroic act, for example, exceeds our expectation, thus arousing our wonder. The strength, sagacity, and boldness of Tarzan always astonish because they rise above what we expect in the normal course of events. But such deeds as there are in fantasy are only gestures made for the sake of their symbolism, because the whole story exists only in the mind.

It is no exaggeration to say that there is more action and suspense in one chapter of Burroughs than there is in a whole volume of Lewis. A plot résumé like that for *Prince Caspian* would take up an inordinate amount of time for any of the Tarzan books. Some aspects of *The Return of Tarzan*, the second in the series, however, would furnish an idea of what I mean. Burroughs had left the reader in suspense at the end of the first volume; so we find Tarzan now facing life without Jane and without the identity he thought he had established. Very little time is given to recapitulating, however; Tarzan meets his new enemy in chapter 1 and he saves a woman's life from this enemy in chapter 2—and the plot thickens, the hero risking his life in nearly every chapter: he kills four lions, swims forty or fifty miles after being thrown overboard, overcomes innumerable human enemies, and saves countless lives, including Jane's. Burroughs has the serial writer's knack of ending each chapter at a point of suspense, often letting the reader and the hero dangle over some unspeakable abyss while the scene shifts to another part of the plot. Lewis, you will remember, also switches from the children to Prince Caspian and back again, but seldom does he leave behind any very suspenseful situation. Aristotle speaks of hairbreadth escapes and dramatic turns of fortune as being wonderful,[18] but, in addition, the element of suspense itself, which is built into the nature of the story, is a cause of wonder, for being in doubt about the outcome of the action is a kind of ignorance that creates wonder. Lewis in his essay on stories spoke rather disparagingly of mere excitement and suspense.[19] Although I will grant that Burroughs exaggerates these devices, much more refined books such as *The Wind in the Willows* and Walter de la Mare's *Three Royal Monkeys* are far more eventful and suspenseful than the fantasies of Lewis.

In my reading of the Narnia books I was disappointed not only in the story but also in the characters. To be successful, the beings of fiction must live in our imaginations and memories. We use the word *vivid* of such beings, often forgetting that the root meaning of that term is simply "alive," the essential quality of real persons or animals—or, for that matter, real ghosts or gods or angels or fairies or griffins. There are many literary devices for achieving verisimilitude, but behind all of them must lie the conviction of the writer, which is really a kind of testimony. The tellers of the old wonder tales did not need any special literary devices to win belief in their supernatural beings: they *knew* they were real and that they might actually be encountered on the road or in the forest. In the Narnia books much is made of the importance of believing in Narnia and its inhabitants, but Lewis himself did not believe in them, not as the wife of Bath or Scheherazade believed in things supernatural. Lewis argued that "it is not necessary to believe in them."[20] But Aristotle thought differently. Lewis tried to solve this problem by saying that the dryads and gnomes are symbols of something real, but there is no way that a symbol can be brought to life. The supernatural beings of Narnia are bookish beings of a scholarly rather than of a poetic imagination.

The human beings in Lewis's books are not as symbolic as the mythological beings, but they fail to live, largely because they fail to act. Mere elaboration of character will not bring a fictional person to life. Hansel is the unforgettable boy who dropped breadcrumbs to find the way back home, and Gretel is the remarkable girl who pushed the witch into her own oven. These two children live in our imagination and memory, too, because they have the fears of real children—the fear of being unwanted by parents, the fear of being lost and abandoned. When I remember the plight of these helpless children, my own old pity for them revives. The children in the Narnia books are often alone and lost in the woods, but they never suffer that aching fear of Hansel and Gretel, nor any very strong emotion for that matter, and the memory of them arouses no emotion in me.

Are the animal characters in Narnia any more successful as fictional creations? Burroughs, Kipling, and Lewis all write about apes. In *The Last Battle*, there is Shift, one of the principal villains; in *The Jungle Book* a band of monkeys kidnaps Mowglie, and, of course, there are the apes who rear Tarzan. Whereas one can learn something about simians by reading Kipling and Burroughs, one cannot by reading Lewis. In both *The Jungle Book* and *Tarzan*, the apes are presented as tribal creatures. Shift, on the other hand, is solitary. Another feature of the apes that Burroughs and Kipling describe in detail and delight is their arboreal life. Shift has a house in a tree, we are told, but that's the end of it; in Lewis the ape is no more arboreal than is a man. The best of imaginative books for children both stimulate and satisfy the desire for knowledge about such things as animals; and, as Aristotle says, the desire for knowledge is wonder.[21]

In both Kipling and Burroughs the apes are not, however, presented simply because of their inherent interest as beasts; they have significance. In *The Jungle Book* the apes, the Bandar-log, are the enemies of all order and law. They have no leader and are the pariahs of all respectable jungle folk. They are the representatives of all that is anarchic and irresponsible in man. In Burroughs the apes represent almost the opposite. They are the very prototype of the brute law of the jungle, red in tooth and claw. In broader terms they are the savage beast in all men, and Tarzan himself is constantly torn between civilization and the life of the ape. In both Kipling and Burroughs, however, this symbolic meaning arises out of the ape as animal. Lewis's villain, Shift, on the other hand, never does exist as an ape at all. I don't mean that Lewis totally neglects this side of him—Shift does scratch himself as monkeys do, and so forth—but such things in Lewis are always perfunctory or at least incidental. Lewis never lets us forget that Shift is the Ape of God, a diabolical figure who deals in craft and illusion.

I could extend my analysis of the Narnia books into other areas, but the results would be repetitious. The landscape of Narnia, including its buildings and artificial objects, is not memorable. There is nothing in Lewis like the secret garden of Burnett's book or the jungle of Tarzan or Badger's home in *The Wind in the Willows*—all places strange and remote and even magical but places as substantial and familiar as our own back yard: "Marvellous places, yet handy to home."

Dorothy L. Sayers, in praising the storytelling ability of Dante, touches upon a quality that lies at the heart of the matter. She says, "If you want the reader not only to follow but to accept and believe a tale of marvels, you can do it best by the accumulation of precise and even prosaic detail."[22] This "trick of particularity," as she calls it, is well known as the secret of those adult books that became children's classics, such as *Robinson Crusoe* and *Gulliver's Travels*. Those two works contain one of the greatest secrets of the literature of the wonderful. All of the activities of Lilliput, which are nothing but the ordinary activities of life, are observed and described in the most exquisite detail, but we look at them in wonder because they are seen in a strange light of miniature. Mary Norton's Borrowers series borrows from Swift this marvelous trick. In Defoe we read with excitement minute descriptions of the prosaic process of making bread because Crusoe is marooned on an island and must, there-fore, learn such elementary things over again. To the Aristotelian imagination, every particular of daily reality is ripe with wonder.

This wonder arises simply because each particular thing *is*. We must recall again that Plato and Aristotle both said that philosophy begins and continues through wonder and that this wonder is some-thing that poets have, too. The primal stuff of philosophy and of poetry is being, the greatest of all mysteries. Beyond this primal fact are others, of course. We may see that things exhibit the marvel of life or of motion or of death. But neoplatonists do not look at the world this way. In *The Allegory of Love* Lewis argued that before the rise of literary allegory there were only two worlds out of which the artist could make his works—the actual world and the world of religion, or nature and supernature—but allegory introduced a third world, the "other world" of pure "fancy."[23] It is clear that for Lewis and his school the actual world and the supernatural world are not enough. Mere reality—mere heaven and earth—is not enough. So be it. But there are consequences. Narnia is a *utopos*, a no place, a shadow-land, and as such, it is unlikely to endure. Dorothy Sayers thought that Spenser managed to induce belief in his world by means of sheer verbal enchantment, as did Keats and Coleridge. Perhaps. Writers of fantasy are themselves often enchanted with words and language, but I don't think anyone will claim for Lewis the verbal gifts of Spenser.

In the meantime, however, the fantasy of Lewis is popular. If his books are as deficient as I claim, how shall I account for this vogue, especially when it exists among highly literate and sensitive readers young and old? It is my view that enchantment with fantasy in general derives in large measure from disenchantment with an all-too-drab modern world. That disenchantment I happen to share with Lewis and his friends, and I share their desire to restore the supernatural dimension to life and literature; but I think the price of fantasy is too high. However besmirched, reality remains full of things enough to make us all happy as kings. Or, to be more theological, how are we to know the reality of God except through the real creation?

Fantasy is harmful to the imagination, and especially to the youthful imagination, because it encourages the reader to turn inward and to distrust if not despise reality. Lewis defended fantasy against the charge of escapism by saying that a child who has read about an enchanted wood may then see enchantment in the actual wood.[24] But fantasy implicitly teaches that there *are* no wonders in the wood; rather, all marvels are in the mind and are of our own making. If we are at liberty to make up marvels, they will no more excite wonder than a surprise party for one's own self excites surprise. Reality is wonderful and surprising precisely because it exists outside of and even beyond our imagination.

According to Plato and Aristotle, the philosopher and the poet are particularly susceptible to this passion of wonder. Because it is the very manifestation of the desire for knowledge, however, it is a passion especially of children, to whom all the world is fresh. To adults the world sometimes seems dull because of habituation or, as in the case of neoplatonists, because ideas seem better; but ideas that lose touch with their source in reality soon go stale, while, as G. K. Chesterton said, "things continue to be fresh." It is the office of the myth-maker by means of his imitative art to cultivate wonder in the young and to restore it in the old. Crusoe and Gulliver, with their fresh beginners' eyes, send us all back to look again—not at illusion but at reality.

### Notes

1. Recent critics have devoted considerable attention to fantasy as a literary genre, notably: W. R. Irwin, *The Game of the Impossible* (Urbana: Univ. of Illinois Press, 1976); Eric S. Rabkin, *The Fantastic in Literature* (Princeton: Princeton Univ. Press, 1976); Tzvetan Todorov, *The Fantastic: A Structural Approach to a Literary Genre*, trans. Richard Howard (Ithaca: Cornell Univ. Press, 1973); and C. N. Manlove, *The Impulse of Fantasy Literature* (Kent, Ohio: Kent State Univ. Press, 1983). For a good recent collection of essays, see *Bridges to Fantasy*, ed. George E. Slusser, Eric S. Rabkin, and Robert Scholes (Carbondale and Edwardsville: Southern Illinois Univ. Press, 1982).

2. E. M. Forster, *Aspects of the Novel* (1927; rpt. New York: Harcourt, 1954), p. 165.

3. See my article, "Donne and the Wane of Wonder," *ELH*, 36 (Dec. 1969), 626–47, and J. V. Cunningham, *Woe or Wonder* (Denver: Alan Swallow, 1954). Some recent critics identify fantasy and wonder. Manlove defines fantasy, in part, as "fiction evoking wonder," p. ix. He gives no definition of wonder, however, and so far as I can determine, he seems to think of it as the response to anything "supernatural or impossible," but how and why the response occurs is not clear. John Gerlach in his essay, "The Logic of Wings," in *Bridges to Fantasy*, basing his analysis of a story of García Márquez on Todorov's definition of fantasy, seems to see wonder in the hesitation or suspense between belief and disbelief in impossible events (p. 129); but that is to identify wonder with doubt or anxiety.

4. C. S. Lewis, *English Literature in the 16th Century* (London: Oxford Univ. Press, 1954), p. 320.

5. Lewis never withdrew his early, but mature, judgment concerning the neo-platonic element in Spenser. He granted Robert Ellrodt's contention in *Neoplatonism in the Poetry of Spenser* (Geneva, 1960) that the neoplatonic influence had been exaggerated. In his last lectures, as they appear in *Spenser's Images of Life*, ed. Alastair Fowler (Cambridge: Cambridge Univ. Press, 1967), Lewis cites Ficino and Pico as having the same iconographical imagination as Spenser (pp. 8–9); and Lewis quotes as being highly expressive of Spenser's view a passage from Nicolas of Cusa that asserts the neoplatonic idea that in the unity of the divine mind created beings lose their differences (p. 15).

6. After his thorough review of recent efforts to define literary fantasy, W. R. Irwin concludes that they have in common "that spirit which seeks liberation from phenomena, and finds pleasure in the nonreal, the fantastic" (*Game of the Impossible*, p. 57). Irwin himself accepts this description, as the title of his work suggests.

7. Cited in W. L. Renwick, ed., *Spenser Selections* (New York: Oxford Univ. Press, 1923), p. 1.

8. Ibid., p. 13.

9. A. C. Hamilton, *The Structure of Allegory in the Faerie Queene* (Oxford: The Clarendon Press, 1961), p. 6.

10. Ibid., p. 13.

11. Ibid., p. 25.

12. Dorothy L. Sayers, *Introductory Papers on Dante* (London: Methuen, 1954), pp. 6–7.

13. C. S. Lewis, *Of Other Worlds*, ed. Walter Hooper (New York: Harcourt, 1975), p. 70.

14. Etienne Gilson, *The Philosophy of St. Bonaventure*, trans. Illtyd Trethowan and F. J. Sheed (Paterson: St. Anthony Guild Press, 1965), p. 88.

15. C. S. Lewis, *The Last Battle* (Baltimore: Penguin, 1956), pp. 153–54.

16. Lewis concedes that Spenser "is only superficially a narrative poet" (*Spenser's Images*, p. 97). In the same work Lewis says that he will "at last" address, in a separate chapter, the question of whether the "story" element in *The Faerie Queene* is worth our attention (p. 112). However, he does not address the question of the story but rather the question of character.

17. Lewis's last lectures, collected in *Images of Life*, stressed the importance of pageantry in *The Faerie Queene*. While he points out the poetic advantages of such pageantry, he overlooks its chief disadvantage, which is the impeding of the narrative.

18. Aristotle, *Rhetoric*, I, 11.

19. Lewis, *Other Worlds*, pp. 17ff.

20. Ibid., p. 13.

21. Aristotle, *Metaphysics*, 982b.

22. D. L. Sayers, *Further Papers on Dante* (London: Methuen, 1957), p. 7.

23. C. S. Lewis, *The Allegory of Love* (London: Oxford Univ. Press, 1936), p. 82.

24. Lewis, *Other Worlds*, p. 15. A recent *TLS* reviewer, T. A. Shippey, while speaking of several new books on fantasy, observed that no one has really made the case that would justify fantasy (*TLS*, May 13, 1983, p. 479). The German romantics, whom Manlove seems to approve, often argue for the fairy tale as an image of real life, but they conceive of "real life" as being chaotic and incoherent (*Impulse of Fantasy*, p. 1). T. E. Apter's study, *Fantasy Literature: An Approach to Reality* (Bloomington: Indiana University Press, 1983), has a promising title but proves to be entirely Freudian in its analysis of fantasy; hence fantasy literature (which is very loosely defined) has therapeutic values that hinge upon the value of psychoanalysis.

# Beyond Explanation, and Beyond Inexplicability, *in* Beyond Silence

Perry Nodelman

A first reading of Eleanor Cameron's *Beyond Silence* confused me. The novel somehow both satisfied what Frank Kermode calls "our deep need for intelligible ends"[1] and did not satisfy it, so that as I finished the novel, I both felt and did not feel that delight in problems solved and suspense fulfilled that I expect from good stories, and that I had felt at the end of her earlier and deceptively similar novel, *The Court of the Stone Children*.

Of these two feelings, the sense of satisfaction the two novels share is easier to explore. Both *The Court of the Stone Children* and *Beyond Silence* begin with a set of three quotations, one about how the past still exists, one about how the future is happening now, and one about the limitations of our conceptions of reality. The idea that the ordinary perception of time's passage ignores a larger reality underlies and gives order to all of Cameron's work. Gil in *The Court of the Stone Children* says, "All time—past, present, and future—is one Time."[2] Dr. Fairlie in *Beyond Silence* agrees: "It's quite possible that all is coexistent."[3] In her discussion of time fantasies in *The Green and Burning Tree*, Cameron herself says, "Time is not a thread at all, but a globe."[4] Furthermore, she praises the English time fantasists for expressing the same idea: "The past and creative magic! Is it the inextricable mingling of these two, the taken for granted presence in their lives of a past thick with myth and legend and fairy tale, that gives the English fantasists, and especially the time fantasists, their depth and their peculiar power of evocation?"[5]

Both *The Court of the Stone Children* and *Beyond Silence* pay homage to that English tradition and its immersion in a living past. But as an American, Cameron cannot take the tradition for granted. In fact, she seems to value it for its distance from contemporary American life, which she finds disorderly and dismisses as incomplete. Of course, life in the past was just as disorderly, just as incomplete; but it was so in a different way, and the difference gives it glamor for

Cameron and for us, a glamor that it did not have for those who were stuck with it.

In English fantasies like Boston's Green Knowe series or Uttley's *A Traveler in Time*, the past comes alive in an old house; in *The Court of the Stone Children* it comes alive in a museum, a reconstruction in San Francisco of rooms from a European house. "These rooms are from my home in France," says Domi, ". . . But it is *not* the same . . . ! This is a kind of strange, twisted dream of my home, the same and yet weirdly not the same" (p. 38). The novel is like its setting, the same as the English time fantasies it is modeled on, and yet weirdly not the same. The difference is that movement across time offers children in the English fantasies a satisfying sense of connection with a place where they already live; but Nina finds completeness by moving away from the jarring anarchy of contemporary San Francisco into Domi's alien and satisfyingly orderly rooms.

In *Beyond Silence* the homage to the order of the past and to the English fantasies that evoke it is even more explicit. Like Tolly in *The Children of Green Knowe*, Andrew hears children of another time sing nursery rhymes. Like Tolly and also like Tom in Philippa Pearce's *Tom's Midnight Garden*, his contacts with the past significantly involve a tree falling in a storm; and in both *Tom's Midnight Garden* and *Beyond Silence*, a woman from the past marries a man named Barty. Above all, Andrew actually leaves California and seems to feel more at home in Scotland; surrounded by relics of the past, he escapes his own confusion by moving across time.

In fact, *Beyond Silence* shares with *The Court of the Stone Children* and with the English time fantasies a resolution that does literally what all novels do formally. In most novels, Frank Kermode says, "Mere successiveness, which we *feel* to be the chief characteristic of the ordinary going-on of time, is purged by the establishment of a significant relation between the moment and a remote origin and end, a concord of past, present, and future."[6] In both of Cameron's novels, meetings of past and present fortuitously solve problems caused by the past's insistence on being over, problems that have concerned characters in both the past and the present. Nina's discovery of the truth about Domi's father in *The Court of the Stone Children* both makes Domi happy and allows Nina to live with those aspects of herself that had previously defined her as a lonely eccentric; Andrew's encounters with Deirdre in *Beyond Silence* both save Deirdre's life and allow Andrew to face his guilt over Hoagy's death. By achieving resolution through such meetings of past and present, each novel literally denies mere randomness.

But for all that, *Beyond Silence* does not seem complete. A quick look back through the novel shows why: Cameron has carefully set up many potentially exciting confrontations that never take place. When Andrew first meets Beth McBride, he says, "I felt a kind of immediate recognition passing between us, some instantaneous knowledge that we were drawn to one another" (p. 7). When I first read that, I assumed Beth would figure prominently either in the mystery about Deirdre or in Andrew's self-recognition: she does neither. Cameron also dramatically sets the stage for Andrew to disburden himself to Dr. Fairlie; she sends him on an exciting trip to Fairlie's house involving missed buses and boats and then lets Fairlie make impressively bald statements about the novel's main themes. I expected Fairlie to perform a miracle, save Andrew, solve the mystery; instead, Cameron kills him off in an automobile accident.

That leaves Andrew with no one to confide in, and Cameron seems to have put Dunstan McCallum in the novel for just that purpose; but Dunstan's mere presence causes problems. Since Andrew meets Dunstan by chance, we can believe his wish to confide in him only if Cameron postulates an instantaneous empathy between the two; and in these cynical times, we tend to assume that all such attractions are sexual. So Cameron has to insert an otherwise pointless paragraph about both Dunstan and Andrew admiring a girl who passes them on the street, which establishes their heterosexuality. My first response was to wonder why she went to all this trouble, when she could easily have settled for one of the two confidants she had already set up and then not used, doing without Dunstan altogether.

Even odder is the way Cameron establishes Andrew's antipathy for Phineas Brock and then unceremoniously drops him completely from the novel. Andrew says, "Phineas became my enemy before I had the least glimmering of why he was. He was nosey, yes. Phineas annoyed the hell out of me. But I felt something deeper; instinctively I felt it" (p. 71). Andrew finds Brock grandly evil, even satanic; Cameron supports Andrew's fear of him even by the name she gives him. Phineas means "mouth of brass," like the biblical image for those who lack charity,[7] and a brock is a badger—it is not surprising that Andrew feels badgered by Phineas. Given all that, I expected a melodramatic revelation of Brock as a true limb of Satan, along the lines of characters in Susan Cooper's *The Dark is Rising* or various novels by Alan Garner, and then Andrew's glorious defeat of him. Alternatively, I thought Brock might turn out to be not dangerous at all, so that Andrew would have to face the cruelty of his false imaginings. But what actually happens is nothing at all. Professor Fairlie dies, and "Phineas had packed up and left before Dad and I got down to breakfast the next morning" (p. 168). He is not heard from again.

Cameron also creates unresolved expectations around the pictures of Deirdre of the Sorrows in the musicians' gallery. Deirdre Cames's letter reports the grandmother of the original Andrew saying that the pictures would mean something special to her; we expect something more than the accident of a name. But Deirdre Cames's life was not filled with sorrow, and she does not seem to have cuckolded her husband. And nothing special happens to Andrew in the gallery, either; when he goes to see those paintings that tantalizingly "had reached out to me when I'd first turned and looked up" (p. 99), all that happens is that Brock relates the story the pictures tell. While that story is about Deirdre Cames's namesake, it has nothing significant to do with events of the novel.

Cameron builds up and then thwarts similar expectations about Andrew's interest in the "Western Sea." He connects his first glimpse of it with the story of King Arthur's death told him by his mother and with his brother's death, for he had once planned to travel to that sea with Hoagy; he also connects it with his recurrent dream of drowning. But nothing remarkable happens when Andrew reaches the Western Sea. Instead of a major breakthrough, an understanding of the truth about himself, or about his brother's death, or a vision of Deirdre or King Arthur or even of Brock, Andrew simply has his old nightmare once more, decides anticlimactically that "I must go inland" (p. 177)—and, astonishingly, falls asleep.

Of course, both the paintings and the Western Sea allude to Andrew's situation, even if they come to nothing in terms of plot. Andrew himself connects them to the poem by Walter de la Mare that Dunstan recites to him; it evokes "the musicians' gallery at the end of the dining hall at Cames: its walls full of rich colors, trees and mountains and figures and, as I remembered, a glimpse of the sea" (p. 88). The end of the poem is, "Across the walls, the shadows / Come and go"; not surprisingly soon after hearing it Andrew overhears a conversation "about the space-time continuum and someone named Minkowski and about space and time vanishing into shadows" (p. 106). So the poem, King Arthur's sea, and the paintings all relate to Andrew's crosstemporal experiences. The problem is clear: what makes sense as an allusion to crosstemporal experience seems to create unresolved expectations is terms of plot.

Ironically, the biggest unresolved mystery in the novel is the easiest to accept. The unexpected death of Fairlie and the departure of Brock made me uneasy; but I had no trouble at all with the unexplained contact between Andrew and Deirdre. The whole point is that it is an infusion of wonderful inexplicability into the repressive understandability of normal reality. Andrew says, "Something had happened, something as impossible of explanation, as far outside the usual run of my life as that visitation on the plane" (p. 26). He asks himself, "Why couldn't I accept it and let all this searching for an unattainable solution sink away so that I would be left in peace?" (p. 131). Eventually he does accept it, and in finding peace beyond explanation, he comes to share an attitude expressed by Loren Eiseley in the novel's epigraph: "Nature contains that which has no intention of taking us into its confidence." It is also expressed by Cameron herself in *The Green and Burning Tree*, when she praises books that "let in almost everything; they make welcome the understandable."[8] *Beyond Silence* seems to do exactly that, but in two quite different ways.

First, *Beyond Silence* shows the limitations of understandable reality by describing experiences that transcend rational explanation and by making the rational scientist, Phineas Brock, the villain of the piece. Brock is called the Quark, "a busy little particle of matter" (p. 17); what Andrew resists most is Brock's attempt to explain, and therefore explain away, Andrew's strange experiences. Brock says, "It would be fatal for you to keep them hidden and unexplained" (pp. 134–35); in Cameron's scheme of things, someone who tries to explain the unexplainable is dangerous.

Cameron may also be confirming her faith in the un-understandable in *Beyond Silence* by deliberately leaving loose ends. All those thwarted expectations may be an attempt to make readers experience for themselves the unsettling state of not understanding something and to have no choice but the one Dr. Fairlie recommends to Andrew: "There's no use wracking yourself over a thing like that. Live with it, Andrew. Accept it. Take it as a wonder—there's so much we can't explain" (p. 158).

If Cameron is indeed doing that, however, there is a tension between her philosophical prejudices and her novelist's craft. For explanations of events and people give meaning to novels and therefore make them pleasurably different from the randomness of mere reality. Seen in this way, life itself is inexplicable, confusingly multi-faceted, and novels satisfyingly explain it; Kermode defines a plot as "an organization that humanizes time by giving it form . . . a transformation of mere successiveness."[9] But in terms of Cameron's ideas about time, life is all too suffocatingly "humanized," all too constricted by the limited explanations of merely human scientists like Brock; deeper perception transcends mere cause-and-effect explicability. In her novels, Cameron transforms "mere successiveness" in two opposite directions, into the inexplicability of cross-temporal experiences and into the explanatory connections of storytelling. In *The Court of the Stone Children*, where there are no loose ends, she creates a satisfying unity that may weaken the unsettling wonder we should feel in face of the inexplicable. But in achieving unsettling inexplicability in *Beyond Silence*, she may have deprived it of its unity. Finally, its various threads do not come together; Brock has nothing to do with Deirdre, nor with Hoagy's death, nor with the separation of Andrew's parents. As a story, *Beyond Silence* seems something like Dr. Fairlie tells Andrew his own state of mind will come to be: "You must realize that even if you *can* connect, this might not be the end. That is, it would be an intellectual resolution while very possibly you would still have some way to go emotionally"

(p. 158). The feeling of incompleteness *Beyond Silence* conveys, even though it solves the central mystery about Hoagy's death, is confirmed by the knowledge that Andrew tells his story "six years later" (p. 2). At that distance he should know what matters and what does not; but he continually misleads us, and ends up unsettling us, in ways that could easily have been avoided—if his creator had wanted to avoid them.

Apparently she did not want to. I believe that *Beyond Silence is* complete, but that the way the loose ends are tied together becomes clear only after a reader has been disturbed enough by its apparent incompleteness to look further.

The key to the unity of *Beyond Silence* is its main difference from *The Court of the Stone Children*—the fact that the story is told not by an omniscient narrator, but by its protagonist. Since Andrew is so disturbed by Hoagy's death, the novel is not just a time fantasy, but a psychological case study; it is similar to Judith Guest's numbingly realistic and thoroughly unconvincing *Ordinary People*, in which an ineffably wise therapist helps a boy confront his guilt over his brother's drowning by teaching this restrained child of restrained WASP parents to become open and responsive—as joyously Jewish as the therapist himself.

If the omniscient narrator of *The Court of the Stone Children* had left loose ends untied, we would have to accuse Cameron of bad craftsmanship. But when Andrew tells his own story, we can assume that Cameron's bad storytelling is quite deliberate—that it reveals his character and his situation. And it does. The central situation of the novel is Andrew's incomplete perception. He has forgotten the events leading up to his brother's death; in the imagery provided by his hypnagogic experience, he has built a wall around that memory. For most of the novel, Andrew does not know the whole truth, and it is his own honest reporting of his flawed perception that creates thwarted expectations. But as Andrew's own voice tells him in his hypnagogic experience, "You can't build the wall high enough—you never can. There'll be a crack in it somewhere" (p. 151). Eventually, the wall cracks; the whole truth Andrew perceives confirms that the apparent red herrings introduced earlier were traps, set by his unconscious to prevent him from making his breakthrough.

Seen in this way, Beth cannot figure importantly in the breaking down of Andrew's walls simply *because* he feels such sympathy with her; as he says himself, "She might, in her good common sense, convince me of something I didn't want to be convinced of" (p. 177). She threatens the walls because her loving concern might break them down. On the other hand, Dunstan is no threat at all because he is so uninvolved with the rest of Andrew's life. Cameron seems to have introduced him so tenuously for just that reason. Andrew believes that Dunstan will listen to him without trying to help, so that he can safely unburden himself "just enough to ease the pressure" (p. 177) without actually cracking the wall. Furthermore, Andrew believes that Dunstan has also built a wall to protect himself: "Maybe he was all right as a man because he had the world he'd made for himself" (p. 87); such a person would understand and respect another's need for walls and do nothing to disturb them.

But Andrew's subconscious understands that Brock, the professional psychological investigator, might. What Andrew most hates about Brock is his desire to help him, which his subconscious sees as a matter of hunting him down. Brock really was only trying to help, and really did not have other things on his mind beside the torturing of Andrew; his unceremonious disappearance from the novel and from Andrew's life, for reasons unconnected with Andrew, is quite natural; and it shows Andrew how distorted his perception was: "I've often thought how I'd hated him—bitterly hated him! And so had been incapable of seeing him as anything but a cold, calculating, impervious little manipulator for his own ends" (p. 166).

Andrew is also blind to the fact that Dr. Fairlie, whom Brock worships, shares scientific prejudices and asks Andrew the same questions. Andrew worries that Brock would "break open the privacy, my secret life" (p. 148), but he allows Fairlie to do just that. Perhaps Fairlie, like Dunstan, is safely distant from Cames castle and can thus feel nothing but professional concern for Andrew. Fairlie's death once more shows Andrew that things are not, however, as he perceives them. Not only does he lose his proposed confidant, but Brock's grief over Fairlie forces Andrew to reevaluate Brock. Yet Cameron also allows Fairlie to die and Brock to disappear from the novel, I suspect, so that Andrew's breakthrough will ultimately come through inexplicable magic, not psychological science. The wall finally breaks down through the hypnagogic experience that provided Andrew with the image of a wall "with the break in it" (p. 187) in the first place.

The expectations aroused and not fulfilled by the paintings in the gallery and the Western Sea also reveal Andrew's unconscious at work. Andrew's flight from the sea as soon as he has his potentially revealing nightmare about drowning suggests how firmly the wall of his resistance stands; his unconscious tells him to leave before any serious crack develops and before he comes to understand what seas and drowning mean to him. But Andrew's unconscious also acts positively, in that it allows the mystical experiences that eventually do break down the wall. Since the paintings in the gallery seem to lose their potential for magic once Andrew hears Brock's dismissing explanation of the story they tell, thwarted expectations about them merely confirm Andrew's unconscious realization that Brock's explanatory mind is deadly to the one thing that can save him.

That one thing is what is still left unexplained—the inexplicable contact between Andrew and Deirdre. But while there is no logical explanation, there is a symbolic one. It involves the idea of going down. Hoagy died going downhill; drowning is going down, and Andrew's recurring nightmare is of Hoagy drowning. Andrew says, "How subtly our dreams express what is deepest: both of us had *gone down*, but only one had survived. As in the sea, so on the mountainside" (p. 189, my italics). On the mountainside, Andrew refused to drive the car, and "Hoagy had *gone down* alone" (p. 189, my italics); that is what Andrew is hiding from himself, and what his nightmare about going down in water expresses, in a disguised way that keeps him from the painful truth. But throughout the novel, Andrew's crosstemporal experiences take him down. When he first walks around Cames, he says that he, "*going down*, left the sunlight and submerged into a dense green shade like a swimmer sinking under water" (p. 36, my italics); once down, he passes Deirdre's house and then reads her letter to the earlier Andrew. Later on, he steps over a wall, and feeling "infinitely remote from all humankind" (p. 93), "*walked on down. . . .* I was lost, because of the gray, drifting, winding obscuring mist" (p. 94, my italics). This is almost like drowning again; but he hears a voice that guides him through the mist and realizes that it "had been Deirdre who'd *led him down*" (p. 96, my italics). Andrew connects the idea of going down underwater with the unconscious—"the unconscious would begin sending up illuminations, rising like bubbles to the surface of simmering water" (p. 186). Deirdre magically guides Andrew whenever he goes down past the wall into his unconscious, so that he does not drown after all. Rather, he comes upon the truth submerged there.

For Eleanor Cameron, the limited world that can be rationally explained is not true, but shifting, insubstantial, illusory. In that world, Cames is not as Andrew's father remembered it; Andrew's girlfriend's "whole life changed, and then she changed" (p. 38); and Beth says, "Never trust that everything will be the same, because it won't" (p. 195). The only permanent truth is in that inexplicable place Deirdre led Andrew down to, which is simultaneously beyond both time and ordinary consciousness. Paradoxically, the explicable workings of therapy do not restore Andrew's memory of the illusory world of reality; inexplicable magic does.

Andrew says of his crosstemporal experiences, "They were mine, of my deepest self" (p. 132). To find those deeps, he goes down into himself just as his mother did in her book, "with time peeled off in layers of reflection so that the whole range of herself as a reading, thinking, feeling, imagining animal was revealed by *going down* and back instead of along in time through the cycle of the year" (p. 112, my italics). And Andrew's father admits that though his "needs will have changed," he will be "always, *underneath*, the same Andrew" (p. 196, my italics)—permanent beyond time and change, beyond ordinary consciousness and beyond explicability. Selfhood is one with magic; both exist permanently outside mere shifting time. Finally, the wrong ideas Andrew has about people in the world of time, the ideas that created our unfulfilled expectations, are just further evidence of the illusory nature of the world we usually perceive.

Whatever one feels about Cameron's ideas of time, the cleverly paradoxical way she expresses them is admirable. Not only does she complete an apparently incomplete fiction, she also presents a psychologically convincing statement about the limitations of psychology. She does admirably what Kermode suggests good novels must do: she falsifies our expectations, and "the interest of having our expectations falsified is obviously related to our wish to reach the discovery or recognition by an unexpected or instructive route."[10] Kermode says we wish to do that because, in the midst of literary conventions, that things we do *not* expect create a sense of reality. But what is most unexpected about *Beyond Silence* is not the way Andrew's psychological difficulties realistically account for the novel's loose ends; rather, it is that inexplicable magic finally dismisses psychological explanations for being as illusory as the incomplete world they describe.

The title of *Beyond Silence* sums it up. The phrase occurs in Dr. Fairlie's statement of faith in wonders: "The thing is, Andrew, we live in a cloud of unknowing, and who knows what lies beyond silence?" (p. 158). Beyond the phenomena we comprehend and therefore can name lies the inexpressible. Not surprisingly, Andrew's mysterious experiences are often voices moving out of the silence, like the voice of the wall builder, or Deirdre's voice in the dumbwaiter. Before Deirdre leads him home, Andrew experiences "utter silence" (p. 92), then moves past a wall into the unknown: "I heard nothing, and so presently I stepped over the wall and continued on down" (p. 93). Once down beyond silence, he is guided by her voice. Later, Andrew's despair about an American who speaks belligerently of Vietnam "stopped whatever words I might have managed to put together" (p. 124). But beyond this silence is an experience in which he shouts to warn Deirdre of danger. The wall Andrew builds around Hoagy's death silences the unspeakable; he remembers "no sound" (p. 32) as he recalls the accident. Dr. Fairlie suggests that Andrew might "see over the wall or through a crack in it" (p. 158); but the wall hides not sights but words, a conversation between Andrew and Hoagy. Other people in the novel also protect themselves with walls of silence. Andrew's mother, "the Quiet One," hides her grief for Hoagy in silence, and Andrew assumes that Dunstan, "big, *quiet*, wounded Dunstan" (p. 177, my italics), has also built a wall around his pain.

Andrew ultimately speaks to Dunstan and remembers Hoagy's words; Dunstan never gets beyond silence. But Nell Cames, whose name is similar to her creator's, finds a way beyond silence that says much about the making of fiction: "Now that Hoagy was gone," says Andrew, "when I'd come in from school at home the house would be silent, or there'd be the faint tapping from her study upstairs of my mother's typewriter: *tap, tap,* silence, *tap, tap, tap,* sometimes long silence—then the tapping again" (p. 55). What lies beyond speechlessness in the face of the pain and unknowing of being alive is the ordered language of imaginative discourse. George Steiner says, "Possessed of speech, possessed by it . . . , the human person has broken free from the great silence of matter."[11] To find the right words is to triumph over the random, chaotic world the words describe; what most truly lies beyond silence is eloquent fiction, fiction like *Beyond Silence.*

## Notes

1. Frank Kermode, *The Sense of an Ending: Studies in the Theory of Fiction* (New York: Oxford Univ. Press, 1967), p. 8.

2. Eleanor Cameron, *The Court of the Stone Children* (New York: Avon, 1976), p. 142. All further references to *The Court of the Stone Children* are to this edition.

3. Eleanor Cameron, *Beyond Silence* (New York: E. P. Dutton, 1980), p. 158. All further references to *Beyond Silence* are to this edition.

4. Eleanor Cameron, *The Green and Burning Tree* (Boston and Toronto: Atlantic/Little Brown, 1969). p. 71.

5. Ibid., p. 131.

6. Kermode, p. 50.

7. Corinthians 13. 1.

8. Cameron, *The Green and Burning Tree,* p. 134.

9. Kermode, pp. 45–46.

10. Ibid., p. 18.

11. George Steiner, *Language and Silence: Essays on Language, Literature, and the Inhuman* (New York: Atheneum, 1977), p. 36.

# A Response to Perry Nodelman's "Beyond Explanation"

## Eleanor Cameron

Books for children and youth are rarely accorded the full-page, or even longer, reviews that books for adults are given in the major reviewing media, reviews sometimes gathered later as collections of critical essays. Therefore the truly critical pieces on single works found in *Children's Literature* would, I should think, be of considerable interest to their authors. Of course it is a curious and even unsettling encounter to read the objective remarks of the critic who has taken apart and keenly penetrated this creative experience, because it is one which has, more than likely, been completely private, very often the work of the writer's unconscious fully as much as his conscious self. And it is the unusual reviewer who will have had the time or the space to cut through to whatever deeper levels of meaning the work might have beneath the surface of story.

Therefore, what Perry Nodelman has written on *Beyond Silence* is something to make the author of it reread with close attention, so as fully to take in the way in which Nodelman's insights were gained over a period of time and then made clear through the three-part structure of his essay. (I say "over a period of time" because in his initial letter to me he said, "I wrote the first draft of my paper a few months after reading the book, having been unable to stop thinking about it.") It is a structure that reveals first of all the critic's exploration of his approval, then of his confusions, and with these two layers finally excavated, of the arrival at his resolution of both approval and confusions. It is an unusual approach, born of Nodelman's apparent desire to be honest in confessing he had difficulties in arriving at his resolution, rather than stating at once his final understanding, as if it had been there all along.

To begin with, I will get past a few quibbles. When Nodelman says that my work affirms the "idea that the ordinary perception of time's passage ignores a larger reality," an idea that "underlies and gives order" to all my work, we first come upon that world *order*. We then come upon it a second time in its negative aspect when he says that "she seems to value [the English tradition and its immersion in the living past] for its distance from contemporary American life, which she finds disorderly and dismisses as incomplete," and also in the following sentence where Nodelman speaks of the "glamor" the past has for us. We come upon it a third time and in a still different form when he speaks of "Domi's alien and satisfyingly orderly rooms" in the French Museum in *The Court of the Stone Children*. And there it is a fourth time in the following paragraph: "In *Beyond Silence* the homage to the order of the past and to the English fantasies that evoke it is more explicit."[1]

I must say that the idea that I pay homage to the *order* of the past is entirely Nodelman's, not mine. Perhaps he may unconsciously have got onto this false track when he first used the world *order* in connection with my conviction about the globe of time, the eternal moment, saying that it gives "order" to all my work (not all of it, actually, but certainly to the two time fantasies). It gives order to the works of any time fantasist, as a matter of fact, as the genre of time fantasy requires the intermingling of the past and present, and sometimes the future in one way or another. But when Nodelman says that I seem "to value [the English tradition and its immersion in the living past] for its distance from contemporary American life, which she finds disorderly and dismisses as incomplete," I must take issue.

I do value the *sense* of the past one feels in the British Isles and have acknowledged in *The Green and Burning Tree* (as Nodelman observes) that undoubtedly that vivid and immediate sense of innumerable layers of history one feels there so strongly could be responsible in part for the richness of British fantasy, the quality of which we in this far newer country seem rarely able to approach. But this doesn't at all mean that I find value in *anything* simply for its distance from contemporary American life, per se—which would have to take in so much, so many vastly differing aspects of it—or that I find American life disorderly in comparison with the English tradition and therefore dismiss it as incomplete.

I am not sure what Nodelman means by "incomplete." The American scene assuredly lacks a sense of the ancient past, but I don't dismiss it for that reason. I wonder in which one of my books I

appear to have done so, any more than any other writer of time
fantasy appears to have dismissed the present. (As for my books of
reality, I often go back to my childhood as far as circumstances, if not
happenings, are concerned, but this is because the possibilities offered create an intriguing and fruitful soil.) Somehow a non se-
quitur has been committed here, a leap from a true apprehension in
Nodelman's mind to a complete misapprehension. On the whole,
one could say that all of life, or rather what humanity has made of it,
is disorderly everywhere: we are constantly being confronted in our
news of the world with the most tragic randomness and mischance.
And I cannot believe that many of us look on the past, with all of its
differences from our own time, as having much glamor—except as
set forth in the popular historical romances. At least I do not.
Different as the past might have been, man's appalling inhumanity
to his fellow creatures, human and animal, has always been a common characteristic.

    Nor can I rest content with an implied relationship between
"Domi's alien and satisfyingly orderly rooms" and my supposed
"homage to the order of the past." Here again we are led from what
is true to another misapprehension. There has to be order in the
arrangement of a museum's relics of the past or we could not look at
the collection with any understanding or pleasure (in the case of
Domi in *Court*, the rooms and their furniture and bibelots from her
chateau have been reassembled in the French Museum, an imagined
place in San Francisco). But this necessity in a museum does not in
any way carry over to the notion that in my mind the past was more
orderly than the present. And I should much regret if anyone
believed that because I have written a time fantasy about a museum
and because Andrew in *Beyond Silence* finds resolution of his difficulties through contacts with the past in Scotland, far away from re-
minders of grief in present-day California, I am yearning or nostalgic for some kind of "orderly past" that never existed.

    In fact, as I am brought to think about it, I see that there is always a
war in the background of my novels written after *Tree:* the First
World War in *To the Green Mountains* and the three books about Julia,
a war in which her father is killed; the French Revolution in *The
Court of the Stone Children*, in which Domi's father is court-martialed

as a subversive; and in *Beyond Silence* the Boer War in Africa and the war in Vietnam, between which I wanted to draw a parallel, especially in the reactions of the two young people: Deirdre seeing the Boer War and Andrew the Vietnam War as wrong from the beginning. I do not believe it can be taken from these facts that I pay any least sort of homage to "an orderly past," nor that I see it as glamorous.

My second point is indeed a quibble, but it leads to interesting details about time fantasy. Nodelman says in that same paragraph that "like Tolly [in *The Children of Green Knowe*] and also like Tom in Philippa Pearce's *Tom's Midnight Garden*, [Andrew's] contacts with the past significantly involve a tree falling in a storm." Actually both the fir tree in Pearce's novel and the shaped yew called Green Noah in Boston's are struck by lightning: Green Noah disappears, while the fir tree falls and is cut up for firewood. But no tree is struck by lightning in *Silence*; a branch falls in great wind storms in both Deirdre's time and Andrew's, seventy years later—or are the storms coexistent?

For Tom, the fir tree's presence or absence in his midnight garden tells him that he is seeing the garden at confusingly different moments in time; it is there one night, then it is struck by lightning and falls on what is to him a night only a little later, yet on a succeeding night it is there again. It serves an entirely different purpose from those served by the superficially similar events in the other two novels. For the presence or absence of the fir tree in *Garden* is an almost unnoticed sign in the background of the story as to where we are in Hatty's life—whether she is child or adult—and this is not understood until the very end. For Tolly, the death of Green Noah by fire simply means that an evil presence has been removed from Granny Oldknow's loved surroundings. But the falling of the branch in *Beyond Silence* is an event in Andrew's and Deirdre's lives which brings them together under such extraordinary circumstances that Andrew is for the first time brought face to face intellectually with an unanswerable proposition (unanswerable to him at his stage of understanding), one that is symbolic of the meaning of all he has experienced and absorbed emotionally, before the branch's falling, without the frantic, desperate questioning he now undergoes in his own mind. A crisis has been reached which forces him to seek help outside the circle of family and friends.

As for Deirdre in *Silence*, her marriage to a man named Barty assuredly echoes the marriage of Hatty in *Garden* to "young Barty"; and I will go even further in echoings. In all four novels, Boston's *The Children of Green Knowe*, Pearce's *Tom's Midnight Garden*, and my own *The Court of the Stone Children* and *Beyond Silence*, there is a *loved* place where the inexplicable events occur: the protagonists, Tolly, Tom, Nina, and Andrew, solitaries and newcomers every one, literally fall in love with a house (or the museum in *Court*) and with a garden (the wild hill country around Cames in *Silence*). The tremendous power of place over the imagination and sensibilities of a child or adolescent is evoked in each case. But always the love of place is deepened and enhanced by its ghostly and human inhabitants. Tolly falls so deeply in love with the children of Green Knowe that when Granny Oldknow tells him finally that they are dead, something he had not previously understood, he "sat dumbfounded, with his big black eyes fixed on her. He must have known of course that the children could not have lived so many centuries without growing old, but he had never thought about it. To him, they were so real, so near, they were his own family that he needed more than anything on earth. He felt that the world had come to an end.[2]

Tom, who hated the idea of leaving his brother Peter (ill with measles during vacation) to go and stay with his stuffy aunt and uncle in a stuffy apartment some distance from his own town, changes over a period of time after discovering his garden and Hatty. Eventually he works every device he can manage to put off the unhappy hour of departure for home, for he has become utterly devoted to a place out of his own time, a house as it once was, and a garden that no longer exists. And if he has not actually fallen in love with Hatty herself, he has certainly fallen wholly in love with the idea of her, of her situation, and with his relation to her and to the garden. So that when, just before leaving, he discovers that for some unexplainable reason he cannot recover his midnight garden, he screams, "Hatty, Hatty!" His uncle hears. "Alan Kitson jumped the last few steps of the stairs and ran forward and caught Tom in his arms. The boy sobbed and fought as though he were being taken prisoner. Then his uncle felt his body go limp, and he began weeping softly now, but as though he would never stop."[3]

Nina in *Court*, like Tom, changes from positive dislike of the new place—in her case San Francisco—to the point where, because of the French Museum and its ghostly inhabitant, she is determined that she and her mother and father shall stay. Meanwhile, her father has gradually been changing the other way and has begun to think of leaving. Nina, upon realizing that Domi, in the end, will not return from some other level of existence or awareness, calls out to her in the silence of the court of the stone children:

> "*Domi . . . Domi, do you hear me? I'm ready. Let me come—*" Still with her arm around Odile, she held her body poised, willing herself over the brink, her breathing caught, in the concentration of her desire to follow Domi, without consciousness of need for breath, and her eyes opened to their widest while she waited for that moment when her angle of vision might be changed by the minutest degree and she could see Domi again.[4]

Andrew at the end of *Silence* is with Beth, the owner of Cames, to whom he has promised he will come again the following summer. But she reminds him of how he will change between the ages of fifteen and sixteen, of how his needs will change, and he thinks, in acute sorrow, "No, but it wasn't possible I wouldn't need to be here. I couldn't bear to think it would become unnecessary. Or—could it be it was Deirdre alone who was making me want to come back? Yet who knew if I would ever see her or hear her again, and why did I feel as I stood there with Beth that I probably never would?"[5]

Then there are the greenhouses. Surely both Green Knowe and the French Museum must have had greenhouses on the property, because no large gardens can be kept up through the seasons, with their changing flower beds, without them. But a greenhouse is central to place and in a way to story as well, in both *Tom's Midnight Garden* and *Beyond Silence*. I always saw the greenhouse behind Cames, at the back of it and up beyond the walk that led down to the lane where Deirdre's house stood. And the reason I knew it was there and always saw it in that particular location was because there *was* an old, broken-down, dilapidated greenhouse at the side of the

path leading to a lane, there at the back of the huge house beside a
loch where my Scottish husband and I stayed for our vacation in the
lake country in the west of Scotland.

And there is one more parallel, this time again between *Tom's
Midnight Garden* and *Beyond Silence*: in each the idea of relative time
is acted out. As I have said, Tom is confused by seeing Hatty as a little
girl in the beginning, then later as a very small girl, and even later as
the girl he saw in the beginning. But over the period of the whole
novel, while Tom himself remains a boy of about ten during the
weeks he is with his aunt and uncle, Hatty grows to young woman-
hood—a change Tom is not really aware of until his brother Peter,
on one strange occasion, points the fact out to him. And in *Silence*
(though I did not think of *Garden* as I wrote my book), Andrew sees
Deirdre, during his hypnagogic experience on the plane carrying
him to the British Isles, as a young girl, hears her three times as a
small girl later on, and sees her out in the hills as a young woman.

Indeed, quite unconsciously, I could have been paying tribute, as
Nodelman suggests, just as Philippa Pearce could have been paying
tribute to the art of *The Children of Green Knowe* in creating her own
loved house and garden with its own ghostly presences (or was Tom
the ghostly presence in Hatty's time?), after reading the story of
Tolly and his much loved house and garden and the ghost children
who came and went according to their own mysterious whims.
*Children* was published in 1954 and *Garden* in 1958.

Furthermore, as in the writing of sonnets, where there are certain
givens in structure, meter, and rhyme scheme, so there is a certain
given in the writing of most time fantasies, apart from the intermingling of two or possibly three time periods. Yet this need not
prevent each fantasy from being quite unlike every other in its
overall plot structure, its meaning, in the impressions the place and
the characters make upon us, and in the evocation of feeling. The
given I speak of is that the protagonist, or the reader, or both,
usually find out the truth about the past in one of three ways.

One way: in *The Children of Green Knowe* it is Granny Oldknow
who is the communicator by means of the stories she tells Tolly
throughout the book, just as in *Tom's Midnight Garden* old Mrs.
Bartholomew tells Tom a fuller story of the past than he could ever

have known without her when he ventures upstairs to say goodbye just before going home.

A second way: in *The Treasure of Green Knowe*, as also in K. M. Peyton's *A Pattern of Roses*, Nancy Bond's *A String in the Harp*, and William Mayne's *A Game of Dark*, scenes of the past alternate with scenes of the present, and the protagonist may or may not be a part of what is going on in the past. In Penelope Lively's *The House in Norham Gardens*, scenes of other times in the world of the hidden valley in New Guinea are given in brief paragraphs, indented, in smaller type than the text, and in italics, at the beginning of each chapter.

A third way: in Jill Paton Walsh's *A Chance Child*, Christopher goes to the local library to find out what eventually happened to Creep in records of the early part of the Industrial Revolution, records in the form of statements by various men and women who worked in the mines and potteries and mills in the area to which Creep went out of the present into the past. In *The Court of the Stone Children*, Nina at first learns of Domi's past during the French Revolution when Domi tells her the story of it (the first way), and then about Odile's past through her journal, which was published in France and the translation of which the curator of the French Museum has in her library. In *Beyond Silence*, Andrew learns of Deirdre's life through a letter she has written to the Andrew of her time, a letter which was among the rubbish Beth was clearing out of the old house when she and her husband bought it for a hotel. And the reason she kept it is a part of the philosophical-scientific problem enunciated throughout the book.

Ideally, this particular given, brought out by whatever method, speaks under the flow of movement of the feeling of inevitability the story had for its author: how it seemed to have grown as a part of the writer's private vision of his novel, characteristic of it, *right* for it, embedded so deeply within the structure that it could not be torn out and replaced by some other method of dealing with the problem of communication of the past without ruining the delicate net composed of all the elements of the novel interrelating. Delicate, yes, but a net which must at the same time be so firmly woven, with so satisfying an inner logic, that one never stops to think, as one reads, of the technique by which this firmness and sense of satisfaction for the reader were attained.

I come now to a third and last quibble: that of Nodelman's view of the Quark's—Phineas Brock's—relation to Andrew, his intentions toward Andrew. Nodelman says of Dunstan McCallum, Andrew's friend, that he "would understand and respect another's need for walls and do nothing to disturb them." This is quite true. However, Nodelman then adds, "But Andrew's subconscious understands that Brock, the professional psychological investigator, might. What Andrew hates most about Brock is his desire to help him, which his subconscious sees as a matter of hunting him down."[6] I would replace that word *might* with the words *was determined to*. And it wasn't a matter of Andrew's subconscious alone seeing Brock as the hunter, the cold, single-minded breaker of walls of privacy for his own self-centered ends; the consciously aware Andrew was fully convinced that Brock was on his trail, though he did not know why. And it took the words of Professor Fairlie to shed a hard light on just what Brock was up to.

Nodelman argues that "Brock really was only trying to help, and really did have other things in his mind beside the torturing of Andrew."[7] *But Brock is not benign.* Andrew does admit, after he hears Brock weeping over Fairlie's death, that he *had* "been incapable of seeing him as anything but a cold, calculating, impervious little manipulator for his own ends."[8] But then Andrew adds, "And he *was* that—he *was*." Yes. That is the way Andrew and I see the matter. And Brock's grief over Fairlie does *not* force Andrew to reevaluate Brock. Andrew sees him in the end just as he had before. Of course Nodelman has every right to view the matter as he wishes, maintaining that Andrew isn't remembering correctly, but I am puzzled to know why he interprets Brock as he does, as a helpful little man of pure, comradely motives, when, as I believe, the text points to a quite different understanding of him.

Concerning *Ordinary People* by Judith Guest and its similarities to *Beyond Silence* in certain turns of the story—in both novels a boy loses his older brother, by drowning in *Ordinary People* (Andrew's nightmares in *Silence* echo this) and by a suicidal auto accident in *Silence*, and in both the boys are overcome by guilt and get help from psychologists—I can only say that I had not read *Ordinary People* at the time I was writing my novel, had never heard of it, nor have I seen the movie. I did finally read the book recently, feeling that I should know what two reviewers, a friend, and Perry Nodelman were talking about. In my estimation, aside from the likenesses mentioned above, the novels appear as different from each other as it is possible for them to be.

We go now, beyond quibbles, to Nodelman's comments on the naming of Phineas Brock and Nell Cames. The whole subject of names in novels is fascinating. Roland Barthes tells of Proust who, in order to write *Remembrance of Things Past*, which had begun to blossom in his mind as early as his terms at the lycée, underwent years of "groping," as if the true and unique work were being sought, abandoned, resumed, without ever being found, "until at last he came upon that federation act which would permit Proust to write *Remembrance* without flagging, from 1909 to his death."[9] What was the "federation act"? Barthes answers that "the (poetic) event which 'launched' *Remembrance* was the discovery of Names; doubtless, since his *Contre Saint-Beuve*, Proust already possessed certain names (Combray, Guermantes); but it was only between 1907 and 1909, it appears, that he constituted in its entirety the onomastic system of *Remembrance*: once this system was found, the work was written immediately."[10]

Further along, Barthes speaks of the proper name "as sign . . . and a precious object, compressed, embalmed, which must be opened like a flower . . . a voluminous sign, a sign always pregnant with a dense texture of meaning."[11] And one of the most vivid examples of Barthes's conviction is the example Leon Edel gives in his essay on Hugh Walpole's last novel, *The Killer and the Slain*. It was a novel Walpole had had in mind for years before he was finally compelled to write it at the behest of an unconscious which perhaps knew that Walpole had not much longer to live.

Walpole dedicated it to Henry James twenty-five years after James died: "This macabre is dedicated in loving memory and humble admiration to the great author of *The Turning of the Screw*."[12] And the error in that dedication, the misquotation of the title of James's novel, Edel reveals as central to the evidence that led Walpole to

open out, as one might open out a flower, that "voluminous sign . . .
pregnant with a dense texture of meaning," the name Walpole gave
to one of his two protagonists. This is the initial villain of the novel,
James Oliphant Tunstall. In other words, as Edel eventually came to
understand, James Old Elephant Turnscrew was what Walpole's
unconscious was actually saying deep beneath the level of his conscious hearing. The name James is obvious. And Old Elephant was
the name Henry James had often given himself in letters to Walpole,
whom he loved, but whose novels he always deprecated and was
condescending about, acts which caused Walpole the deepest humiliation and which aroused in him a bitter, continuing resentment
(that is, the *turning* of the screw). Turnscrew, melded into Tunstall,
speaks of the title of the tale Walpole greatly admired and which
held an element repeated in Walpole's novel, the corrupting of a
small boy by a cynical elder.

Having set down the results of his detective work on that name,
Edel was told, from evidence in Walpole's diaries, that he was indeed
correct and that Walpole, in his last novel, had written out the
submerged hostilities, harbored all these years of their friendship
and afterward, toward the author he had loved in return. Walpole
died on June 1, 1941, twenty-one days after reading the final typescript.

There is nothing at all so fascinating or mysterious in my own
naming. Nodelman is quite right as to the meaning of Brock, the old
Celtic word for badger; and also, as I came to find out, for a dirty
fellow, a skunk. However, I hadn't realized that Phineas means
"mouth of brass" in Biblical terms, apt as that is. In the beginning I
had called him Alpheus but saw, as I got into the novel, that Andrew,
Alpheus, and Alex would boggle the mind. Thereafter Phineas
came to me, a much better name, I thought, and looked it up. Yes,
Phineas blinded by his own ambition, as Phineus in mythology was
blinded by Zeus. As for Nell Cames echoing Eleanor Cameron, that
is very acute.

Why I chose Cames for the name of the castle, I have no idea. In
1971, my husband and I went to Scotland and stayed in the old
residence, built in the 1700s, that became my castle. And while we
were there a novel came to me, complete, but as the years passed the

whole thing changed into its present version. Meanwhile my husband went back again some time later, while I stayed home because of a broken knee; he joined our son there and played golf with a young woman we had met on our first trip. But here everything falls apart as far as the novel is concerned: our friend is happily married and the Camerons and the Harknesses write to each other two or three times a year.

In Nodelman's perceptive discussion of the use of actual and symbolic walls in *Silence*, he speaks of inexplicable magic and psychological science, and their opposition. In the beginning I though that I was writing a time fantasy. But as time went on I could see that two other genres would come up as possibilities, and so it turned out. Ethel Heins, in her review in the *Horn Book*, said of it, "A kind of psychological science fiction, the novel presents a warping of reality, explained in terms of theories of the unconscious mind and precognition as well as of revised notions about space-time, cause and effect, and coincidence."[13] Others rejected the idea of science fiction vigorously and said that it is a psychological study of a disturbed boy, while still others spoke of speculations as to the true nature of time. But a good many saw it, as I had in the beginning, as time fantasy.

Nodelman, apparently, sees it as fantasy, for he speaks of Fairlie's death as necessary because Andrew's breakthrough "will ultimately come through inexplicable magic, not psychological science." Yet, oddly enough, he goes on to say in the next sentence that "the wall finally breaks down through the hypnagogic experience that provided Andrew with the image of a wall 'with a break in it' in the first place."[14] For me, this is true. The break must come through his own efforts, his own perceptions, while he still keeps his secret. On the other hand, the break couldn't have come if Andrew hadn't heard Deirdre, as a woman, speaking of her own guilt, which brings us back either to "inexplicable magic" or possibly to a psychologically troubled boy hearing voices.

But of course there is a third possibility, with reference to speculations as to the true nature of time. If, actually, all of time *is* one time, all times being coexistent on a level of experience beyond our comprehension, and if Andrew, in a state of intense, vulnerable sensitivity, has been allowed briefly to experience that oneness and,

because of this experience, is brought to a realization of the underlying truth of his own situation, then this is a book neither of fantasy
nor psychological science fiction, but of time and reality.

In any case, I respond to Nodelman's words, "Beyond the phenomena we comprehend and therefore can name lies the inexpressible"[15] *Yes.*

## Notes

1. Perry Nodelman, "Beyond Explanation, and Beyond Inexplicability, in *Beyond Silence*," above, pp. 122–23.

2. L. M. Boston, *The Children of Green Knowe* (New York: Harcourt, Brace, 1954), p. 75.

3. Philippa Pearce, *Tom's Midnight Garden* (Philadelphia: Lippincott, 1959), p. 212.

4. Eleanor Cameron, *The Court of the Stone Children* (New York: E. P. Dutton, 1973), p. 191.

5. Eleanor Cameron, *Beyond Silence* (New York: E. P. Dutton, 1980), p. 196.

6. Nodelman, above, p. 129.

7. Ibid.

8. Cameron, *Beyond Silence*, p. 166.

9. Roland Barthes, *New Critical Essays*, tr. Richard Howard (New York: Hill & Wang, 1980), p. 57.

10. Ibid., pp. 58–59.

11. Ibid., p. 59.

12. Leon Edel, *Stuff of Sleep and Dreams* (New York: Harper & Row, 1982), p. 309.

13. Ethel Heins, Review of *Beyond Silence*, *Horn Book*, 56 (Dec. 1980), 646.

14. Nodelman, above, pp. 129–30.

15. Ibid., p. 132.

*Reviews*

# Bringing Shakespeare to Young People,
# and Young People to Shakespeare

Sidney Homan

*Macbeth*, by William Shakespeare. Illustrated by Von. New York: Workman Publishing, 1982.
*Tales from Shakespeare*, by Charles and Mary Lamb. Washington, DC: The Folger Shakespeare Library, 1979.
*Shakespeare and His Theatre*, by John Russell Brown. Illustrated by David Gentleman. New York: Lothrop, Lee and Shepard Books, 1982.

A comic-book version of *Macbeth*, an early nineteenth-century retelling of twenty of the plays, and a book on Shakespeare's theater and company—at issue here are the ways in which we can introduce and attract young people to Shakespeare. Or perhaps the real issue is what such approaches exclude, no less than what they include.

We know from comic-book festivals that the genre is not confined to the young, and Workman's *Macbeth* capitalizes on such widespread interest, preserving the entire text of the play—though no specific edition is mentioned—yet placing that text in the old Classic Comics format, a series of illustrated panels by the Brazilian artist Von, carrying the reader/viewer through the ongoing scenes of Shakespeare's play. In one sense, this very act of visualizing the play represents an interpretation that is by definition exclusive. Though the cartoonlike panels set an appropriate mood for the dark world invoked by the Macbeths and duly register a thought-tormented husband and a satanic wife, the "interpretation" itself is, I think, mostly superficial. It offers a variety of long shots and close-ups of the play's various sets but hardly penetrates the minds of the characters as a good performance can, when the actors complement Shakespeare's text with their own subtext of emotions made manifest in stage movement and the very act of delivery. Still, this *Macbeth* does establish the external, if not the more significant internal, world of the play: the witches close the opening scene by dissolving into a murky cloud that itself threatens to engulf a rainbow-colored sky; Von's camera zooms in on Lady Macbeth as she reads her husband's letter; there is a nice juxtaposition of the Macbeths immediately after Duncan's murder with four vertical panels showing a hand frantically knocking on the castle gate; Hecate's bloodshot eyes and distorted hand loom at us from the center of the page; and there is a marvelous pastoral backdrop for the conversation in Edward the Confessor's peaceful kingdom between Malcolm and Macduff.

Still, the faces, for the most part, are too formal, stylized, too confined to a few predictable emotions. At times the pictures become only a backdrop for the text, pushed to the periphery, while Shakespeare's blank verse—here printed as prose—commands our attention. And for the many striking panels, such as those mentioned above, there are an equal number of pedestrian ones. In a curious way, the Workman edition does little more than the Classic Comics did, confining itself to "picturing" the plot, thereby conveying the story and transporting the reader/viewer from one set to the next. This works well for an action story, and I think here of the *Ivanhoe* of the Classic Comics. When that "action," however, is ultimately interior, symbolic, when the "story," as in Shakespeare, is enacted through a productive tension between the verbal and the visual dimensions of a stage production, this method is much less effective. Perhaps the judgments of my college-bound son and high-school daughter, however, are more significant than my own: they found the Workman *Macbeth* a good tool in helping them move from the printed text to that larger text sustained by what we see as well as hear at a performance. Given our visual culture and the complexities of character and plot that a Shakespearean play presents to a contemporary generation, this is no mean achievement.

The Folger Library has reprinted the Lambs' 1807 *Tales from Shakespeare* and added a good number of eighteenth-, nineteenth-, and twentieth-century illustrations from the plays, many in color, and representing several styles as well as media ranging from watercolors to engravings. These illustrations, placed alongside those of the Workman *Macbeth*, are accordingly a much more profound expression of the art; and, while readers of the Folger edition will have favorites that best translate their personal views of the plays, it is safe to say that their presence here, coupled with the Lambs' own *Tales*, provides something of a double bonus. In all honesty, though, while I value the Lamb's *Tales* as a historical document, I cannot recommend this handsome edition for the young reader. The Lambs' intentions are the best: to capture the magic of the stories, to make them, in the author's words, "easy reading for very young children," and especially for young girls since boys are "generally permitted the use of their fathers' libraries at a much earlier age than girls are." The Lambs' prose *is* engaging, often eloquent and witty, as when they comment on the wrestling match in *As You Like It*: "In those times wrestling, which is only practiced now by country clowns, was a favourite sport even in the courts of princes, and before fair ladies and princesses." It is refreshing to find *A Midsummer Night's Dream* retold by the Lambs as a tale of magical adventures, of mysteries, after that same play has been allegorized by scholars into a weighty debate between reason and passion. The chapter on *Hamlet* is a model of condensation, and when the Lambs paraphrase Shakespeare's language the effect can be engaging: "Now was the middle of night, when over half the world nature seems dead, and wicked dreams abuse men's minds asleep, and none but the wolf and the murderer is abroad." As stories in themselves, apart from their sources in Shakespeare, they will surely delight young readers eager for adventures.

But not all the play is here, and I think this is a fault, if the goal of such retellings is to move the young reader through the Lambs to Shakespeare: the guides here, to put it bluntly, should not be the goal. The Fool in *King Lear* is introduced well into the story, almost as an afterthought; and missing are the gravediggers in *Hamlet* and Autolycus of *The Winter's Tale*, not to mention the Christopher Sly scenes in *The Taming of the Shrew*. There is also a problem of proportions. The second scene of *The Tempest*—Prospero's conversation with Miranda—takes more than one-fourth of the narrative, and we seem to spend more time getting to the forest of Arden than we actually spend there. As often as *Tales* is a valuable document revealing a sensitive and no less typical early nineteenth-century view view of Shakespeare—a sentimental response to Lear, an Iago of rather ordinary motives, a basically decent Macbeth overwhelmed by his wife—it is also a refined plot summary, and not always a complete summary at that. And this division is further reflected in the three styles of the stories: the Lambs' own prose that alternates between interpretation and narration, lengthy quotes from Shakespeare, and paraphrase of his poetry. I would think it no less important, perhaps even more important, for young people to be introduced to the Shakespeare of our age, as he exists in performances and in the classroom. That Shakespeare is surely no better, or worse, than that of the Lambs. Still, he is somewhat different and he is what we currently have.

I have no such qualifications about John Russell Brown's *Shakespeare and His Theatre*. A distinguished scholar who is also associate director of the National Theatre in London, Brown brings a world of information and experience to such topics as how the Globe was built, what the interior looked like, the organization and personnel of Shakespeare's company, the activities onstage and backstage, the private theaters, and the rebuilding of the Globe after the 1613 fire. Brown stays with the facts or at least keeps to those areas in which Shakespeareans and theater historians have some consensus, and he does all of this in a style that is personal, often rather eloquent—and never condescending. Some of the parallels to twentieth-century entertainment, such as comparing the stage to a large boxing ring, should be particularly helpful to high-school readers; and Brown is especially clear when handling the technical dimensions of the theater, introducing commentary on the stage from Elizabethan writers, or imagining what an actual production of *Henry V* looked like to the audience. The prose is calm, businesslike, and yet Brown also allows himself some liberties of imaginative flight, as when he describes the clown Tarleton peeking at the audience from behind the curtain (p. 24). This is easily one of the best books on the technical as well as the psychological dimensions of a production. The illustrations by David Gentleman, even when mostly decorative, are always accurate and thereby complement Brown's narrative. Some of those illustrations are very fine indeed; I think particularly of those showing the Globe being built, the actor facing the galleries, the stage set for Juliet's tomb, and the burning of the theater.

Indeed, the success of this last approach, when considered in the context of the illustrated *Macbeth* and the Lambs' *Tales*, makes one wonder if someone could present for the young reader the entire "world" of Shakespeare, giving some sense of the age itself, the physical theater, the craft of playwriting, and—most important— the actual plays. It would be an approach that, while not avoiding interpretation and hence bias, would be as inclusive and as sugges- tive as possible. And it would at length be pedagogically liberating, launching the reader into the plays, arming him with all the tools necessary for this most difficult and therefore most rewarding of playwrights, and yet at length releasing the reader and thereby allowing him to re-enact the play in the "text" of his own mind and heart.

# Childhood's Companions

Gillian Avery

*A Nursery Companion*, by Iona and Peter Opie. London and New York: Oxford University Press, 1980.

The truth that emerges from the corpus of Iona and Peter Opie's work on the lore of childhood, written and spoken, seems to be that children take little interest in themselves, their taste being for a violent if not lawless world beyond the playground, a world that most of us who write books for them prefer not to represent. Richard Lovell Edgeworth, in his preface to *The Parent's Assistant*, quotes Johnson to this effect and then repudiates him. "Dr. Johnson says, that 'Babies do not like to hear stories of babies themselves; that they require to have their imaginations raised by tales of giants and fairies, and castles and enchantment.' The fact remains to be proved, but supposing that they do prefer such tales, is this a reason why they should be induldged in reading them?"

This was 1795, when the publication of books aimed specifically at children had been a commercial proposition in England for some decades, and there was consequently a deal of dry, didactic stuff around. For it is a sad but indisputable fact, evident to anyone who considers the history of children's books, that authors writing for the prestige end of the juvenile market write with their eye on the parent, teacher, or librarian who is going to do the buying (and even more on the reviewer). Richard Lovell Edgeworth was by no means the first person to say, in effect, "Find out what they want to read and stop them." Thomas Boreman's *Curiosities of the Tower of London* (1741), a little book that was admittedly far more entertaining and bloodthirsty than anything on Richard Edgeworth's list of recommended reading, contained the following lines:

> The author, doubtless, aims aright,
> Who joins instruction with delight.
> Tom Thumb shall now be thrown away,
> And Jack, who did the giants slay;

> Such ill concerted, artless lyes,
> Our British youth shall now despise.

But heroes like Tom and Jack are not so easily dislodged; they have, after all, been part of the mythology of childhood for centuries whereas the children's book proper is a relative innovation. That is to say, up to the mid-eighteenth century the same sort of literature was enjoyed by the unsophisticated of all ages—heroic and violent deeds, farce, all preferably laced with a boisterous if not crude humor.

In their introduction to *The Oxford Dictionary of Nursery Rhymes* (1951) the Opies point out the adult nature of the genre: "It can safely be stated that the overwhelming majority of nursery rhymes were not in the first place composed for children; in fact many are survivals of an adult code of joviality, and in their original wording were, by present standards, strikingly unsuitable for those of tender years." They were verses that a mother or nurse, without thought of their origin, would use to soothe or amuse a child, and since little difference was seen in the natures of adult and child, few before the nineteenth century saw reason to bowdlerize them. The Opies' introduction lists some of their origins: fragments of ballads or folk songs; remnants of ancient custom and ritual, some of them perhaps holding the last echoes of long-forgotten evil; ditties from taverns, pot-houses, or barrack rooms; songs that poke fun at religious practices, or contain rude jests and coarse innuendos. "We can say almost without hesitation, that, of those pieces which date from before 1800, the only true nursery rhymes (i.e., rhymes composed especially for the nursery) are the rhyming alphabets, the infant amusements, and the lullabies."

Similarly the fairy tales. *The Classic Fairy Tales* (1974), where the Opies examine the origins of twenty-four of the best-known tales and print their texts as they were first published in English, breathes violence and cruelty, qualities that are reflected in the illustrations, even though these are all taken from nineteenth-century books designed for the nursery. There are ogres with gleaming, pointed teeth about to devour children or cut their throats, screaming giants in their death agonies, a giant slitting his belly, the yellow dwarf having his head cut off, and (from *Favourite Stories for the Nursery*, 1900) Red Riding Hood's wolf poised for his first meal of the day—he is crouched with slavering jaws on the grandmother's bed, about to devour her. It seems clear that the compilers were at pains to stress the savageness of a tradition that is now associated with children only, but which was once the property of all who enjoyed the story.

In *The Lore and Language of Schoolchildren* (1959) the authors observe that whereas nursery rhymes are preserved and propagated by adults, and can therefore be said to be adult-approved, the playground jingles are invented by the children themselves and are not intended for adult ears. Indeed, adults may try to suppress them. But though the style is not polished, the basic emotions remind us of the sources from which the nursery rhymes and the fairy tales sprang. They are crude, ribald, violent. The book's chapter headings convey that much: "Parody and Impropriety"; "Nicknames and Epithets"; "Jeers and Torments"; "Partisanship"; "Pranks." And a random sampling confirms it:

> Don't care was made to care,
> Don't care was hung.
> Don't care was put in a pot
> And boiled till he was done.

And with perhaps the solitary exception of Shirley Temple, the playground does not commemorate children but legendary folk heroes like Davy Crockett, Charlie Chaplin, Betty Grable, or oppressors such as Napoleon or Hitler.

*A Nursery Companion* (1980) is the latest book compiled by the Opies, and, since Peter Opie died two years later, probably the last that will appear under their joint names. Here they are dealing with children's books proper. Twenty-seven little books are reproduced in it, the earliest dating from 1807, the latest 1827. They are all light-hearted, and many of them have as well that earthy vigor that is the mark of the older tradition, but they differ strikingly from any books that had gone before in that they are delectably and colorfully illustrated. The older tradition of illustration was, in contrast, dispirited and gloomy. Thackeray was born in 1811, and though he could have known some of Harris's contemporary publications, he was evidently reared, as so often happened when books were expensive and children were not indulged, on the products of an earlier generation. In 1846 he remembered how the books of his childhood appeared: "Such picture books as we had were illustrated with the most shameful, hideous, old woodcuts which had lasted through a century, and some of which may be actually seen lingering about still as head-pieces to the Catnach ballads." "When the verve of nursery literature a hundred and sixty years ago is observed," the Opies write in the introduction, "how is it that educationalists and others have kept talking about the dreariness of books for the young in the past?" Their guess is that the books that survive are the expensive and the unreadable, whereas those that gave delight were mostly read to pieces. There is truth in this; comics, books for small children, are soon in shreds; the sober, hard-backed stuff is more indestructible.

And it is true as the Opie's collection reveals that there was for twenty years or so at the beginning of the last century a sudden splendid splash of picture books. But even so it has to be said that the Regency age was for children—and indeed for the ordinary household—sedate and sober, whatever it may have been for George IV and court circles. The evangelical revival was well underway; the words of Richard Edgeworth, Mrs. Trimmer, Mrs. Sherwood upon what children might read (and, more to the point, what they might not) had long ago made a deep impression on the impressionable minds of anxious parents; and, though the tone of children's books was not necessarily uniformly religious, as it was with the early Victorians, it was generally very serious, dismayingly rational. Charlotte Yonge, for instance, born in 1823, was brought up on the Edgeworth system ("though modified by religion and good sense") and read the books of her parents' childhood that Edgeworth himself would have recommended: Mrs. Trimmer's *Fabulous Histories* and *Sacred History, Sandford and Merton*, Rollin's *Ancient History, Perambulation of a Mouse.*

For every one of the delicious little trifles reprinted by the Opies there was a shelf full of drab volumes that one can only describe (in the words of marginalia I once found in a library book) as "cursed prosy." Volumes, for example, by lady moralists such as

Mary Robson, Priscilla Wakefield, Mrs. Budden, Mrs. Pilkington, Elizabeth Sandham, with enticing titles such as *Precept and Example, Claudine or Humility, Moral Truths, The Twin Sisters of the Advantages of Religion* (note the coolly rational approach, the *advantages* of religion), *Mentorial Tales, Sacred Elucidation.*

Of the twenty-seven books that the Opies show, eighteen are from the publishing house of Harris, and this is perhaps the important fact to note. Harris was the prime mover in what Harvey Darton has described as "the dawn of levity." Yet, to my mind, it is not so much a dawn as a sunset, the last beams of light from the folk tradition that had put children and adults on the same level. It was, for instance, Harris who published in 1805 *Old Mother Hubbard,* verses that, if we did not know the author Sarah Catherine Martin and her history, as recorded in *The Oxford Dictionary of Nursery Rhymes,* we well might suppose to have sprung from the soil, like the Old Woman and her Pig. Up to that time John Harris had not, in the Opies' words, displayed any great entrepreneurial skill since he had taken over the firm of Newbery. Now he hit the jackpot and it was not just with children. "Peter Pindar," in a tetchy collection of satires published in 1806 under the title of *Tristia,* deplored the level of general taste, and particularly the craze for nursery rhymes:

> Or where wert thou, O Goddess of the Fiddle?
> To suffer Air to join with Goosy Gander,
> Cock Robin, Horner, and High-diddle-diddle;
> And turn a tuneful prostituted pander.

He finishes:

> In vain I preach—in vain in scorn I smile—
> In vain my pen the giant vise assails;
> Herculean labour to reclaim an Isle
> Where Rapture dotes on Mother Hubbard's tales.

By this envious lament one may infer that of the 10,000 copies that Harris said he had sold in a few months (to say nothing of the 20 additions the following year) a great proportion had gone to adults.

*A Nursery Companion* includes *Mother Hubbard,* and also *Dame Trot and her Cat* (1819), *Cock Robin* (1819), *The House that Jack Built* (1820), and *The Old Woman and her Pig* (1827), all published by Harris, all traditional stories far older than the nineteenth century. These verses and pictures are links with the country life of pre-enclosure times when the cottager was sturdy and independent and beholden to no one, and was not the squire's obedient tenant he would become. The illustrations in themselves are of great interest to the social historian. Look at the drawing on page 96, of the old woman sweeping her house ("Too small for a giant, too big for a mouse") with its detail of a spinning wheel between the bed and the fire, the hourglass on the shelf, a candlestick and a teapot on the chimney-piece.

"Fine illustrations were indeed the secret of John Harris's success," Marjorie Moon says in her 1976 catalogue of the Harris publications. "Very often the text of his picture books shows every sign of having been written by untalented hack writers, but the engravings, or woodcuts, and their colouring are of a higher standard than those of most of his contemporaries." This is borne out if one compares, for instance, the illustrations in the compilation of limericks—the first of their kind—published in 1820 under the title of The History of Sixteen Wonderful Old Women with the coarse draftsmanship and crude coloring in *Anecdotes and Adventures of Fifteen Gentlemen*, which Harris's rival Marshall published in imitation the following year.

Not everybody, however, appreciated these vivid little books. A long article in the *London Magazine* in 1820 deplored present-day picture books and picked out Harris as the worst offender. The writer looked back with nostalgia (unlike Thackeray) to the crude drawings he remembered in the books of his youth: dark and shadowy, blotched, clumsy and irregular, often nearly indistinct; they had, he said, more mystery and interest than the flashy pictures now given to children that left nothing to be imagined.

The same writer picked out particular Harris publications for censure, notably *Peter Piper's Practical Principles of Plain and Perfect Pronunciation* (1813), a zestful collection of tongue twisters (included by the Opies) that he dismisses as degrading trash. "A decent nurse," he says roundly, "would now blush with shame to repeat what is daily put into the hands of her charges to read!" His greatest sense of outrage, however, is felt when he contemplates *The Dandies' Ball*, published this time by Marshall, and "ringing the charges on all the diverse topics of street vulgarity." Perhaps that was why it appealed so much to Richard Brinsley Sheridan's eleven-year-old granddaughter, for she followed it up with *The Dandies' Rout* which Marshall published in 1820 (and the Opies 160 years later). It is a sparkling piece with some fascinating glimpses contributed by Robert Cruikshank of a Regency dandy's toilette: stays, false calves, tall collar, hooks to get him into his tight boots, and bootjacks to get him out of them.

*A Nursery Companion* concentrates on Harris's racier and more subversive publications. He was in fact an eclectic publisher, who had studied his markets and therefore had on his list authors like Mrs. Trimmer, Mrs. Pilkington, Mrs. Budden, and their kind, as well as the sort of books that Thackeray remembered as "abominable attempts made to make useful books for children, and cram science down their throats as calomel used to be administered under the pretense of a spoonful of currant-jelly." But in *A Nursery Companion* it is as if the Opies have set out to display examples of the qualities they have found to characterize the child's own taste. You could call it the culmination of their thirty years of research into childhood. They have certainly included some of Harris's lesson books such as *The Paths of Learning Strewn with Flowers* (1820) and *The Chapter of Kings* (1818), yet both are delightfully pretty; the second has a history rather like the common one of a nursery rhyme, in that it originated as a popular song sung by the eighteenth-century actor John Collins. The overwhelming impression of the Opies' collection is therefore of a universality of taste, of humor that would cut across class and age groups and has not been in the least dated. It is, in short, a book that will be enjoyed as much as the originals once were, and, as then, by children as well as adults.

This volume, the sixth of their presentations of aspects of childhood, beautifully rounds off the Opie achievement. It is a pendant, if you like, to their weightier works, but presented with the same consummate yet unobtrusive scholarship, the same wisdom and humor. In the breadth of their knowledge and in their wideranging interests they dwarf everybody else in the field. They have explored child-hood, as George Steiner wrote of one of the books, "where it is most guarded and lives with secret laughter." All of us who study children and childhood are immeasurably in their debt.

# *The Grimm* German Legends *in English*

Jack Zipes

*The German Legends of the Brothers Grimm,* edited and translated by
  Donald Ward. 2 vols. Philadelphia: Institute for the Study of
  Human Issues, 1981.

It is somewhat of a mystery why the English-speaking world has had
to wait until 1981 for the first translation of the *Deutsche Sagen*
(*German Legends*) by the Brothers Grimm. After all, the *Legends*,
which first appeared in 1816 and 1818, were translated into French,
Danish, and even Rumanian in the nineteenth century and have
always been considered a vital source book for folklorists and critics
alike. Perhaps we have always assumed that the *German Legends* had
been translated since many of them are known through romances,
novels, adaptations, selective translations, films, comic books, and
references in critical studies. The two most famous examples are
Richard Wagner's *Tannhäuser* and Robert Browning's *The Children of
Hameln.* The *Legends* have been very much with us, albeit in some
very unusual forms which confuse their meaning and origins. Now,
thanks to the efforts of Donald Ward and his excellent English
rendition, we can finally clarify some mistaken assumptions and
appreciate the *Legends* in their proper context.

Ward's accomplishment does not stop with the translation, which
maintains the singular styles of the colorful legends. Indeed, he has
also provided copious notes, bibliographical references, and an epilogue that sheds light on the historical significance of the Grimms'
work. Since this epilogue is essentially an introduction to *German
Legends,* I should like to begin by discussing the major points and
then to point to the relevance of the *Legends* for various scholarly
disciplines.

After documenting the source which he used for his translation,
Ward divides his epilogue into four sections: "Precursors of the
Brothers Grimm," "Lives of the Brothers Grimm," "The Brothers
Grimm and the Emergence of the Study of Folklore," and "The

German Legends." Throughout this long essay Ward endeavors to distinguish fact from fiction about the Brothers Grimm; for, despite a few general accounts of their lives, there is no exhaustive critical biography of the Grimms to date. The two biographies in English, *The Brothers Grimm* by Ruth Michaelis-Jena (London: Routledge and Kegan Paul, 1970) and *Paths through the Forest* by Murray B. Peppard (New York: Holt, Rinehart and Winston, 1971), leave a great deal to be desired, and even in German there is a real lack in this area, despite the source book by Ludwig Denecke, *Jacob Grimm und sein Bruder Wilhelm* (Stuttgart: Metzler, 1971). Furthermore, there have been major revisions in the interpretations of their tales due to discoveries about their method of research and the historical reception of their findings. Heinz Rölleke's important research is surprisingly *not* discussed by Ward. (See Heinz Rölleke, ed., *Die älteste Märchensammlung der Brüder Grimm* [Cologny-Genève: Fondation Martin Bodmer, 1975] and Gerd Hoffman and Heinz Rölleke, eds., *Der unbekannte Bruder Grimm. Deutsche Sagen von Ferdinand Phillip Grimm* [Cologne: Diederichs, 1979]). In addition, Rölleke has recently edited the significant 1819 edition of the Grimms' tales and written an epilogue which contains new material about the research methods of the two scholars: *Grimms Kinder- und Hausmärchen*, 2 vols. (Cologne: Diederichs, 1982).

All this has had a bearing on the status of the Grimms as folklorists and the importance of their *Legends* as well. Thus, Ward does well to begin cautiously by explaining that the Brothers Grimm were *not* the founders of modern folklore as has been commonly believed, but that they were a part of a broad movement in the eighteenth century when numerous scholars were undertaking ethnologically based studies of folk customs. Moreover, even the philological orientation taken by the Grimms had been initiated in Germany by Herder and the early romantics (particularly the Schlegel brothers, and also Tieck, Novalis, Fichte, Schelling, and Schleiermacher, all of whom Ward unfortunately slights). Nevertheless, the Grimms did set new standards for field research and textual analysis once they realized the significance of their work on folktales and legends, and they became the foremost pioneers in the field of comparative folklore and mythology in the nineteenth century.

Ward devotes the biographical part of the epilogue to a survey of how the Grimms developed an interest in folklore and mythology. Here, in a few pages, he admirably transmits a vivid picture of their lives and concerns. The more salient points pertain to the Grimms' background in law under the influence of Karl von Savigny, who saw judicial codes as an outgrowth of culture and the same forces that generated customs, rites, and manners; the relationship of the Grimms to other romantic writers such as Brentano and Arnim, who were endeavoring to reinvigorate German popular culture; the Grimms' strong desire to provide the German people with an understanding of their *common* language and culture; the Grimms' contributions toward the democratization of the German states; and the differences between the two brothers, who conducted many separate studies and had contrasting lifestyles (which, unhappily, Ward does not fully portray). We tend to forget that Jacob and Wilhelm were not one and the same entity even though they shared the same roof for most of their lives. Their personalities were markedly different, as were their political and philosophical outlooks. Here Ward might have dared some psychological probing that could have produced some interesting results in regard to both the tales and the legends. For instance, their distinctly patriarchal leanings influenced their choice of subject matter, and they often reshaped legends and tales to correspond to their male conservative notions of sexuality and middle-class morality.

Still, in fairness to Ward, there are limits to a short biographical account. He is more interested in the cooperative work of the Grimms and how the two scholars set standards for future folklorists both by synthesizing their research from literary documents, books, manuscripts, diaries, logs, chronicles, and histories and by gathering oral material from the lower classes—peasants, itinerant workers, servants, craftsmen, market women, housewives, and governesses. Ward stresses that the Grimms were among the first German intellectuals to take popular culture seriously: they developed a historical comparative method so that the German people could know more about their cultural tradition and affirm it.

The *German Legends* were collected about the same time as the folktales were being gathered (1808–16), and it became apparent to the Grimms that it was important to distinguish between the two genres. Essentially, they believed that the legends were based on actual events and were more historical than the poetic folktales. Unlike the folktale or fairy tale, there is no tight narrative structure to the legend, which, they discovered, was often introduced as an aside to make a notable point in the middle of a conversation within a story. Ward characterizes the legend as "newsworthy": legends are simply accounts of events that are interesting enough to warrant telling and retelling. Moreover, according to Ward, they express or reflect the "most dominating concerns and cherished values of the members of the communities in which they are told." Indeed, he details with great care how closely the legends are tied to the experience of the German people, and thus it is not only Ward's "working definition" of the legend but his own historical research which is invaluable in these two volumes.

It is obvious that, in many cases, it was and is still difficult to distinguish between legend and folktale. For instance, the Grimms' collection, divided into local and historical legends, contains narratives with witches, werewolves, fairies, water spirits, dwarfs, dragons, and giants. Many of the characters and incidents are directly related to *German* culture, ancient beliefs, and historical incidents, which are exaggerated but often believed by the German people. In general, the Grimms endeavored to retain the frank tone and style of the oral local legends while they rewrote the historical legends from documents and known texts such as *William Tell* and *St. Genofeva*. (In contrast, Wilhelm constantly revised and stylized the folktales to make them more suitable for the conservative taste of parents, who were to transmit them to children.) The result is an unusual and rich compendium of "noteworthy" legends, which both belong to and transcend German culture.

Aside from the particular aesthetic and historical appeal of each legend itself, the publication of the entire canon can serve many different purposes. Ward has documented each legend with ample references so that one can trace its roots and do further research on the subject matter or the motif of the story. For instance, the specific functions of Mother Holle, dwarfs, miners, or water spirits can be analyzed within the German tradition and can then be related to other cultures. Here it is possible, for the first time in English-speaking countries, to study the relationship of the legends to the folktales gathered by the Grimms. A comparative study can also help elaborate the similarities and differences between the two genres. In the field of children's literature the two volumes of legends could stimulate writers to rewrite and expand some of the unusual stories. Certainly, since they emanate from the concerns of German communities, they shed light on childhood and are good examples of the types of stories, other than the fairy tales, to which children were exposed. Furthermore, since many of these legends such as *The Faithful Eckhart, William Tell, The Stable Boy and the Kitchen Boy*, and *Lohengrin* served as the source for novels, stories, dramas, operas, and ballets for young and old alike, it is now possible to do interdisciplinary and comparative analyses of the way the legends have been transformed to strike a universal chord in audiences of different nations. Here it is remarkable to observe how the Grimms' initially nationalistic purpose in collecting the legends has contributed to and continues to contribute toward international understanding of cultural differences.

The "national question" of the *Legends* is important, and Ward carefully distinguishes between the Grimms' nationalist yet democratic aspirations and purposes in collecting the *Legends*, in contrast to those purposes of later, more chauvinist German folklorists. Perhaps we have another reason here to explain why English-speaking scholars did not think about translating the *German Legends* until this late in the twentieth century: the chauvinism and racism of German folklorists cast a shadow over the democratic intentions and attitudes of the Brothers Grimm. Fortunately, the narrow philological and ideological work of German folklorists has been exposed and surpassed by scholars inside and outside Germany since World War II. Certainly, Ward's fine translation and research is an example of how folklore scholarship can retain its humanistic and international quality while focusing on a particular national culture.

# Illustrated Classics in Facsimile

Feenie Ziner

*Facsimile Editions of Early English Children's Books from the Osborne Collection, Toronto Public Library.* Distributed in the United States by Merrimack Books, Salem, New Hampshire; in Great Britain by The Bodley Head, Covent Garden, London, 1982. 35 volumes, boxed.

An international enterprise in which Canada and Japan played the leading roles has reproduced a treasury of early English illustrated children's books, selected from the great Osborne Collection of the Toronto Public Library. These thirty-five facsimiles come handsomely boxed and individually slipcased and are offered only as a set—a core collection.

American families who would not hesitate to spend as much on home computers for the education of their young are not likely to come forward in any great numbers to purchase this collection at $695. Indeed, many public libraries will find it too heavy an investment. But it is interesting to note that two editions of these English books sold out in Japan before the negotiations for British or American distribution were even completed.

The earliest and in some ways most absorbing of the rarities is *Orbis Sensualium Pictus,* by J. A. Comenius, whose name in his native Moravia was Komensky. First published in 1657 and in use for 200 years, *Orbis,* or *The Visible World,* served as a model for Diderot's *Encyclopedia,* influenced John Locke, and in our own time furnished inspiration to Piaget. Comenius was a religious radical, a member of the sect called the Unity of the Brethren. He believed that peace and prosperity depended upon universal understanding of the intrinsic order and unity of reality, and his book demonstrates that belief. Subtitled, "All the Chief Things That are in the World, and Men's Employments therein," *Orbis* is an illustrated nomenclature, in English and Latin. Through pictures and text it purports to include all the knowledge a person might need to lead a useful and well-informed life. Undaunted by abstraction or complexity, Comenius

devised pictures little over two inches square to show objects in
relation to their use and in their contexts, thus anticipating the
insights of Gestalt (context) psychology by several hundred years.
The elements, heaven, metals, tame fowls, the seven ages of man,
butchery, burial, the making of honey—the scope is breathtaking.

Properly speaking this was not an English book but a book which
was exceedingly popular in England. Translated from High Dutch
by Charles Hoole in 1658 for use as a Latin text, it went through
twelve English editions, the last of which is the one reproduced. It
was still used as a school text in Prague, in 1845. Recently the
University of Sydney, Australia, published a facsimile of *Orbis Pictus*,
but until now it has only been available in this hemisphere in such
collections as the Osborne, the Library of Congress, or the Pierpoint
Morgan Library. It is interesting that the nomenclature continues to
prosper as a literary form in our own day. Richard Scarry's books for
children have adult counterparts in the proliferating books of lists,
and in such widely read works as the *Whole Earth Catalogues*. Apparently the nomenclature offers the browser an enormous range of
facts from which fancy may take wing, unimpeded by visible inter-
ference from an author.

One hundred years intervene between *Orbis Pictus* and the second
oldest book in the collection. *Goody Two-Shoes*, which first appeared
in 1765, is usually identified as the first fictional narrative written
expressly for children. Having seen only bowdlerized versions before the present edition, I understood for the first time why the
book has had such lasting appeal. Goldsmith (for it probably was he)
endowed his schoolmarm heroine with want and tragedy at the
outset of his story and gave her an undefatigable spirit with which to
overcome them. The little book, small enough to be carried about in
a child's pocket, is enriched with spirited illustrations whose drama is
not diminished by their minuscule size. The reprint is bound more
soberly than the original, which was encased in colorful flowered
Dutch paper boards. Actually, it is a facsimile of a facsimile, but it is
based upon an edition published only a year after the first.

Unfortunately, none of the books that follow chronologically pos-
sesses a literary quality comparable to *Orbis* or to *Goody*. For the most
part they are either inspired textbooks or beautiful artifacts. They

are primarily illustrators' books, though occasionally, as in the work of Walter Crane, they approach the level of fine art.

Historically, games and chapbooks come next. Though a good many chapbooks (or cheapbooks) were calculated to appeal to prurient interest, those included here were intended to educate the poor, to elevate public taste, or to spread religion. Cruikshank's designs for *Jack and Jill* are tiny gems. *Scripture Histories* condenses the Old and New Testament into a dozen pages. *The Butterfly's Ball* and *Cock Robin* are boldly and brilliantly illustrated. A board game called *Mansions of Bliss* offered "Honey-tongued Instruction for the Infant Mind." Instead of *Monopoly*, the goal of this step-by-step route across an illustrated surface is "to inculcate in the Minds of Youth the most necessary Virtues . . . by choosing the Good and avoiding the Evil . . . [in] the Hopes of a brighter Reward hereafter."

Thomas Bewick, the eighteenth century's most illustrious wood engraver, is poorly represented by a tiny book of pictures without text called *A New Year's Gift for Little Masters and Misses*. Like another book of this period, *A Birthday Gift*, it was presumably chosen, for its historical interest, both books being among the first true picture books for children. But many of the engraved wood blocks from which the work was reproduced were either worn or broken, and this little book is very far from being Bewick at his best. Another puzzling inclusion is *A Visit to the Bazaar*, a compendium of mercantile intelligence calculated to furnish children of the middle class with knowledge of price and value. Poor children added color to the engravings on a piece-work basis, by the sheet.

By the mid-nineteenth century the books for children became larger and more elaborate. *Traditional Fairy Tales* (1845) by Felix Summerly, pseudonym of Sir Henry Cole, is an exquisite volume, gilt-edged and illustrated by members of the Royal Academy. Sir Henry, himself the father of eight, believed in providing children with the best possible art. He was a good writer, and though he prettied up the ending of *Little Red Riding Hood* by extricating her from the wolf's stomach (but leaving Grandmother in the beast's digestive tract), his text shows him to be a keen and unsentimental observer of behavior. Cole, who headed the British postal service, is also known as the originator of the Christmas card and of the warmly remembered penny post card.

At about the same time Cole began publishing his Home Treasury Books the firm of Darton and Clark issued a series of equally impressive books of instruction for children. *The Ocean and its Inhabitants* (1844) engages the natural curiosity of the child with information of intrinsic interest. Its language is straightforward and devoid of condescension. Polysyllabic words are hyphenated, but the author never talks down to the reader, stating in his preface that there is no basis for the common assumption that it is easier for children to recognize short words than long. *Ocean* is still a delightful book, rich in detail and sparked by an occasional anecdote, such as one about a sly harbor seal who often played with a band of children and once stole their dog's supper.

Three historical romances in elegantly gilded paper wrappers satisfy the yearning of the nostalgic swashbuckler in this collection, but this reviewer could have done without another *Patient Grissel*.

Another mid-European book that is included under the English umbrella is by the German Nicholas Bohny. *The New Picture Book* (1858) picks up where Comenius left off a hundred years earlier, "Being Pictorial Lessons on Form, Comparison, and Number, for Children under Seven Years of Age." Designed for active involvement of the child reader in study, the book poses questions of increasing difficulty and complexity. Three hundred and fifty categories are presented in comic-strip format. The text begins with simple counting and progresses to simple reasoning. "How many trees do you see in this row? Why have they been uprooted? What part of the tree is visible? What are the woodcutters doing? For what purpose does one need the wood? What instruments are they using to cut the wood?" Then, back to simple arithmetic: "Five from five and nothing remains." Bohny's book was based upon the educational theories of Froebel and Pestalozzi, later championed by Maria Montessori (and earlier by Mrs. Goody Two-Shoes), who believed that learning ought to be pleasurable, that play was worthwhile and creative, concepts still considered to be revolutionary a hundred years ago. The English translation of Bohny's book had great popularity in England, a fact which presumably explains its inclusion. Unfortunately, the translated typescript is quite difficult to read and it is likely that many of Bohny's most evocative questions were rarely asked.

Charles H. Bennett was the cartoonist-illustrator of a Mother Goose called *The Old Nurse's Book of Rhymes and Jingles.* Had he lived longer, it is likely he would have found a place among the immortals of children's book illustrators, for each of the characters in this charming book has been depicted shrewdly, from life. At the far end of the fantasy scale is "Dicky" Doyle's *In Fairy Land: A Series of Pictures from the Elf World.* This handsome edition has an inane text by John Allingham, added—in order to make a book—after the illustrations were completed. I have never known a book in which this sequence of composition succeeded, and *In Fairy Land* is no exception.

In the Department of Gentle Whispers we find *Sing Song,* a book of poems for the very young by Christina Rossetti. It is a fragile work full of melancholy musings on the death of babies. Better poems of Rossetti have been published, but here, as in the other books in this collection, it is the illustrator who carries the day. Arthur Hughes's engravings are subtle and packed with emotional power.

Among the best exponents of the craft of illustration is an unidentified artist who drew the pictures for *The Dog's Dinner Party,* a shilling toy book originally published around 1870 by George Routledge and Sons. It is a social satire worthy of W. C. Fields. A limpid-eyed spaniel invites all the better dogs in the neighborhood to an elegant soirée, only to be disgraced by the uncouth behavior of a dirty old bulldog, "This shows how careful we should always be in avoiding low company," the book admonishes, but not before we have seen the upper and lower classes of English society putting on—and being put on by—the dog.

Walter Crane, whose vigorous designs were inspired by his study of the Japanese wood block, is represented by *The Baby's Own Aesop, Puss in Boots,* and *The Alphabet of Old Friends.* Crane was a socialist and he had a deep commitment to making fine books available to all classes of the population. There is a certain breadth of conception in his work, even in the books for very young children. Each of his pages conveys an entire thought, including all its ramifications and implications.

Randolph Caldecott's *Journey of John Gilpin* and his *Babes in the*

*Woods* make clear all the reasons for his preeminence. *Gilpin* is genuinely comical and wonderfully drawn. His rendering of the sinister story of *Babes in the Woods* is done, remarkably, without bitterness or terror.

It was a relief to find a few poems in Kate Greenaway's lovely *Under the Window* in which she actually pokes a little fun at the formal creatures of her imagination. It isn't much, but "The Twelve Miss Pelicoes," a family of well-turned-out little girls of evenly graduated size,

> Were always most polite—
> Said, "If you please," and "Many thanks,"
> "Good morning," and "Good night."
> The twelve Miss Pelicoes
> You plainly see, were taught
> To do the things they didn't like,
> Which means, the things they ought.

Nothing more can be said of the magic of her vision except that some of it has been dissipated by too-frequent exposure. It is work better come upon with a fresh eye. The inclusion of her Calendar of 1884 is a puzzle, for it was an unsuccessful work when it was first published; deservedly, it seems.

Temperamental Charles L. Dodgson criticized John Tenniel's colored engravings for *The Nursery Alice* for being too gaudy. The color was toned down in later editions of the work, and here they seem benign and pastoral rather than fierce and fantastic, as they are in black and white. Dodgson wrote *The Nursery Alice* in the hope of further enlarging his readership by appealing to the very young, but his text does little beyond describing the pictures. The book's failure demonstrates, as does *In Fairy Land*, that it is the text and not the illustration that determines the quality of the work. *The Nursery Alice* was a failure when it was published, and it remains a disappointment. And while I am busy about sacrilege I found Lear's elegantly bound *Book of Nonsense* as funny as an ethnic joke, its content not improved by the fact that there is so much of it.

Considering the collection as a whole, several questions arise. Since these thirty-five books were selected from a collection of

18,000 volumes, one would have thought the widest possible representation would have been the major consideration. But there are three Cruikshanks, three Cranes, two Greenaways, and two Caldecotts. Ought not space to have been made for one William Blake? What history of nineteenth-century book illustration can leave out William Morris?

Although we rarely see these books in the United States, many of them are still obtainable in second-hand bookstores in London. A comparison of the Osborne fascimile with late editions of many of the originals reveals a considerable difference between "the real thing" and the photographic derivation. Even with the best reproduction, some of the definition produced by the imposition of a metal plate on paper is lost when that picture is subsequently photographed. Its artistry is diluted. A degree of distortion enters—the darks are too dark or not dark enough, and the reader who has not seen the original can only guess at the quality that made it nonpareil. Still, as between an approximation and nothing at all, one can only choose the approximation.

The final volume in the series is a book of commentary, "English Illustrated Books for Children," which describes the genesis of this publishing project and gives background information about each of the books. An erudite work by Margaret C. Mahoney, head of the Osborne Collection, it is the most essential element in the set, for without it the ordinary reader would not understand the significance of most of the books included. If anything can be criticized about Mahoney's meticulous account it is her caution and restraint. Ironically, her very objectivity makes it more difficult for the reader to appraise the works. The decision to reproduce these books exactly, without individual introductions, makes it necessary to seek background information in the Mahoney volume, and it reinforces the rationale for selling the books only as a set.

It is regrettable that the price of the Osborne facsimiles is such that few American children will have the opportunity to see and handle them. A young Doyle enthusiast is more likely to find a counterpart in Osaka than in Omaha. But if these children's books will not be much used by our children, who will benefit by their publication?

One hopes that every university library will acquire the set, though there is the danger that, in the parochial mentality of universities, Library Science, History of Childhood, Book Illustration, Education, and Social History people may overlook it because "it belongs in the English Department." It would be invaluable, of course, to students of children's literature. One would also hope that textbook publishers would make this set required study for their designers.

A final note on the history of this publishing venture. Some years ago a number of noted Japanese authors, artists, and critics of children's books visited the Osborne Collection at Boys and Girls House, in Toronto. One result of the friendships formed was the publication by the Japanese publishing house of Holp Shuppan of an Osborne manuscript, a facsimile of an 1831 book, *The Story of the Three Bears*, which subsequently won the Nakamori Prize as one of the "four best books for Japanese children from the world." Since World War II there has been a flourishing market for contemporary American and English children's books in Japan, which their presumed simplicity of language does not explain, for the *Encyclopaedia Britannica* also sells like hotcakes in that country. Officially, the publication of the Osborne Collection books was undertaken to celebrate one hundred years of friendship between Japan and Canada and to commemorate the International Year of the Child. Personally, I think Makito Nakamori, president of Holp Shuppan, simply fell in love with the Osborne Collection and saw in this project an opportunity to demonstrate the exquisite capabilities of the printing crafts of Japan. For his ardor, and for the existence of organizations like the Osborne Collection, dedicated to preserving the best in books for children, we can only be grateful.

# Alice's Adventures,
## *the Pennyroyal Press Edition*

Leonard S. Marcus

*Alice's Adventures in Wonderland,* by Lewis Carroll. Illustrated by Barry
Moser. Preface and notes by James R. Kincaid. Text edited by
Selwyn H. Goodacre. Berkeley: University of California Press/The
Pennyroyal Press, 1982.

For more than one hundred years, a parade of artists like hopeful
suitors in the fairy tale about the glass mountain have tried their
hand at illustrating one or both of Lewis Carroll's *Alice* books. For all
that time the woodcut engravings by Sir John Tenniel, prepared for
the earliest published editions under Carroll's watchful eye, have
somehow remained so nearly synonymous with Wonderland-and-
Looking-Glass reality as to seem the inseparable twin of Carroll's
elusive art.

Yet if none of Tenniel's successors—excluding for the moment
the artist to whose work we will soon turn—can be said to have
supplanted him altogether as the *Alice* illustrator of record, memorable images, garden-glimpses as it were of alternative Wonderland
visions, have come down to us in the versions of Harry Furniss,
Arthur Rackham, Charles Robinson, Willy Pogany, Salvador Dali,
and Ralph Steadman, among others. Pogany, for example, working
in a jazzy Art Deco–related graphic style, made the printed double
page a more active field for Carrollian chaos than has any illustrator
before or since. (If only his Alice were not such a simpering twenties
ingenue, the least believable character or detail in the artist's imagined world!) In theory any number of convincing visual interpretations, each distinctly different from the rest, are conceivable given
the singular nature of Carroll's text. For as James R. Kincaid in his
sensitive and sensible preface to the Pennyroyal *Alice* has said:

> The book opens itself to all sorts of models: it is satire, a novel, a
> mathematical-political-logical-theological allegory, a dream vi-
> sion , and an elegy all at once; both a comedy and an irony; a

work with rich and directed meaning and one without any
whatsoever. . . . No work is directed more relentlessly or with
more subtlety to the questions we habitually ask, the models we
use to structure, understand, and make bearable our world and
our lives. Carroll applies continuous pressure to the forms and
models we use to think about such things as space, time, logic,
language, meaning, authority, and death. Under such pressure,
these structures explode, their naturalness disappears, and only
the paltry skin remains.

It may well be that illustrators since Tenniel have themselves
tended to become overly committed to one or another interpretative
model of the story to the exclusion of all others. Steadman's leering
satire does not, for example, encourage us to feel even slightly
sympathetic toward Carroll's at times charming, mercurial heroine;
Robinson's decorative color plates tame Alice and Wonderland of all
menace. Thus and again, to illustrate these books, as much as to
write about them or to read them, is to find oneself relentlessly
drawn into the retiring Oxford don's masterful game.

The Pennyroyal *Alice's Adventures in Wonderland*, in both its trade
and limited editions, is a tall, elegantly designed and produced book,
illustrated with finely rendered, black-and-white woodcut engravings by Barry Moser. Moser, who is also its designer, is proprietor of
the Pennyroyal Press and director of the Hampshire Typothetae of
Northhampton, Massachusetts. Among the many other books he
has illustrated are the University of California Press *Dante* and the
Orion Press *Moby-Dick*.

Certain visual details of the Pennyroyal *Alice* recall details of the
author's life and of *Alice's* earliest published editions. The shade of
blue in which chapter headings are printed, for example, is Oxford
blue. The spine of the trade volume and the complete binding and
slipcasing of the deluxe limited are red cloth, a festive allusion to the
bright red covers of the first printings overseen by Carroll—and to
his attendant notion that of all colors, red is the one children find
most pleasurable.

Tireless child-observer that he was, Carroll may well be expected
to have arrived at this last conclusion on his own, though it is worth

remarking that a century earlier Jean-Jacques Rousseau had by the same reasoning urged parents to provide children with red garments and crimson-colored playthings. Late eighteenth- and nineteenth-century European and American child-portraits attest to the widespread acceptance of this bit of plausible child-rearing advice. Once supposed to have been an attentive reader of *Émile*, Carroll may also be imagined to have had Rousseau's memorable assault on the drabber ranges of juvenile literature in mind—"I detest books. . . . Reading is the scourge of Childhood. . . . What do books teach? . . . Words, words, words!"—when he supplied Alice with her own more temperate, though no less sharply expressed, opinion about literature as a whole: "And what is the use of a book . . . without pictures or conversations?"

Carroll, in any case, wasted no time in assuring readers that *his* book was well supplied with pictures and dialogue worth the trouble of lingering over. Moreover, having overseen his collaborator's progress with a fastidiousness that Tenniel would eventually find maddening, Carroll, as much Wonderland's impresario as its author, had made certain that in image and text *Alice* would be all of a piece. Wonderland chaos is chaos of a highly ordered variety.

For readers encountering Lewis Carroll's fantasy for the first time through the Pennyroyal edition, comparison between Moser's art and Tenniel's may be of little concern. But, the Tenniels being as widely dispersed throughout the world as they are—in advertising, on theater posters, on rubber stamps and drinking mugs as well as in editions of Carroll's actual writings—relatively few readers are likely to experience the Pennyroyal without some prior knowledge of the earlier Wonderland graphics. Children of course are somewhat more likely to do so than adults, and the Pennyroyal, at least in its trade version, is not so much of an *edition de luxe* that older children cannot relax with it and be entrusted with it (though it is plainly not a book to be handled with sticky fingers except at one's peril). From a critical standpoint, the main question to ask about the book remains how well it succeeds on its own terms, but comparison to Tenniel is inevitable and so must also be considered. Moser himself seems to have been mindful of this reality as he went about his task.

Many features of the Pennyroyal *Alice* work exceedingly well on terms distinctly (and perhaps intentionally) different from those laid down by Tenniel. On the level of pure graphics, the predominance of black-over-white in Moser's woodcuts is an ingeniously apt Looking-Glass inversion (if not merely a pleasing chance reversal) of the white-over-black impression of the earlier artist's images. And whereas Tenniel's characteristic line is incisive, steely clear, a stylistic mirror-equivalent for Carroll's lucid, marksmanlike prose, Moser's line is rougher, ruder, more tactile, less predictable, engaging us at gut level in Wonderland's labyrinth of unsettled meanings and fugitive emotions. Illustrations in the Pennyroyal *Alice* emerge from rigorously ordered bundles of these nervelike textural incisions, with certain bundles set against others in contrapuntal rhythmic patterns, or forcefully juxtaposed with solid areas of black or white. In the most effective images—the portraits of the Caterpillar, the Duchess, and the Queen, among others—this skillful linework results in a shimmering moiré effect similar to that achieved by the nineteenth-century French illustrator Gustave Doré in his visionary engravings for (among other works) Coleridge's *Rime of the Ancient Mariner*. The moiré illusion, thus exploited, charges Wonderland with an aura of the uncanny and implies for the characters portrayed a swarming, turbulent inner life or under-life. Readers become enmeshed in a dimly lit chimera-world, a nightmarish vision that strongly hints at the probability that Wonderland, if discoverable at all, must lie somewhere along the trunkline to the Inferno.

Moser's most ambitious departure from Wonderland-according-to-Tenniel, however, consists of his abandonment of a traditional approach to illustration that is so often the one chosen that we tend to think of it as the only possibility the illustrator has; namely, the convention of illustration as theatrical tableau, under the terms of which scenes from the author's imagined world are presented for an ideal observer perched as it were (and as Carroll often found himself during day trips to the London theater) in one of the house's preferred stalls.

The Tenniels not only conform to this theatrical convention but accentuate it, leaving vague or altogether omitting background scenery so that the page itself can become the primary scene. Carroll's artful use of dramatic dialog, of descriptive writing so finely compressed as to approximate stage directions for the reader's imagination, and of slapstick routines directly inspired by the contemporary English Harlequinade—all contribute to Wonderland's subtly theatrical edge and flavor. The Tenniels' staged quality likewise quickens our sense of Wonderland as an illusion-world of a particularly ambiguous kind: equally a cunning mirror on reality and a manic negation of reality. In the Tenniels, all the world's a stage within a stage within a stage . . . onward to infinity. It is thus (and in the unsparing precision of the artist's caricature, the bite of his satire as of his line) that Tenniel's woodcuts merge so fully with Carroll's elliptical tale.

Moser, like certain experimental theater directors of the sixties and seventies who felt the urgent need to abolish what they perceived to be an artificial barrier separating the actors from their audience, has taken a more confrontational approach to representing Carroll's fantasy. He has attempted to have us come face to face, as Alice herself does, with the towering Caterpillar, the absurdly menacing Hatter, the imperious, murderous Queen; to illustrate Wonderland in the first person. The artist explains:

> To illustrate *Alice* entails a certain indelicacy, for *Alice* is a story of loneliness. Its illustrators, beginning with Carroll himself and including Tenniel, Rackham, Steadman, Pogany, Furniss, and Dali have intruded on the privacy of Alice's adventure, standing apart and observing Alice in her dream. They have been voyeurs, and yet there can be no voyeurs in dreams. In the Pennyroyal *Alice*, the images of Alice's dream are always seen from Alice's point of view, for after all the dream *is* Alice's dream . . ."

These observations, which seem novel enough both as a critique of earlier attempts at illustrating Carroll's work and as a program for a new edition, overlook one essential feature of the Wonderland narrative: that Carroll interposes himself as an all-seeing presence, an observer looming Cheshire Cat—like at the very edge of Alice's dream. For example: "'Curiouser and curiouser!' cried Alice (she was so much surprised, that for the moment she quite forgot how to speak good English)." "'You ought to be ashamed of yourself,'

"The Mad Hatter" by Barry Moser. From *Alice's Adventures in Wonderland*. Reproduced by permission from the University of California Press.

said Alice, 'a great girl like you,' (she might well say this), 'to go on crying in this way!'" "'Who cares for *you?*' said Alice (she had grown to her full size by this time). 'You're nothing but a pack of cards!'"

The intrusiveness to which Moser objects is thus actually an element of the author's tale. One may of course call this "voyeurism," too. ("Call it what you like," as the Cheshire Cat, sorting out growls and purrs, chillingly advises Alice.) But one would still be left to ponder what purpose such deftly planted dramatic asides—stage whispers more pointed at times than the Duchess's chin—serve in establishing the peculiarly convincing tone and atmosphere and world of the most memorable dream episode in modern literature. Carroll's asides are unsettling, and they disrupt our capacity for believing in the Wonderland dream and more especially for identifying ourselves with Alice.

Adventure fantasies, generally, arouse an overwhelming wish for identification with the hero, for the essence of all such tales of escape is the impulse *to see what happens next* as only the hero is in a position to do; to venture farther into the unknown than one has yet gone in one's own experience. This of course is the motive which impels Alice down the rabbit hole, and, once in Wonderland, sustains her from one puzzling encounter to another, despite periodic doubts suffered at the hands of a well-developed Victorian conscience and of the less time-bound human fear of being overwhelmed by chaos.

Yet Carroll would disturb this wish of ours to escape *like* Alice and *as* Alice, reminding us sharply, as he does at many turns, of the foolishness of certain of her thoughts, actions, and remarks; praising her tongue-in-cheek for her struggles to remain good in a world where goodness has no apparent referent or value; or merely witnessing her predicament with an amused detachment and unflinching objectivity such as one might well expect of the accomplished and disciplined logician and portrait photographer that Carroll also was, but hardly of an author intent on transporting us deeper and deeper into a conventional type of escapist fantasy. We recoil from Alice emotionally at such moments, though only to be drawn back to her moments later by her next casual leap into Wonderland's rarefied state of pure possibility.

Carroll's purpose in thus dividing our loyalty toward her would seem nonetheless to be dramatic in nature, an attempt to involve us more directly in her ambiguous plight. In dreaming, the self at times adopts the double role of actor and observer, the better to sort through its dilemmas from a clarifying distance; Alice's adventure is essentially a dream of this kind. In Wonderland she becomes radically divided over the matter of her self-identity: "I can't explain *myself* . . . ," she says in one of many expositions of her situation, "because I'm not myself, you see . . ." As readers we find that out of our own confusion of feeling toward her comes a strangely immediate insight into Alice's central predicament. It is as though Carroll, turning Coleridge's formulation on its head decided that it is not so much art as the self which is a fiction requiring of us a "willing suspension of disbelief." Paradoxically, it is in not being quite certain how to feel toward Alice that we as readers experience Wonderland firsthand.

Moser's premise that there can be "no voyeurs in dreams" turns out, then, to be misleading in nearly all its consequences; for not only does Carroll observe Alice's dream; Alice herself does. Illustrating Wonderland from her point of view (in the literal sense of what she saw) does not necessarily yield a more faithful impression of her dream than do the Tenniels; in fact the Tenniels may themselves be said to represent Alice's vantage point—that is, that side of it which consists of detached, intensely concentrated self-observation. Moser's work does not so much correct the earlier illustrations as complement them as no previous *Alice* edition has done. The Pennyroyal also leads us to imagine some future Wonderland that will somehow accommodate both aspects of Alice's double dream.

Even within the limits proposed by Moser, however, more inventiveness might have been shown in illustrating Alice's psychic dislocation, the inner division she experiences between body and mind, as for example when she grows so tall that her feet no longer seem a part of her and she is led to consider sending Christmas presents down to them. Except for one fugitive glance of her catching sight of herself in a mirror, no such instance of Alice looking at Alice has been recorded.

Instead, and as if to emphasize the pervasive mood of loneliness that Moser has found at the story's emotional core, his heroine perceives Wonderland as a series of isolated details—the White Rabbit's watch and gloves, the key to the garden, the bottle standing before a mirror—and as a gallery of monolithic, masklike heads of ferocious intensity edged with whimsy. Few dramatic scenes or actions are portrayed. Characters, rarely seen much below the neck, do not often meet within an illustration's or a double spread's frame.

Alice's reeling contortionist changes of physical size are cleverly implied in the shifting scale of certain images. The Caterpillar appears, end-to-end, both as the immense and billowingly lugubrious overlord first encountered by shrunken Alice, and as the three-inch creature more familiar to her, and ourselves. The giant puppy that tiny Alice meets after escaping from the Mad Hatter's inhospitable table is depicted close-up—all eyes, nose, and fangs to the bewildered little girl. This last image, intended to make us relive Alice's fright, is however too abstract—*too* close-up—to be very menacing. More visual information is needed for us to accept the dog's menace as real. In certain instances, then, seeing Wonderland from Alice's viewpoint actually becomes a hindrance to imaginative sympathy. Nearly all of Moser's more fully rendered portraits are by contrast bracingly immediate in their claims on our attention. We find ourselves staring at them, warts and all; and one by one they return our gaze.

From the Pennyroyal illustrations, a deep sense of loneliness emerges as from all the failed Wonderland attempts at even the slightest forms of social contact. But in Carroll's text, more so than in Moser's engravings, the feeling is modified, lightened somehow, by the mad persistence with which all press onward with their wildly wrongheaded experiments at society. One misses in the Pennyroyal an illustration of the assembled Tea-Party and the Queen's Croquet-Match. (Moser's cursory depiction of the trial is among the least effective images.) Although lonely, Alice is scarcely overwhelmed by her loneliness. "I almost wish I hadn't gone down that rabbit-hole," she shrewdly remarks early on, "and yet—and yet—it's rather curious, you know, this sort of life!"

Comic characters, Mary McCarthy has observed, are the "incorrigible" ones, those characters who do not learn. Wonderland society is made up entirely of incorrigibles—comic to us and isolated from each other precisely because their experience teaches them nothing.

In the *Alice* books, society is comic theater, as much a fiction to be credited by a "willing suspension of disbelief" as is the self, that mysterious phenomenon which conventional middle-class Victorians so confidently aspired to under the grave rubric of "individual character." For Carroll, character does not exist, only characters. Alice, dreaming, discovers all sorts of characters within herself: a Mad Hatter and a savage Queen as well as an Alice. All are her and not her. To accept such difficult self-knowledge requires a tolerance of more chaos than Alice apparently can bear. She prefers to wake up, to "grow up," to insist that her dreams are her dreams alone.

# *Lives and Letters*

## Elizabeth Segel

*Kate Greenaway: A Biography*, by Rodney Engen. New York: Schocken, 1981.

*Beatrix Potter's Americans: Selected Letters*, edited by Jane Crowell Morse. Boston: The Horn Book, 1982.

One cannot contemplate the lives of Kate Greenaway and Beatrix Potter, preeminent female contributors to the development of illustrated children's books, without being struck by certain similarities—and substantial differences. Born a generation apart, both were raised in London, yet holidays spent in the rural countryside provided for both of them intense childhood happinesss and lifelong nourishment for their creative art. Both expressed reluctance to grow up and leave childhood behind and possessed as adults a remarkable ability to recall in vivid detail scenes and experiences of their earliest days.

The divergences in their artistic careers stem primarily from their birth into different classes. Given the constraints of Victorian gentility, this meant that the nominally privileged child of wealthy parents, Beatrix Potter, was denied the artistic training that was available to the working-class child, Kate Greenaway, and thus found it more difficult to develop her gifts and pursue art as a career. As is often the case with self-taught artists, this provides both a blessing and a handicap.

While Kate Greenaway worked hard as an artist all her life to raise herself and her parents from near-poverty to a more comfortable life, Beatrix Potter used her royalties to buy property in the north of England. In time, she gave up her artistic career for the work of a sheep-farmer and made a comfortable marriage. Greenaway's need to support herself and her parents in a respectable quarter of London, on the other hand, kept her toiling away in her studio after imitators and changing public taste had eroded her popularity.

The name Kate Greenaway conjures up visions of quaint frocks

and flowers, innocent children, and sunlit rural scenes. Reading
Rodney Engen's biography of Greenaway, one soon finds the source
of her visionary world in the idyllic countryside of Nottinghamshire,
where she spent happy childhood summers on the farm of relatives.
All her life she could call up these scenes at will. "I suppose I went to
it very young before I could really remember and that is why I have
such a wild delight in cowslips and apple blossoms. . . . They always
give me the strange feeling of trying *to remember*, as if I had known
them in a former world," she wrote (p. 24).

She was born in 1846, daughter of a wood-engraver and a shop-
keeper. An apparently observant and introspective child, her shyness and sensitivity made her miserable at one dame school after
another, but she soon evidenced an interest in and aptitude for her
father's work. When she begged for art lessons, her parents enrolled
her (at the age of twelve) in art school. She studied for a least twelve
years, first at Finsbury School of Art (one of Henry Cole's schools
"geared to teach uniformity in technique and design principles,"
Engen reports), and then at the National Art Training School. She
was a star pupil, winning major prizes, but was not satisfied with the
rigid, copyist approach of these institutions. She subsequently enrolled at two schools which provided an atmosphere of greater
freedom and direct study from nude models. Here she was not as
successful as before, her rigid early training inhibiting her figure
work, as it was to do all her life. Engen's description of Greenaway's
training enables one to better appreciate Beatrix Potter's comment
in her May 1929 *Horn Book* essay: "I am glad I did not go to school; it
would have rubbed off some of the originality (if I had not died of
shyness or been killed with over pressure)" (Morse, p. 209).

Rodney Engen is a knowledgeable historian and critic of Victorian
illustration, and his account of Greenaway's developing career is
detailed and convincing. Under the guidance of her father and the
patronage of Sir William Loftie, the ambitious, hardworking young
woman slowly evolved her distinctive style and subject, as she fulfilled commissions for greeting cards and book illustrations. Her
father introduced her to the eminent Edmund Evans, and Evans
agreed to publish *Under the Window*, a collection of quaint Greenaway verses and designs. When the book appeared in 1879, the

20,000-copy first edition sold out quickly, a critical, popular, and financial success.

The book came to John Ruskin's attention and, urged by another of Greenaway's mentors, Stacy Marks, the great art critic was persuaded to advise the artist and help promote her work. From his first letter to her in 1880, the biography is dominated—as was Kate Greenaway's emotional life—by the figure of John Ruskin. The correspondence he initiated was sporadic on his part but of increasing intimacy. In 1883, with trepidation on both sides, the two first met, when Greenaway spent nearly a month at Ruskin's lakeside estate. Largely in the company of Ruskin's distant cousin and companion, Joan Severn, they talked, boated, and walked the shores of Coniston. Ruskin withdrew for days at a time to work or brood; Kate was then free to explore the estate and its library and, of course, to sketch. It was a blissful time for her. Unfortunately, her growing but unreciprocated love for the unstable Ruskin made her emotionally dependent on him for the rest of her life, and she devoted much of her time and strength to pleasing him, though they met infrequently.

Greenaway was only one of many young women Ruskin adopted as his "pets"—in what Engen aptly calls "semi-professional, semi-flirtatious relationships" (p. 67). Actually, his preference was for protégées younger and fairer than Kate, who had always been plain and was now in her mid-thirties. But in her pictures of roses and fair maidens, he found embodied his fantasies. It is clear that Ruskin did admire Greenaway's work and felt he could help her correct her faults of perspective and figure drawing. Unhappily, his mental instability and deviant sexuality (evidenced by his unconsummated six-year marriage and a subsequent passion for the child Rose la Touche) made a normal mentor relationship impossible. Ruskin had experienced mental breakdowns before he met Greenaway and his fear of their recurrence intensified his moody narcissism.

While these moods were destructive of Greenaway's confidence and caused her much emotional pain, she wrote him nearly every day for many years, often enclosing sketches of the Greenaway nymphs he craved (her "girlies," he called them). For special occasions, she labored long hours over finished watercolors for him.

Ruskin kept her at a distance, in spite of "elaborate postal kissing games," and chided her for "wasting time drawing feasts of pretty girls to please me, who are of no use to publish" (p. 136). He urged her repeatedly to perfect her skills by drawing from nature, "the coalscuttle or the dust pan" (p. 105); yet in his frequent depressions, he wrote that only her drawings and the fantasies they inspired gave him any comfort. Allowing full credit to Ruskin's achievements as critic and thinker, one nevertheless concludes that not only were his erratic pronouncements of scant benefit to Greenaway's work, but his obsession with "Greenaway girlies" was partly responsible for the artist's failure to develop new subjects as the public tired of the old.

Though Greenaway had a few other friends in her last years, loneliness, self-deprecation, and melancholy color the verse and letters she wrote at this time. She realized little profit from paintings she entered in London gallery exhibits, and attempts to earn needed money by portrait painting and writing were unsuccessful. Ruskin died in January 1900; due to his severe mental deterioration, it had been five years since their last meeting. Greenaway herself was now suffering from the spread of breast cancer, which took her life the following November. Few, it would seem, have had better reason than Kate Greenaway to look back on childhood scenes with wistful pleasure.

Engen's biography, the first authorized life since the Spielmann and Layard 1905 volume, is without question a major contribution. The author had access to family papers and a massive unpublished correspondence, and he interviewed descendants of the Greenaway family and friends. Although he does not belabor the matter, his account of the early years illuminates the sources of the famed Greenaway style: the pastoral plenty and quaintly garbed laborers of the Nottinghamshire summers, the treasured doll collection, the child's fascination with the fashionable clientele of her mother's millinery shop and with her father's craft. On the Ruskin-Greenaway relationship, Engen is invaluable. (Not surprisingly, Joan Severn had censored all of Ruskin's letters before passing them on to Spielmann.)

The book's format is attractive and Engen's use of Greenaway's verse as chapter epigraphs adds an effective dimension to the narrative. An authoritative list of books illustrated by Greenaway is appended to the text. Unfortunately, the book's illustrations, though well chosen, are not keyed to the text, so that when a painting or sketch is described, one never knows if it is reproduced in the volume and, if so, where. And while the color plates are satisfactory, the many colored illustrations which are reproduced in black-and-white bear little resemblance to their originals.

Engen's book is unlikely to be soon rivaled in its account of Greenaway's education, career, and achievement. If he lacks the narrative gifts of a Margaret Lane or a Justin Kaplan, his is nevertheless a workmanlike account of a poignant and important life.

Jane Crowell Morse's selection of Beatrix Potter's letters to American friends covers only the later years of her subject's life, beginning in 1921 when Anne Carroll Moore, Superintendent of Children's Work for the New York Public Library, was granted a meeting with the reclusive figure. Moore was invited to stay on for tea, a tour of Hill Top Farm, and then—such was the rapport established—to spend the night. Mrs. Heelis (as Potter preferred to be called after her marriage at the age of 48) so enjoyed the company of her intelligent American visitor that she encouraged other Americans to call when in the Lake District, and she corresponded with many of them until her death in 1945. From this correspondence Morse has gathered a volume of engaging letters and presented them with succinct and helpful editorial comments.

Beatrix Potter was the sheltered daughter of leisured upper-class London parents whose strict notions of what constituted a proper life for a young lady did not include formal education, serious art lessons, a life-work, or a marriage beneath her. It is difficult to explain briefly, then, how their daughter became first a celebrated author and illustrator of children's books and later a sheep-farmer and wife of a Lancashire county solicitor. Suffice it to say that by 1921, the fifty-sixth year of Beatrix Potter's life, farming and conservation—of land, of ancient cottages, of sheep breeds, and of old oak furniture—had superseded the making of children's books in her life. Even so, these letters from that period help us understand the original and enigmatic figure who put her mark so firmly on books for the young.

Running though all the letters is Mrs. Heelis's thorough enjoyment of the intelligently appreciative Americans who found their
way to her door. "I feel that you take me seriously!" she wrote (p. 31).
She found that American admirers valued her writing, with which
she took great pains, as well as her illustrations. And while her own
favorite, *The Tailor of Gloucester*, was neglected in England, she knew
from her friends across the Atlantic that American storytellers were
sharing it with children.

Her high estimation of the Americans contrasts with her complaints about the English scene, dominated, she felt, by "gaudy, ugly
toy book style" (p. 192). "I think the vogue of children's books in this
country is far too much governed by the shop keepers," she confided
(p. 31), and she much preferred the cultivated librarians and children's books enthusiasts who sought her out. They were a select
group, of course—she met only those who valued children's books,
not their numerous countrymen who, then as now, dismissed them
as trivial.

She appreciated the books that Mrs. Perry and others sent her:
"The writers take more pains with juvenile literature in America.
[The books were a select group, too, we realize.] They seem to think
anything is good enough for children . . . here" (p. 66). Her comments on such books as Cather's *Shadows on the Rock* bespeak her own
aims as a writer: "I think I never read a more beautifully written
book. The atmosphere, and character drawing are perfect . . . Not
many can write such clear cut sentences in so polished a style without
its becoming cold or finicky" (p. 45).

Although in the last years of her life she thought of Peter and his
relatives as "those wearisome rabbits" (p. 175), her speculations in
several of the letters as to the reasons for Peter Rabbit's preeminent
success are instructive. She came to believe that her first book came
nearer to oral "live speech story-telling" than its successors, even
though she insisted that its illustrations were "bad; the rabbit on the
cover I have always thought a horrid monstrosity out of all drawing" (pp. 81–82). A good many of the letters throw light on the
genesis and publication of her later books, *The Fairy Caravan* and
*Little Pig Robinson*.

Nearly every letter, it should be noted, includes news of her sheep;

identifying herself as a sheep-farmer at this period was no empty pose.

The second half of the volume is more sombre, as the impending war brings to a halt the pleasant visits. In spite of repetitious passages when she reports the same news to different correspondents, a narrative urgency is imparted by the accounts of bombings, black-outs, refugees, and rumored invasion. American friends are found to take in two young Potter relatives, if need be, and food parcels make their way from New England to Sawrey.

Beatrix Potter Heelis did not live to celebrate the war's end, but she wrote six weeks before her death, "I hope to do a bit more active work yet—and anyhow I have survived to see Hitler beaten past hope of recovery!" (p. 202). With the importance of wool to the war effort, she was able to lead the useful life she valued right up to her final illness.

A number of charming sketches and paintings, Mrs. Heelis's gifts to her American friends (sometimes in return for contributions to the Windermere Fund), are attractively reproduced in the volume, and two *Horn Book* articles by Potter, which grew out of her American correspondence, are reprinted in an appendix.

One comes away from reading these two books regretting that Kate Greenaway, in the last bleak years of her life, lacked the kind of sympathetic and understanding support, free of emotional demands, which Beatrix Potter Heelis received from her American friends. It is ironic that, though these friendships were personally rewarding to Mrs. Heelis, they bore little artistic fruit, coming as they did when other interests had taken priority in her life over the creation of children's books. Kate Greenaway, who devoted her entire life to her art and badly needed the money that renewed critical and popular success would have brought, could well have used appreciative and perceptive correspondents who were less difficult than the towering, tormented John Ruskin.

# Literature and the Child Reader

Carol Billman

*Cushla and Her Books,* by Dorothy Butler. Boston: The Horn Book, 1980.

*The Cool Web: The Pattern of Children's Reading,* ed. Margaret Meek, Aidan Warlow, and Criselda Barton. New York: Atheneum, 1978.

*On Learning to Read: The Child's Fascination with Meaning,* by Bruno Bettelheim and Karen Zelan. New York: Alfred A. Knopf, 1982.

Reading is the subject of the hour in a variety of places these days. In the last decade or so, literary theorists and critics have flaunted the New Critical notion of the affective fallacy and attended more and more to the reader's part in giving meaning to a piece of literature. Psychologists interested in children's development—aesthetic as well as cognitive—are discussing the patterns and the value of both storytelling and the perception of stories by the young. Researchers, from those whose approach is psycholinguistic to those who observe the reading practices of a particular child in a particular social context, have worked to describe the skills necessary for reading and the processes involved. The appearance, in the last year alone, of a handful of practical guides for sharing literature with the young suggests that the current attention to reading and children is by no means restricted to the academic community. Thus it is an exciting time for those of us interested in thinking specifically about children's literary reading. The three books on reading reviewed here approach the subject from decidedly different directions. Together, they not only indicate the heterogeneity of contemporary reading inquiry but also spell out many of the important considerations for critics of children's literature now ready to pursue the subject that Robert Louis Stevenson explored in his own way nearly a century ago—how children play in the land of storybooks.

The story behind Dorothy Butler's *Cushla and Her Books,* originally presented by the author in 1975 as her dissertation for the Diploma of Education at the University of Auckland in New Zealand, is by this time rather well-known. Butler's granddaughter, Cushla Yeoman, was a baby born with an array with physical problems, the most serious of which were a perforated heart and a deformed kidney. Later, others emerged: Cushla had little control of her arms, and she could not focus properly. Mental retardation was presumed by some of her doctors. When she was four months old, Cushla's anxious parents, in the face of these distressing facts and still more unknowns about their daughter, began to read and show her books because they were determined "to keep her in touch" with the world and to keep themselves in touch with her. Butler recounts the friendship that evolved between Cushla and her books from that time until the age of 3 years 9 months, documenting the little girl's concomitant physical and cognitive and language development, in addition to her amazing personal and social growth.

In literary acumen Cushla soon *exceeded* her peers, though at thirty-five weeks her growth in other areas was greatly retarded. Early on, Cushla responded to and incorporated into her own speech scraps of poetry and stories read to her, and by the age of approximately one year she had already demonstrated an unusual perceptual interest in symbols on the page, both printed words and shapes in pictures. To corroborate this record of achievement, Butler provides narrative accounts of Cushla's specific responses to a number of her favorite books, from Edward Lear to Lois Lenski, Brian Wildsmith, and Paul Galdone. But it should be pointed out that Butler's (and Cushla's parents') emphasis is not on literary development per se, but rather on the child's gradual acculturation, which was accomplished almost exclusively through books, the "friends who went with her into the dark and lonely places where others could not follow." Indeed, *Cushla and Her Books* is as much hortatory literature, told "in the hope of recruiting more human links between books and the handicapped children of the world," as it is a descriptive and analytic study for professionals. (In a final chapter Butler does, however, discuss Cushla's maturation in the light of the developmental theories of Jean Piaget, L. S. Vygotsky, et al.)

Set alongside other studies of individual children as they learn the ways of literary books, most of which have appeared since the publication of *Cushla and Her Books*, Butler's work proves less helpful than some in understanding the actual development among the young of literary competence and preferences. I think especially of the work of Maureen and Hugh Crago on their daughter's mastery of the conventions of picture books, and the pioneer study in this field, *Books before Five* (1954), by Dorothy White, whose thorough though discursive accounts of her daughter Carol's first reactions to books are immensely beneficial in providing *facts* about one young reader reading. (The latter is acknowledged by Butler time and again and is even used as a point of comparison for Cushla's story.) Butler does include a reprint of Cushla's mother's informative diary for one day in the girl's life, as an appendix to *Cushla and Her Books*. Here we learn of Cushla's particular responses to stories and, what is more, see how literary experience not only fits into Cushla's daily schedule but also completely permeates all other aspects of her life. Through this diary readers realize that literature shapes Cushla's response to the people and events of her life, by giving her the language and points of comparison she uses to comment on them. Had Butler offered more such systematic information about how literature was interwoven into Cushla's life, her book would have been extraordinarily useful to those concerned with aesthetic development and its social context. But, again, this was not her primary intention.

Finally, by its very nature Butler's study presents an important caveat for those critics who turn to this burgeoning genre of reading records and diaries in hopes of finding hard evidence concerning children's interaction with literary narrative. She is always quick to emphasize that Cushla's psychological and literary development, and the social setting in which they occur, are unique. For that matter, so are any other child's—so we must hold back from generalizing from a sample of one or even a few young readers. When, but not until then, more reading records have been compiled and accurately and fully reported, this body of literature will serve to counterbalance and ground the influential work by Aidan Chambers and others on hypothetical young readers, as implied by various literary texts.

Bruno Bettelheim's most recent contribution on children and the literature they encounter, *On Learning to Read*, coauthored by Karen Zelan, is another investigation of real readers reading. Like Butler, the authors consider the contextual aspects of reading; *how* reading and literature are introduced to the child is what matters, they say. But *On Learning to Read* concentrates on the "public" context for reading—that is, the schoolroom—rather than the highly individualized environment of the home. What Bettelheim and Zelan (and the six others on the research team) found in their four years of observation of some 300 children was a uniformly unsupportive context for reading, though they make it clear that they intentionally visited only the schools deemed the best by the administrators of their respective systems. A variety of factors, the authors contend, contribute to the negative atmosphere in which most American children learn to read: the low value implicitly placed on reading as an aesthetic experience; repetitive and ultimately deadening methods for teaching reading; and—most significant—the insipid primers generally used for the task. The last three chapters of this book, and fair amounts of the opening ones as well, are an impassioned exposé of American reading texts (in contrast to those in use in Austria and Switzerland) and an energetic plea for meaningful reading matter.

As for their analysis of what actually goes on when a child reads, Bettelheim and Zelan discovered to their surprise the all-pervasive and all-important phenomenon of misreading. "Not all errors," they suggest, "are due to a lack of skills, knowledge, or attention, but . . . they may reflect important processes going on in the child's mind." Accordingly, much of *On Learning to Read* is the unrelenting application of this explanation to individual children's reading behavior. Word substitutions, blocking or hesitation before a particular word, reversals and other perceptual errors—all are attributed to subconscious pressures that interfere with the basic cognitive processes of the conscious mind.

Since these subconscious pressures vary from one reader to the next, Bettelheim and Zelan are not interested in the common denominators of the reading process. Like Butler's account of Cushla, then, this book offers a healthy reminder that while children are alike in the limited experience they bring to reading, they are nonetheless idiosyncratic readers. In fact, *On Learning to Read* is to reader-based criticism of children's literature as the works of Norman Holland and other psychoanalytic critics are to the current theoretical debates about readers' responses to literature: both caution against simplistic statements about "the reader" by underscoring readers' basic psychological differences. Bettelheim and Zelan spend considerable time reporting and analyzing individual readings—for example, the girl who consistently substituted *Tigger* for *tiger* (because, they say, she is afraid of real tigers and is comforted by Milne's character) and the boy who read *was* for *saw* (because he was having trouble coming to terms with the past tense of his own life experience). These portions of the book are too anecdotal and conjectural to be persuasive. This is unfortunate, for a strong case needs to be made against the idea of a "generic" reader—that is, a homogeneous readership. "Between the lines of every story there is another story, and that is one that . . . can only be guessed at by the people who are good at guessing," says Frances Hodgson Burnett in her essay preceding *A Little Princess*. And child readers, like their more mature counterparts, will guess differently.

Another salient feature of child readers according to these authors is their active response to the task; reading, they convincingly show, is anything but a passive skill applied by rote. (In this recognition Bettelheim and Zelan align themselves with other influential students of the reading process, from psycholinguist Frank Smith to literary theorist Wolfgang Iser.) Even the most boring "Dick and Jane" story, they say, can elicit readerly efforts to improve upon the dull material. And they see misreadings as the young child's effort to communicate personal responses to texts probably not personally chosen.

Yet despite these basic insights and the author's praiseworthy intentions in conducting their study, *On Learning to Read* is a book that wants to address both the layman and the professional and suffers as a result. For one reason, there is the irony that, while the study purportedly argues for imaginative, meaningful stories for young readers, its focus is on children's psychological responses to what they are given, not on the potential literary or psychological effects of reading worthy material. Lay readers come away having learned far less about the mind-opening possibilities of the best children's literature than they did in *The Uses of Enchantment*. Likewise, academic and professional readers will probably not be satisfied with the meager and occasional references to other studies of reading and children's cognition and development. Other researchers, for example, have addressed the subject of mistakes in reading—Frank Smith and Kenneth Goodman most notably. And Bettelheim and Zelan say nothing of and seemingly have not profited from the abundant research now in progress among psychologists and reading specialists in the area of aesthetic development, more specifically, in the "narrative grammars" employed by the young as they tell, listen to, and read stories during their childhood and adolescence.

Other analyses of the psychological aspects of reading are found in *The Cool Web: The Pattern of Children's Reading*, a collection of fifty essays by British and a few American authors. Most of the work printed or reprinted in this volume does not speak of a specific child reader whose encounter with literary texts has been directly observed, but rather of that generalized child reader often posited by writers and critics of children's literature. It should be noted, however, that these essayists certainly allow for the ongoing development of this hypothetical child, both as a person and as a reader, as is seen clearly in James Britton's contribution on the young reader's changing response to fantasy, or in fantasist Alan Garner's comments on the writer's job to show, not tell, adolescent readers narrative worlds they must learn to envision for themselves. Not surprisingly, then, the three editors include Randall Jarrell's "Children Selecting Books in a Library," a poem which concerns, above all else, the power of literature to transform every child reader. Indeed, the selection of material and the editors' ample transitional commentary emphasize the special opportunities for growth that the young derive from literature.

Like the other two books under review, *The Cool Web* is polemical as well as descriptive. In their introduction, the editors assert: "It would be difficult to justify another collection of essays [such as their own], unless it opened up a way forward from the minority cult which children's literature can so easily become if the authors and

the critics . . . lose sight of the readers." To support this stand on the
preeminence of the *reader*, they have mustered the forces of such
students of the psychological processes of reading and storying as
Britton, D. W. Harding, and Arthur Applebee; poets and novelists
like C. S. Lewis, Philippa Pearce, and Lucy Boston; and, occasionally, literary critics such as W. H. Auden and Barbara Hardy. This
very inclusiveness is, in fact, the most problematic feature of the
book. *The Cool Web* consists of four major sections—one on the
reader, one on the writer, one on critical approaches to literature,
and a final and somewhat ambiguous one entitled "Ways Forward."
Within each section are at least nine essays. Inevitably they are
uneven in quality, and the best ones lose force by juxtaposition with
superficial journalistic pieces from *Catholic Education Today*, *Redbook
Magazine*, and *New Society*. Fully a third of this collection could well
have been omitted in order to include longer excerpts from the
choicest writing—Auden and Britton, for example—thereby high-
lighting the editors' central concern with the nature and benefits of
children's literary reading. As it stands, other matters continually
diffuse this purpose (I am thinking of the by-now-shopworn defense
of the validity of children's literature qua literature).

Despite its patchwork quality, *The Cool Web* is, to my mind, the
most suggestive of the three books in its frank acknowledgment of
the diverse ways literary reading is being and must continue to be
studied. The annotated bibliography and marginal glosses within
the text further encourage readers to continue their exploration of
the massive and still growing body of research and commentary on
reading. Within the selections themselves are found, to summarize,
an introduction to the reading diary (with an excerpt from White's
*Books before Five* and one from Kornei Chukovsky's *From Two to Five*);
classic and new studies on the process of reading (by Barbara Hardy
and Aidan Warlow); and more than a dozen essays that underscore
the contribution of the writer to the "cool web of language" that
weaves together writers, young readers, and books. "Unless we pay
attention to all of these people," the editors remind us both explicitly
and through their collection as well, "discussion of children's fiction
will remain narrow, elitist, and inadequate." Thus, while not really

showing us a particular "way forward" for future study of child readers, *The Cool Web*, an ambitious survey of recent research and commentary, certainly guards against a monaural, overtly textual critical response to children's literature.

# Thirty Writers Talk about Writing

Perry Nodelman

*The Signal Approach to Children's Books*, edited by Nancy Chambers. Metuchen, NJ, and London: Scarecrow Press; and Harmondsworth, Middlesex: Kestrel Books, 1980.

*The Openhearted Audience: Ten Authors Talk about Writing for Children*, edited by Virginia Haviland. Washington: Library of Congress, 1980.

*Celebrating Children's Books: Essays on Children's Literature in Honor of Zena Sutherland*, edited by Betsy Hearne and Marilyn Kaye. New York: Lothrop, Lee & Shepherd, 1981.

Writers can be their own worst readers. They can tell us what they intended, but their finished work might not fulfill their intentions. Their secret reservoirs of private associations with the words they write are just as likely to mislead them as they read those words as ours might mislead me and you; and their secret knowledge of how the words they eventually chose came to be chosen might actually confuse them. Jill Paton Walsh's discussion of how she writes in *The Openhearted Audience* suggests one version of the problem: "Whereas the reader and the critic are confronted simply with the way the author did go, the author himself was confronted with an immensely elaborate network of interrelated choices. No one but a writer ever looks at a literary problem in quite this way." I doubt that anyone can ever look at a finished book in quite the way its writer does.

In adult literature, the recognition that writers are biased readers of their own words has led to a sensible division of labor. Those who can write literature, write literature; and, we hope, those who can read literature well become readers and writers about reading—that is, literally critics. When it comes to children's literature, unfortunately, that division is not so firmly made. Editors and organizers of conferences and lectures often ask children's writers to discuss their own work; and what they have to say about it often takes the place of criticism by more objective readers. In the three books in question, there are twenty-five pieces about writing by writers and illustrators of children's books—thirty, if you count the nonfiction writers.

The presence of writers in *The Openhearted Audience* is not surprising, since the book's subtitle quite fairly announces its contents— "Ten Authors Talk about Writing for Children"—and like the British magazine its contents have been chosen from, *The Signal Approach to Children's Books* contains essays by professional critics as well as authors. *Celebrating Children's Books* is a different matter; in addition to selections by fourteen writers and illustrators, and other pieces by a mixed bag of librarians, editors, and publicists, it contains a short section called "Understanding the Books," in which the difficult art of writing about reading is represented by a grand total of two essays, both by reviewers.

Now reviewing is no more criticism than writing fiction well automatically qualifies one to write wisely about it. In the *Signal* collection, John Rowe Townsend says that, when it comes to children's literature, "there is little writing that . . . could be dignified by the name of criticism." It is sad to report that these three books do little to correct that. It is even sadder to report that, with the partial exception of the *Signal* collection, they do not particularly even try to correct it. Their editors have simply accepted the convention that what children's writers have to say about their books should interest readers of those books; they all contain numerous discussions of the creative process and little in the way of critical analysis.

Perhaps I should not be angered by that. Discussions by children's writers of how they came to write their novels are, indeed, an established genre; these three books do little that is different from many earlier books. But they do anger me. They anger me because they are so similar to those earlier books, and because they keep the focus of discussion of children's books on the creative process rather than on the results of that process. I suspect children's literature will not get the respect it deserves until it is read carefully by readers whose only bias is their pleasure in reading children's literature, without having necessarily written it first.

But many of these writers seem to believe that that sort of careful reading is dangerous. In fact, dismissive comments on criticism seem to be a significant aspect of the genre, almost *de rigueur* for writers writing about their own work. (As Eleanor Cameron's gracious response to my critical discussion of her novel *Beyond Silence* in this issue reveals, not all writers are hostile to criticism.) Even John Rowe Townsend, who is a critic as well as a writer, expresses a surprising disdain for critical analysis: "I have never greatly cared for laying works of art out on the slab and taking them to pieces; it is all too easy to finish up with nothing but dead remnants." It would also be all too easy to accuse Townsend himself of laying children's books out on the slab in his own critical writing; but despite his negative metaphor, I suspect he has done more illuminating of them than permanent damage.

If even a critic feels the need to make dismissive comments about criticism in the context of a discussion of how he writes his novels, then it should not be surprising that writers who are not critics often seem to be quite proud of their critical ineptitude. In *Celebrating Children's Books*, Arnold Lobel unashamedly announces that "in the matter of my work and children's books in general, articulate I am not." He is right; he is not articulate. I don't blame him for that; but I see no logic in the apparent assumptions of the editors of this book: first, that he could perhaps be articulate, and second, that his declaration that he isn't might be useful information. I also find little use in Lloyd Alexander's true statement in the same book that everything he says could be learned "in greater detail better expressed from any book on narrative technique"; and I am annoyed when, having admitted his own inability to describe the distinguishing qualities of good literature, Alexander says he is "not at all sure they can be defined." Many other writers share his disdain for the possibilities of critical understanding. In *The Openhearted Audience*, Pamela Travers says that the qualities of good writing "can't be described," and Ivan Southall says they are "almost impossible to define"; and in *Celebrating Children's Books*, Robert Cormier says, "Too much theorizing worries me," and Susan Cooper asks, "How can we define what we are doing? How can a fish describe what it's like to swim?

I doubt that a fish can, or should. But I am not a fish. As an unrepentant critic and analyzer, I may even be a fisherman (although I try to keep my catches alive enough to throw them back in after I've caught them, rather than laying them out on slabs for filleting). The point is, I am a reader, not a writer of fiction. My annoyance with all these anticritical pronouncements of writers is that, consciously or not, they seem to be recommending to their readers an attitude that might well be essential to their own continuing creativity as writers but that is unnecessarily limiting for readers. We can, and should, think about the qualities of good books, even if their writers can't or don't want to.

Because many of them don't want to, what they have produced here is not often illuminating. As self-analysis, it is of special interest to the self doing it. Virginia Hamilton wonders *why* she chose to write about eccentrics; as a reader, I am more interested in *what* she writes about them, and *how* she does it. And what am I, as a reader, to do with Maurice Sendak's idea that his characters' attitudes represent his own activity "as a creative artist who also gets freer with each book and opens up more and more?" That matters to Sendak; for other readers of his books, it's just gossip.

If discussions about how books came to be written don't often throw much light on the finished books themselves, they might nevertheless offer insights into the act of writing. In fact, the frequent agreement among the writers represented in these books to a few central ideas does suggest that there is something distinct about the creative processes of those who write for children. One of those ideas is the conviction that writing is not a conscious act, that stories and characters come from somewhere below the conscious mind. Eleanor Cameron says in *The Openhearted Audience* that "there is nothing more mysterious than the ability of the unconscious to present the writer with his characters"; numerous others suggest that their books come from "the depths," or "somewhere lower down in the less accessible regions of mental experience," or "at the deepest roots of being," or "from deep sources within." Furthermore, many of them seem to equate these depths with childlike feelings. In *The Openhearted Audience*, Maurice Sendak says, "I have the mind of a child," Ivan Southall says, "I become a child," and

Eleanor Cameron makes a specific connection between childhood
and the unconscious: "All the impressions of childhood are still
there in the depths."

Many of these accomplished children's writers also insist that they
don't write for children, neither the children they know nor children
in general. Rather they write for themselves. But they almost always
add the proviso that the self they write for is some aspect of the child
they once were and believe they can still contact: the child of the
depths.

The frequent reiteration of such ideas does say something about
the distinct sort of imagination needed to write children's books. But
it does something else, too. Despite the fear expressed by many of
these same writers of critical analysis, it suggests how critics might
come to understand the significant differences between children's
books and other sorts of writing. In other words, these discussions of
writers about how they write, while unilluminating in themselves,
might help critics to better understand what children's writers have
written.

A series of three perceptive and stimulating discussions by critics
in the *Signal* collection suggests how. First, Charles Sarland does
a detailed analysis of the prose of William Mayne, to show how
Mayne's evocation of childhood implies a reader who is not childlike. Peter Hunt builds on Sarland's conclusion, and finally, Aidan
Chambers adds to it the conception of an "implied reader," borrowed from Wolfgang Iser, in a stimulating attempt to define the
audience implied by children's fiction. These three articles show
what criticism of children's literature might be; the one by Chambers
was the deserving recipient of the first award for critical writing
given by the Children's Literature Association. But they are more
than just good criticism, for the light they cast, quite unintentionally,
upon the many comments of children's writers about how they write
points the way to an even deeper understanding of children's literature, a literature peculiarly governed by the inevitable gulf between
those who write it and the audience it implies.

If such an understanding emerges, it will be from the critical
writing of readers, not from writers' discussions of how they came to
write their books. That is not to say writers cannot be critics; books by

John Rowe Townsend and Eleanor Cameron show that it is possible to be good at both these different pursuits, and many of the other writers represented in these three collections express the sort of insight that can only come from much reading and much thinking about what one has read. But such insights must necessarily come only occasionally in discussions that focus on the creative process rather than on the works that result from it; and we have to acknowledge, finally, that even a writer's pronouncements about his own work come after the fact, that when writers talk about their books they are talking as readers like the rest of us, and not writers. As Alan Garner insists, "Everything I say *about* writing is with hindsight."

Garner makes that statement during an interview with Aidan Chambers, included in the *Signal* collection, an interview that sums up what it is about the attention paid to the creative process in discussions of children's books that distresses me. Garner is a fine writer, and Chambers a fine critic. But Chambers is so convinced that writers ought to have valuable things to say about their books that he badgers Garner about it, in a most unseemly fashion. After fifty pages or so, Garner finally admits to Chambers's ideas about the implied reader and such. He ought not to have had to do that. His writing speaks eloquently for itself, to sensitive readers, and Chambers's critical ideas are persuasive enough to have no need of a writer's acceptance of them. Nevertheless, Chambers did do this interview, and Garner did agree to do it; their mutual acceptance of a longstanding pattern in discussions of children's literature suggests an important reason for the relative inadequacy of the criticism of this one particular sort of writing.

*Varia*

# A Blind Child's View of Children's Literature

Craig Werner

Those who overcome fear and shyness often ask me questions about what it is like to be blind. "What is it like to read Braille?" they ask, or "What is your understanding, if any, of color?" I do not mind such questions, and I answer them as well as I can. Recently, I was asked, "Did you never wonder as a child what the pictures in the books read to you looked like?" I may have, but I cannot honestly recall ever inquiring. Certainly, the Braille children's books I read contained no raised-line drawing reproductions of the pictures in the print editions. The people who read to me did not describe the illustrations to me, perhaps believing their efforts would be fruitless. I grew up, then, nourished by words alone, and any images I gleaned from children's books had to be triggered by those words. Now, as an adult, I am teaching children's literature and must grapple seriously with this problem of the applicability of illustrations in children's books to blind children. I now realize that to make a story come to life for me I had to create pictures in my own mind. In pondering this problem, an even more provoking question arose: What kinds of images did I form? In other words, what was my childhood view of children's literature? Although my mental drawings were undoubtedly more tactile than visual, I assume my perception of literature shared ample common ground with that of my sighted friends.

I need, though, to sound one note of warning before going on. I am trying to reconstruct memories of twenty-five or more years ago, memories of a congenitally blind boy, the only child of a devoted mother and father in Connecticut. Childhood speaks the language of emotions and feelings, not always of rationality, and these emotions are often elusive and ill understood by the child. The pressure on adults to stop acting and thinking like children facilitates and even encourages the erasure of such memories. Calling them into the present demands patience, thinking, and constant questioning. Even when we think we have them successfully conjured up, how can we be sure we are recalling them accurately? Once youthful innocence is lost, it is no easy matter to resurrect it. We can only guess intelligently as to what it must have been like and rely for security on those relatively few unshakeable memories from childhood which will die only with us. It is hard, for example, to recreate exactly the feeling of a child when encountering for the first time the wicked fairy in "The Sleeping Beauty," the ogre in "Puss in Boots," or the glass mountain in "The Seven Ravens."

To suggest that a blind child's perception of literature must be radically different from that of a sighted child is misleading. All of us, blind and sighted, read stories ourselves as children or had stories read to us, and all these stories were composed of words. Many words do not have visual connotations, and the sighted and the blind child should both arrive at the correct meaning of these words without difficulty. The wolf's "I'll huff and I'll puff" depends not at all on sight for proper comprehension. Indeed, perhaps more than any other subject, literature lends itself to the blind person's understanding with a minimal amount of intermediary aid. Consider geometry, physics, or chemistry. These disciplines cannot adequately be understood and learned without the help of raised-line drawings and modified equipment. Literature, on the other hand, needs no outside assistance before it can effectively enter the mind of a blind receiver. The blind child gets the words from the reader or the Braille book he is reading or the taped text, and then he processes them to the best of his ability. Admittedly, it is the processing of some of these words that is responsible for what must be termed a difference—the only difference, perhaps—between a sighted child's view of literature and a blind child's outlook. One of the most incomprehensible word groups deals with colors. For the child who has never seen, color must always be largely a mystery. Attempts to correlate color with musical pitch or temperature must needs be inaccurate. Colors depend upon visual recognition: either you can see them and understand or you don't see them and don't understand. Since I could not see, I could not grasp color.

What I *did* see (blind people freely use the word without embarrassment, so common is it in our language) were objects that I knew contained the color in question. I vividly recall my mother reading to me Andersen's "The Red Shoes." The tale triggered memories of a pair of shiny shoes I had when I was about three years old. These shoes I knew were red, since my mother always referred to them as my red shoes. Although the shoes of the little girl in the story were not red to me, the shoes themselves were very authentic. In connecting the girl's shoes with mine, I was merely doing what any sighted child would have done.

With "Little Red Riding Hood," however, the case was somewhat different. As a child, I possessed both a cap and a hood for my jacket, so I clearly understood the meaning of the hood, and of the cap in the story of "Little Red Cap." I do not know now, and I do not think I knew then, whether my cap and hood were red. In any event, the connection between the girl's possession and one of mine was not so clearly defined as in "The Red Shoes." Nevertheless, not being able to see the girl's cap or hood did not significantly diminish the image of the item in my mind. Her wear resembled mine to a sufficient degree to allow for comfort; of this I was certain. Hers felt furry, just like mine; and of this, too, I was certain. I had an adequate understanding of the basic items *cap* and *hood*, and that did well enough for me. My curiosity was satisfied. Admittedly, I minimized the importance of the color red, and red thus became incorporated into my understanding of the girl's name as Littleredridinghood. I ceased to worry about red and about the hood. What interested me was the foolish little girl at the story's center. Her name, Littleredridinghood, was a single expression, a unified whole, if you will, much like the compound in chapter 1 of *The Wind in the Willows* that is formed with the names of all the foods in Ratty's lunchbox.

Although red was something I could not fathom, it is well to note that there are comparatively few visual words having no tactile analogs. Chris Senden, a blind writer, suggests that a blind child will look for a touch-orientated way of perceiving what might at first glance be considered a visual experience. Even a sunrise, which one might think would completely escape a blind child's cognition, can be grasped, albeit in a limited sense. A blind child feels the sun on his face, and feeling the warmth is the child's understanding of sunrise. Moreover, for sighted and blind child alike, sunrise begins a new day, full of excitement and worlds to conquer. To exclude the blind child from perceiving sunrise, even if his understanding is a partial one, is to deprive him of all the anticipation and joy associated with the dawn; and this deprivation is not only misleading but also unnecessary.

Granted, then, that a blind child is able at least in part to partake of a visual image by transformation, it is much less difficult to believe in the obverse: that pictures depending for their understanding on senses other then sight can be grasped with total ease. The cold of the Snow Queen's palace and the taste of the gingerbread house were no less real to me than to my sighted friends. In fact, the gingerbread taste may have been even more tantalizing for me than for my playmates, since gingerbread, especially that made by my grandmother, was one of my most favorite foods. My other grandmother lived in an ever increasing circle of stray cats for whom she provided a home, and many of these cats were on intimate speaking terms with me. It did not, therefore, require much thought to place one of them in aristocratic boots. Voilà, the Master Cat! The Snow Queen's palace, the witch's gingerbread lure, and the cunning Puss—all these I could easily share with my sighted friends, and common experience brought rich rewards. After all, it is not always the image restricted to the comprehension of a select few that is most prized. Despite lack of sight, I still possessed in my childhood the most important faculty involved in understanding and appreciating a good story, that catalyst which brings literature to the mind's eye: imagination.

A story without imagination working upon it is like a musical score with no one to execute the notes. The tale lives only as vibrantly and as vividly as the listener's imagination will allow. Although I could not see—perhaps because I could not see—I longed to reach out far and wide for all the images I could handle. Whenever possible, I reinforced these pictures with people and objects from my real world. Puss, for instance, was naturally wearing a pair (or was it two pair?) of my very own boots. Andersen's steadfast tin soldier marched stiff-shouldered out of a box of *my* tin soldiers that made a wonderful clinking sound when you struck two together. I will never forget that martial, metallic sound. Plastic soldiers could not duplicate this sound and were quite useless to me. Soldiers they might have been, but warriors they surely were not. The fierce voice of the troll under the bridge in "The Three Billy Goats Gruff" needed no visual image to make him terrible. For him, my imagination created a voice decidedly terrible and inhuman. The story is told (I cannot recall the source) of Richard Strauss conducting one of his own compositions in rehearsal. At a moment of extreme volume and intensity, Strauss stopped the orchestra and told his musicians to play more softly, stating that the music was loud enough as it was. His statement can be easily applied to my conception of images in fairy tales; I did not have to see the characters and objects in a story, since my imagination already made them real enough.

When, however, I encountered stories with no familiar objects such as tin soldiers or stray cats, I occasionally ran into temporary trouble. Witches, dragons, and ogres did not issue from my grand-mother's house or from my toybox. I must have wondered what a witch or giant might have looked like. The physiognomy of people never interested me as a child, so I did not bear out the belief that blind people feel the faces of their acquaintances in order to deter-mine what they look like. Consequently, it was not the hideous face of the witch that frightened me, but rather her trappings: her bubbling pot, her winged broomstick, and her perpetually mewing black cat. I imagined her den full of the most hateful creatures my liberated imagination could summon. As was the case with the troll in "The Three Billy Goats Gruff," I did not overly concern myself with a giant's facial features or immense proportions. His voice, deep like thunder and bordering on the inarticulate, was much more horrible than anyone's attempt at mimicry. What I am point-ing to amounts to saying the child is an inventor. If one door opening to an image does not function, there is always another that will yield satisfaction.

My imagination was at the peak of exercise when I allowed it to create something entirely new, something I could not at all connect with my own experiences. This situation would occur when I had only a dim idea, or none at all, about the exact nature of the object being described in the story. I had not the slightest notion of what a castle looked like. When faced with a blank of this kind, the child has two alternatives. He can request information, or he can create his own concept. Although asking for a definition or a description satisfies his curiosity, the child may not always choose this easy way out. Ignoring the so-called right answer may occur because the child resents having to appeal to a higher authority, but more likely he manufactures his own concept because he feels that idea is superior to anyone else's. This conscious choice gives the child autonomy over a brand-new world. Returning to our castle, I decided that *all* castles must have huge rooms, all of which must echo for many seconds. This prejudice persisted until 1972 when visits to several castles in Scandinavia convinced me that my assumption was largely untrue. Many castle rooms, I learned, were fairly small and acoustically dead. Similarly, I never visited a palace as a child. The fairy tale descriptions portrayed them as beautiful, and beautiful must mean, I thought, lovely to the touch. Accordingly, I constructed in my mind a new palace whose walls and floors were made of a substance that felt like a very hard and shiny marble. Since beauty in tapestry or carpeting is largely a visual matter, I took not the slightest notice of them and allowed my palace walls and floors to shine in their naked splendor. That a palace room could resemble a spacious livingroom in someone's home never crossed my mind. I reveled in such imaginative forays as a child because they were mine alone. No one could take them away from me. Indeed, no one even knew of them.

Creation of the nontransferrable picture reminds me of a point. Might it not be that, given the blind child's lack of sight and comparative lack of prejudice, he is in a better position to allow his imagination full sway than the sighted child is? Deprived of data available to those with sight, the blind child's mind must work overtime, if you will, to force the other senses to create a full picture of fairy tale objects. Of course, imaginative zeal cannot be quantified, so my theory cannot ever be scientifically proven. But just as radio drama appeals to the mind's eye of the listener to create a picture that television automatically builds for him, so might stories without visual illustrations (either those read by the blind child or those read to him) kindle and develop an imaginative capacity outstripping that of children for whom pictures in books do much of the work.

The obvious key to enjoyment of a story, then, is its appeal to the imagination or creative spirit. The stories that appealed most to me during childhood were those offering thrilling and novel experiences that could be perceived, or at least that I perceived, through tactile means. Not in the least terrified by overtones of violence in *Alice's Adventures in Wonderland*, the book became a favorite upon first hearing, only to be surpassed a few weeks later by *Through the Looking-Glass*. How hilarious it would be, I thought, to hold and try to manipulate a flamingo croquet mallet in perpetual motion. I owned a real croquet set, so I could better appreciate the incongruous mallet in *Alice*. Since it was shiny, hence beautiful to me, the little glass table atop which lay the key to the garden offered great attraction to me. I imagined the White Knight in *Looking-Glass*, perhaps my favorite character in the *Alice* books except Alice herself, to be a metal chess piece shaped exactly like a standard chess knight with no arms and legs. How such a piece would manage to stay astride his horse I neither knew nor cared. In fact, the White Knight cannot ride well.

For me, Alice's White Knight was more a chess piece—a toy, so to speak—than someone with real human physical features. Perhaps because of this liking for toys and gadgets, I favored Andersen's tales. I loved animals, and I still do; and Andersen's tales abound with them. I have already mentioned my special tin soldier, and I would add to my list of favorite characters the ugly duckling, the swans in "The Ugly Duckling" and in "The Wild Swans," and the little mermaid, who transcends humanity both in spirit and in physical beauty. I enjoyed the Grimm stories, of course, but perhaps because of their terse economy they never sparked my imagination to the degree the Andersen stories did. My mind seemed to thrive on those sprawling descriptive passages Andersen carried off so well, such as that at the beginning of "The Little Mermaid." That many of the images in this opening are visual is no matter, since I struggled to touch everything in them that could be handled. Once again, it comes down to tactile perception of the visual. The tactile imagery of the icy Snow Queen's palace in Andersen's "The Snow Queen" is heightened and protracted to almost unbearable lengths by the deliberate pace of Andersen's prose. Deliberate the Grimm Brothers never were. Perhaps their world was too stark, too cut-and-dried for my thirsty imagination to grasp. At any rate, I have come to appreciate as an adult what I think I more or less tolerated as a child; Andersen still remains my favorite story teller.

What, then, can we conclude from the interaction of a blind child with a pictureless tale? My experience indicates that I handled images in three ways. I adapted them as well as I could, as in the case of the sunrise, or I disregarded the visual component entirely and concentrated instead on nonvisual traits such as the troll's and giant's voices, or I created an entirely independent picture, as in the case of the castle or palace. The question of whether the image was complete for me without sight does not interest me. Honestly speaking, there can be no such thing as a complete image, since any image can be further strengthened through active and careful thought. It is not the mere possession of five senses that assures enjoyment of a tale, but rather the mind's ability to perceive substance and spirit through verbal cues. All of what I have said amounts to this: If you respond to words, you will respond to literature.

All literature is constructed from words, but it is important that it did not begin with the written word. It began instead with something that was later to be represented visually, and that something is a vocal utterance. Chris Senden reminded me recently that it is "important to remember that much of the literature we read evolved from the verbal practice of storytelling. Likewise, our first personal encounter with stories probably came from being read to as children. I think we should make an effort to read aloud—both to ourselves and to each other—in order to enhance our enjoyment and appreciation of a particular work." Homer, says tradition, was blind, and the blind minstrel is still a common figure in many countries, although not in ours. For that matter, sighted storytellers are rare in the United States. I am not making a case for the superiority of the blind storyteller over the sighted one, nor for the blind person as better able to understand a tale. I am saying, though, that the blind child, or adult, is not as limited by lack of sight as one might at first think. The best literature, after all, is not based on one sense, but upon the universal bank of experiences, both physical and spiritual. The blind person is equally able to understand emotions such as fear, joy, or despair. Feelings go beyond the senses in their appeal to all of us. We do not merely look at the reality literature presents to us. Each tries in his own way to grasp it, to embrace it, and to make it his own.

# Dissertations of Note

Rachel Fordyce

Abookire, Noerena. "Children's Theatre Activities at Karamu House in Cleveland, Ohio 1915–1975." Ph.D. diss. New York University, 1982. 375 pp. DAI 43:306A.

Karamu Children's Theatre has been active since 1915 when it was founded by Rowena and Russell Jeliffe as a neighborhood settlement house. Abookire's study shows the variety of activities at Karamu, analyzes the numerous directors, and assesses its impact on children's theatre in the United States. Included are reproductions of many original photographs, programs, posters, press releases as well as the results of extensive interviews.

Adamson, Lynda Gossett. "A Content Analysis of Values in Rosemary Sutcliff's Historical Fiction for Children." Ph.D. diss. University of Maryland, 1981. 176 pp. DAI 42:3475A.

Realizing that what most parents and teachers look for in a "good" children's book are values that reflect their own, Adamson analyzes *The Eagle of the Ninth*, *The Shield Ring*, *the Witch's Brat*, and Carnegie-medal winner *The Lantern Bearers* to see if they reflect "positive values of Western contemporary society." While comparing types of protagonists, settings, conflict, tone, point of view, and theme in the five novels, Adamson concludes that Sutcliff's novels, despite their Roman setting, and probably because of the complexity of their characters, do reflect value systems of western civilizations.

Amandes, Joanne Beran. "A Study of Adaptations for Young People of the *Iliad*, the *Odyssey*, and the *Aeneid*." Ed.D. diss. Texas Tech University, 1982. 194 pp. DAI 43:1024A.

Analyzing the treatment of plot, narration, characterization, and theme in thirteen adaptations of Greek and Roman mythic literature, Amandes attempts to show teachers how to discriminate as well as how to approach the use of myth in class.

Anderson, Dorothy Jean. "Mildred L. Batchelder: A Study in Leadership." Ph.D. diss. Texas Woman's University, 1981. 404 pp. DAI 42:3332–33A.

"Based on voluminous existing records, interviews with Batchelder's contemporaries, and with Batchelder herself," this dissertation in library science traces Batchelder's career with the American Library Association from 1936 through 1966 and highlights her impressive influence on the improvement of library services for children and young people.

Antczak, Janice. "The Mythos of a New Romance: A Critical Analysis of Science Fiction for Children as Informed by the Literary Theory of Northrop Frye." D.L.S. diss. Columbia University, 1979. 376 pp. DAI 42:208–09A.

Extrapolating from Frye's list of basic literary images, Antczak "explores the role of the genre [of science fiction] as a contemporary romance form" implicit in the mythology of the modern world. She is concerned with models of heroes, quest forms, whether or not settings conform to typical romance styles, and archetypal images in modern romance as well as older mythologies.

Barron, Pamela Patrick. "The Characterization of Native Americans in Children's and Young Adults' Fiction, with a Contemporary Setting, by Native American and

Non-Native American Authors." Ph.D. diss. Florida State University, 1981. 191 pp.
DAI 42:234–43A.

Barron includes 114 books in her study of stereotyping of North American Indians in contemporary children's and young adults' literature. She is particularly concerned with "story setting, attitudes of author in relation to Native Americans, use of dialect, author's portrayal of the values and ethics of Native Americans, author's portrayal of contributions of Native Americans, author's portrayal of contemporary Native American life, characterization of the Native American character, stereotype with regard to characterization, and stereotype with regard to storyline." She concludes that while the most blatant of the stereotypes of Indians have generally disappeared, they have been replaced by more subtle stereotyping and a portrayal of Native Americans as totally devoid of humor.

Barros, Maria Dirce do Val. "Monteiro Lobato and the Renewal of Children's Literature in Brazil." Ph.D. diss. Tulane University, 1982. 142 pp. DAI 43:704A.

Barros analyzes Monteiro Lobato's substantial contribution to children's literature and, most important, shows how he has contributed to the overall revitalization of children's literature in Brazil. Her thesis is that "Monteiro Lobato's works were a direct response to a need to lead the development and writing of children's literature in Brazil down new, diverse and relevant paths."

Beasley, Mary Lord. "The Effect of Death Awareness on the Protagonists of Selected Adolescent Novels." Ed.D. diss. University of Tennessee, 1981. 160 pp. DAI 42:3851A.

The works that Beasley is concerned with are Annixter's *Swiftwater*, Zindel's *Pardon Me, You're Stepping on My Eyeball*, Collier and Collier's *My Brother Sam is Dead*, Richard Peck's *Something for Joey*, Lowry's *A Summer to Die*, Guest's *Ordinary People*, Gunther's *Death Be Not Proud*, Lund's *Eric*, Klein's *Sunshine*, and Beckman's *Admission to the Feast*. Her ultimate goal is to demonstrate that death education "should be part of the English curriculum."

Bennett, Priscilla B. "Humorous Children's Literature and Divergent Thinking." Ph.D. diss. University of South Florida, 1982. 120 pp. DAI 43:662A.

This dissertation in elementary education is concerned with whether children perform more creatively if they have been exposed to elements of humor, particularly from children's literature.

Bernard, Joy Hubbard. "The Image of the Family in Young Adult Literature." Ph.D. diss. Arizona State University, 1981. 257 pp. DAI 42:4271A.

Bernard studies the image of families in transition by analyzing young adult literature produced from 1967 through 1979. She is primarily concerned with family size, parents' careers, a sense of belonging, leadership, conflict, the urban poor, and rural families.

Bolton, Randy. "Peter Schumann's Creative Method Used in Making Plays with the Bread and Puppet Theatre." Ph.D. diss. Florida State University, 1981. 311 pp. DAI 42:3347A.

The dissertation, directed by Gill Lazier, looks critically at Schumann's "unique creative process and his unusual mixture of sculptured shapes, movement, sound, and space." Bolton concludes that Schumann "like other rebellious figures in the development of contemporary theatre, contributes specifically and generally to our theatre's growing eclecticism."

Brett, Betty Marion. "A Study of the Criticism of Children's Literature 1969–1979." Ph.D. diss. Ohio State University, 1981. 501 pp. DAI 42:1947A.

Focusing on criticism in the United States, Canada, and Great Britain, Brett demonstrates that there is "convincing evidence of the existence of an extensive and impressive body of criticism of children's literature which may be categorized as work-centered, child-centered, and issues-centered." She is certain that criticism is becoming more serious and that the subject of children's literature is being treated with respect "both within the university community and among scholars in general."

Cardwell, Patricia Brown. "Death and the Child: An Historical Analysis of Selected Puritan Works of Children's Literature with Implication for Modern Education." Ph.D. diss. Catholic University, 1982. 431 pp. DAI 43:1067A.

Cardwell demonstrates that Puritan children's literature "emphasized death because the ideas of sin and salvation were matters of intense concern. Yet they also stressed spiritual values to conquer and overcome death." By contrast, modern children's books, "more diverse and pluralistic, . . . speak to a child's emotional and intellectual understanding, and rarely seek to further spiritual understanding." The implications are that modern education might profit from addressing "death in a manner to help children enhance the quality of life," and that modern children's literature should confront the realities of personal death and terminal illness.

Dittrick, Anne Margaret Triba. "An Adolescent Novel: Art and the Computer." Ph.D. diss. University of Nebraska–Lincoln, 1982. 211 pp. DAI 43:792A.

Dittrick's is a mystery novel in which three friends, all involved in computer use in one way or another, must solve problems related to robbery, kidnapping, and computer manipulation.

Dorval, Jeffrey Harris. "A Comparison of Selected Authors' Intended Ideas and the Actual Understanding by Young Children of Selected Primary Grade Books in which Death is the Main Theme." Ed.D. diss. Temple University, 1981. 114 pp. DAI 42:522–23A.

While Dorval flirts with the fallacy of author intent he analyzes five children's novels whose authors specifically state that they have a personal reason for instructing children about death. His results suggest only partial understanding on the part of the children who were exposed to death through literature.

Garrison, Jean Wood. "A Comparison of Selected Factors in Children's Realistic Fiction Having War-Related Plots Published in England and the United States During World Wars I and II." Ed.D. diss. Temple University, 1981. 193 pp. DAI 42:1930A.

Garrison identifies 300 titles of children's books in Great Britain and 421 titles in the United States and compares them in terms of plots related to the home front, home fronts in countries other than England and the United States, evacuation, flying, sea action, spy stories, land fighting, animals, sabotage, girls in action, training, and miscellaneous themes. The author observes no outstanding differences between American and British publications and says that "series books dominated book production in both countries." Few books were of quality and fewer still remain in print.

Hare, Delmas Edwin. *"In This Land There Be Dragons*: Carl G. Jung, Ursula K. Le Guin, and Narrative Prose Fantasy." Ph.D. diss. Emory University, 1982. 231 pp. DAI 43:165–66A.

Focusing on *A Wizard of Earthsea* and applying the work of Jung, Joseph Campbell, Mircea Eliadee, and David Burrows as well as Frederick Lapides and John Shawcross, Hare concludes that "fantasy has a complex structure with the hero's journey archetype as its nuclear element."

Hyde, Paul Nolan. "Linguistic Techniques Used in Character Development in the Works of J. R. R. Tolkien." (Volumes I–III) Ph.D. diss. Purdue University, 1982. 1230 pp. DAI 43:1979A.

This computer-assisted dissertation in three parts analyzes Tolkien's linguistic aesthetic "as displayed in his invented languages, his use of historical languages, and his patterning of introductory verb and adverbial modifiers for dialog." The works he addresses are "Smith of Wooton Major," "Farmer Giles of Ham," "Leaf by Niggle," *The Hobbit, The Fellowship of the Ring, The Two Towers, The Return of the King, The Silmarillion,* and *Unfinished Tales.* Appendixes contain glossaries of real and invented language.

Jackson, David Harold. "Robert Louis Stevenson and the Romance of Boyhood." Ph.D. diss. Columbia University, 1981. 196 pp. DAI 42:2685A

Jackson treats *Treasure Island, The Black Arrow, Kidnapped,* and *Catriona* as "a four-part romance in which an immature hero [presumably Stevenson] quests, literally and metaphorically towards a goal of bourgeois adult identity." Less attention is given to *Dr. Jekyll and Mr. Hyde, The Ebb Tide,* and *Weir of Hermiston.*

Kauffman Dorothy Mae. "An Identification and Description of Wordless Picture Story Books for Children Published in the United States from 1930 to 1980." Ph.D. diss. University of Maryland, 1981. 222 pp. DAI 42:3478A.

Kauffman uses a variety of rating instruments to evaluate the "literary, visual and format aspects of a sample of 127 wordless picture story books" to establish their clarity of content.

Kaufman, Melissa Mullis. "Male and Female Sex Roles in Literature for Adolescents, 1840–1972: A Historical Survey." Ph.D. diss. Duke University, 1982. 437 pp. DAI 43:750–51A.

To determine whether there are differences in sex roles, the degree of difference, and whether these roles have changed over a 132-year period, Kaufman examines the "relationships between parents and children, relationships between friends, initiation into adulthood, male portrayals in girls' books compared to female portrayals in boys' books, and ideal male and female characteristics." After an exhaustive survey she concludes that stereotypical roles have become more solidified in modern books.

Kennemer, Phyllis Kay. "An Analysis of Reviews of Books of Fiction for Children and Adolescents Published in Major Selection Aids in the United States in 1979." Ed.D. diss. University of Colorado at Boulder, 1980. 156 pp. DAI 42:81–82A.

Kennemer analyzes the effectiveness of publishers' information and aids to published books in assisting school librarians to buy books.

Kolbe, Martha Emily. "Three Oxford Dons as Creators of Other Worlds for Children: Lewis Carroll, C. S. Lewis, and J. R. R. Tolkien." Ed.D. diss. University of Virginia, 1981. 285 pp. DAI 43:1532A.

Kolbe also touches on Ruskin and Auden in her investigation of "some of the motivational factors present in the lives of these scholars that stimulated them in the midst of brilliant academic careers to compose major works for children." Many family, environmental, and personality traits are analyzed to show the similarities among Carroll, Lewis, and Tolkien.

Mitchell, Judith Naughton. "Changes in Adolescent Literature with Homosexual Motifs, Themes, and Characters." Ph.D. diss. University of Connecticut, 1982. 121 pp. DAI 43:133A.

Given the 1973 decision of the American Psychiatric Association to delete homosexuality as an illness, Mitchell explores the possibility that homosexuality in children's literature might be looked at more frankly and honestly after that date than before. She concludes that "after 1973 more characters are homosexual by definition" and that "there may also be some shift in the receptiveness of the social context, the degree of positive self-conflict, and the degree to which homosexual behavior is rewarded or punished."

Osa, Osayimwense. "A Content Analysis of Fourteen Nigerian Young Adult Novels." Ed.D. diss. University of Houston, 1981. 270 pp. DAI 43:3420–21A.

The object of Osa's study is to obtain a composite picture of the Nigerian novel for young adults. Specific analysis is given for Ekwensi's *Juju Rock*, Oguntoye's *Too Cold for Comfort*, and Areo's *The Hopeful Lovers*. Osa points out that Nigerian novels for young adults differ from American novels because of their "hardline moral stance" but that the novels have a high level of relevance to their audiences.

Pascoe, Charles Henry. "Catharsis of Joy in Four Original Musical Comedies for Children." Ph.D. diss. Southern Illinois University at Carbondale, 1981. 485 pp. DAI 42:1378A

Pascoe's dissertation is primarily four scripts for musical comedies, each of which is analyzed for its ability to produce a cathartic joyful effect.

Rockow, Karen Sidney. "The Hero as Fool: The Unpromising Hero in Traditional Literature." Ph.D. diss. Harvard University, 1982. 228 pp. DAI 43:1637A.

Although Rockow's dissertation does not deal strictly with children's literature, the points she makes about the "dümmling" are generally applicable to many tales that have been absorbed into its canon. Chapter 4 glances at the "heroines of the Cinderella and Kind/Unkind stories" and she concludes with an expansion of Freud's and Otto Rank's hypothesis of "the family romance" as well as an analysis of Bettelheim.

Rosenhan, Mollie Schwartz. "Women's Place and Cultural Values in Soviet Children's Readers: An Historical Analysis of the Maintenance of Role Division by Gender, 1920s and 1970s." Ph.D. diss. University of Pennsylvania, 1981. 669 pp. DAI 42:1273A.

Specific Soviet cultural values such as "patriotism, morality, work and the family provide the context" for Rosenhan's discussion of the complexity of sex role treatments in Soviet literature. Despite the radical changes in the Soviet Union over the past fifty years, her readings would suggest that paternalism still flourishes.

Rubeck, Mary Ann. "Annotations Documenting and Interpreting the Reflection of Hans Christian Andersen's Life in His Fairy Tales." Ph.D. diss. State University of New York at Buffalo, 1981. 260 pp. DAI 42:1622A

Although it has been frequently noted that Andersen's life is often reflected in his tales, Rubeck points that no extended study exists. Specifically, she identifies similarity of incidents and background settings, similarity of fairy tale characters with real-life people, Andersen's revelation of his own personality traits, and she identifies "the social conditions, at the time [that] had a profound effect on Andersen and are reflected in his fairy tales."

Rutherford, Wilma Marie. "An Exploration Study of Ageism in Children's Literature." Ed.D. diss. University of the Pacific, 1981. 168 pp. DAI 42:1938–39A.

Rutherford analyzes eight books for children published between 1949 and 1978; she found that aged characters were not, for the most part, stereotyped and that they engaged in a wide variety of roles and life styles.

Schaefer, Emily Susan. "A Children's Book in Perspective." Ed.D. diss. University of Massachusetts, 1981. 207 pp. DAI 42:4712A.

The author's dissertation is essentially a version of her children's novel "Family on the Road" as well as a discussion of the novel's critical reception with children as a listening audience.

Shepherd, Renee Miriam. "Awful Fun: Childhood in Nineteenth Century Children's Literature." Ph.D. diss. University of California, Santa Cruz, 1981. 209 pp. DAI 43:1252A.

Acknowledging the rapid growth of children's literature in the nineteenth century, Shepherd tests Boas's contention that the child is an "exemplar of primitivism" in the context of noble savage and "natural child" theories. Part 1 discusses Rousseau, Calvinism, and eighteenth century backgrounds. Part 2 "examines representative children's texts as an index of the pervasive changes in the nature and status of childhood." Specifically she is concerned with "the moral status of childhood; the degree of autonomy and freedom given childhood; the nature of the subject matter children are exposed to . . . ; and the value of childhood in relation to adult life."

Spaeth, Janet L. "'Over the Horizon of the Years': Laura Ingalls Wilder and the Little House Books." Ph.D. diss. University of North Dakota, 1982. 161 pp. DAI 43:1148A.

Spaeth's thesis consists of five essays that explore themes in Wilder's work that have not been critically analyzed before. These essays deal with family traditions in the books, the westward movement's impact on their subject matter, the portrayal of frontier women, Laura's perception of language and how it reflects her perception of her environment, and Wilder's technique: the use of plot, point of view, tone, theme, imagery, characterization, and personification.

Thorpe, Douglas James. "A Hidden Rime: The World-View of George MacDonald." Ph.D. diss. University of Toronto, 1981. n.p. DAI 43:456A.

To be able to give a unified analysis of MacDonald's world-view, Thorpe briefly surveys his "intellectual, cultural, and religious background" and then focuses on the cosmological, teleological, anthropological, and epistemological aspects of MacDonald's writing.

Williams, Elizabeth Detering. "The Fairy Tales of Madame D'Aulnoy." Ph.D. diss. Rice University, 1982. 297 pp. DAI 43:465–66A.

Williams traces the success of D'Aulnoy's *Contes des fées* and *Nouveaux Contes des fées* through their numerous printings in the eighteenth century. She attributes their success to "the use of popular genre and themes; to a lively style; and to a structure that embodied the transformation taking place in the French outlook" at the beginning of the eighteenth century. She stresses the complexity of the tales and the fact that they are most frequently characterized by the use of magic, enchantment, and metamorphosis.

Wilson, Anita Carol. "Literary Criticism of Children's Literature in Mid-Victorian England." Ph.D. diss. State University of New York at Stony Brook, 1981. 385 pp. DAI 42:4836A.

Wilson looks at criticism of children's literature that appeared between 1839 and 1865 in the *Examiner*, the *Spectator*, the *Quarterly Review*, *Fraser's Magazine*, the *Gentleman's Magazine*, *Household Words*, and *All the Year Round*, beginning with an essay on Catherine Sinclair's *Holiday House* and ending with one on Lewis Carroll's *Alice's Adventures in Wonderland*. She notes the increased complexity of literature for children, the shift from didacticism, the increased use of fairy tale, the heightened sense of responsibility of authors of children's literature, and the acknowledgment of a need to entertain. She feels that the "major challenge confronting mid-Victorian critics of children's literature was the need to assess children's books simultaneously as literature, as entertainment, and as expressions of moral and religious beliefs."

## Also of Note

Balderston, Daniel. "Borges's Frame of Reference: The Strange Case of Robert Louis Stevenson." Ph.D. diss. Princeton University, 1981. 391 pp. DAI 42:1624A.

Degan, James Nerhood. "The Short Fiction of Walter de la Mare." Ph.D. diss. University of Iowa, 1982. 301 pp. DAI 43:1150A.

Dreibelbis, Gary Charles. "A Case Study of Joan Ganz Cooney and Her Involvement in the Development of the Children's Television Workshop." Ed.D. diss. Northern Illinois University, 1982. 182 pp. DAI 43:964A.

Edwards, Bruce Lee. "A Rhetoric of Reading: A Study of C. S. Lewis's Approach to the Written Text." Ph.D. diss. University of Texas at Austin, 1981. 235 pp. DAI 42:3155A.

Gross, Jacquelyn Lee Wagoner. "Differences in Literary Response to a Fairy Tale and an Instructional Story by Fourth-Grade Readers." Ed.D. diss. University of California, Los Angeles, 1982. 111 pp. DAI 43:1098A.

Iacconi, Rosemary R. "Problem Solving Using Children's Literature: A Curriculum Plan for the Primary Grades." Ph.D. diss. University of Akron, 1982. 208 pp. DAI 43:362A.

Koch, Robert Allen. "Gulliver and Dr. Swift: The Issue of the Satirist's Identity." Ph.D. diss. Rice University, 1982. 213 pp. DAI 43:452A.

Macgregor-Villarreal, Mary. "Brazilian Folk Narrative Scholarship: A Critical Survey and Selective Annotated Bibliography." Ph.D. diss. University of California, Los Angeles, 1981. 260 pp. DAI 42:4541A.

Schley, Margaret Anne. "The Elfin Craft: Fairytale Elements in James Stephens' Prose." Ph.D. diss. University of North Carolina at Chapel Hill, 1982. 166 pp. DAI 43:1558A.

Sparing, Margarethe Wilma. "The Perception of Reality in the *Volksmärchen* of Schleswig-Holstein: A Study in Interpersonal Relationships and World View." Ph.D. diss. University of California, Berkeley, 1980. 297 pp. DAI 42:320−21A.

Stahlschmidt, Agnes Dorothy. " A Study of the Recreational Book Reading Habits of Selected Fifth-Grade Children." Ed.D. diss. University of Illinois at Urbana−Champaign, 1981. 108 pp. DAI 42:3009A.

Vanpee, Janie Marie. "The Rhetoric of Rousseau's Pedagogical Discourse in *Émile ou de l'éducation*." Ph.D. diss. Yale University, 1982. 331 pp. DAI 43:1568−69A.

Watson, James Darrell. "A Reader's Guide to C. S. Lewis: His Fiction." Ed.D. diss. East Texas State University, 1981. 135 pp. DAI 42:2692A.

## Errata

*Children's Literature*, volume 10 (1982)
    Title of Michael Egan essay:  *For* "The Neverland of Id" *read* "The Neverland as Id"

*Children's Literature*, volume 11 (1983)
    Page 12, line 14: *For* "the final version of the master" *read* "the final vision of the master"
    Page 12, line 18: *For*, "Burnett atones for her material failings" *read* "Burnett atones for her maternal failings"

# Contributors and Editors

GILLIAN AVERY lives in Oxford, England, and is the author of *Childhood's Pattern* (Hodder and Stoughton, 1975) and *Nineteenth Century Children* (Hodder and Stoughton, 1965), as well as fourteen books for children. She is currently completing a book about nineteenth-century American children's literature.

CAROL BILLMAN, formerly codirector of the Children's Literature Program at the University of Pittsburgh, now lives and works in Kemblesville, Pennsylvania. Her most recent writing project was a book published by Frederick Ungar on American series books for adolescents.

FRANCELIA BUTLER recently directed a summer institute on children's literature for the NEH and is the author of *Masterworks of Children's Literature, 1550–1739*, 2 vols. (Stonehill and Chelsea House, 1983).

ELEANOR CAMERON is the author of a critical study of children's literature, *The Green and Burning Tree* (Little Brown, 1969), and fifteen novels for young people. *The Court of the Stone Children* received the NBA award for 1974. She is currently on the editorial boards of *Cricket* and *Children's Literature in Education*.

JOHN CECH teaches English at the University of Florida and is currently the editor of *The Dictionary of Literary Biography's* three-volume series on American writers for children.

GERALDINE DELUCA teaches at Brooklyn College, where she coedits *The Lion and the Unicorn*. Her interests in fantasy have led to essays on John Gardner, Kenneth Grahame, and other writers of books for children.

RACHEL FORDYCE is an associate dean of the College of Arts and Sciences at Virginia Polytechnic Institute and State University.

JEROME GRISWOLD teaches English at San Diego State University and is the author of a forthcoming study of Randall Jarrell's children's books. He contributes to the *Los Angeles Times*, the *Paris Review*, the *New York Times Book Review, New Republic*, and other publications.

SIDNEY HOMAN, a professor of English at the University of Florida, has written two books on Shakespeare and a variety of essays on Renaissance and modern drama that stress performance criticism. His recent *Beckett's Theaters* (Bucknell, 1983) won a press award for literary criticism.

LEONARD S. MARCUS teaches at the School of Visual Arts in New York and is writing a biography of Margaret Wise Brown.

ALEXANDER MEDLICOTT, JR., a master of English at Deerfield Academy in Deerfield, Massachusetts, has written extensively on early American literature.

PERRY NODELMAN teaches children's literature and science fiction at the University of Winnipeg and is the editor of the Children's Literature Association *Quarterly*.

DENNIS QUINN, a professor of English at the University of Kansas, specializes in Renaissance literature, the history of biblical exegesis, and children's literature. He is currently completing a book on the literature of wonder.

SUZANNE RAHN teaches children's literature at Pacific Lutheran University in Tacoma, Washington. She is the author of *Children's Literature: An Annotated Bibliography of the History and Criticism* (Garland, 1980).

COMPTON REES teaches English at the University of Connecticut and is currently teaching and doing research in London.

ELIZABETH SEGEL, a member of the Core Faculty in Women's Studies at the University of Pittsburgh, is the coauthor of *For Reading Out Loud! A Guide to Sharing Books with Children* (Delacorte, 1983).

MARY-AGNES TAYLOR teaches English at Southwest Texas State University in San Marcos. Her essays have appeared in *Horn Book, Children's Literature in Education,* and other publications.

JEANIE WATSON chairs the department of English at Southwestern State in Memphis. She has published primarily on nineteenth-century British literature and recently received an ACLS grant to study Coleridge's symbolic fairy tales.

CRAIG WERNER teaches children's literature at San Diego State University. He is also an active storyteller in the San Diego area. Other academic interests include Renaissance literature and the interdisciplinary connection between words and music.

FEENIE ZINER teaches English at the University of Connecticut. Her numerous books for adults and children include *Cricket Boy, A Chinese Tale Retold* (Doubleday, 1978). She is currently completing an adult novel based on Arthurian themes.

JACK ZIPES coedits *New German Critique* and teaches German and comparative literature at the University of Wisconsin in Milwaukee. Recent critical books include *Fairy Tales and the Art of Subversion* (Wildman Press, 1982) and *The Trials and Tribulations of Little Red Riding Hood* (J. F. Bergin, 1982).